CLARENDON L

Edited by

PAUL CRAIG

CLARENDON LAW SERIES

THE ANTHROPOLOGY
OF LAW

FERNANDA PIRIE

OXFORD
UNIVERSITY PRESS

OXFORD
UNIVERSITY PRESS

Great Clarendon Street, Oxford, OX2 6DP,
United Kingdom

Oxford University Press is a department of the University of Oxford.
It furthers the University's objective of excellence in research, scholarship,
and education by publishing worldwide. Oxford is a registered trade mark of
Oxford University Press in the UK and in certain other countries

Published in the United States of America by Oxford University Press
198 Madison Avenue, New York, NY 10016, United States of America

British Library Cataloguing in Publication Data
Data available

Library of Congress Control Number: 2013945299

ISBN 978–0–19–969684–0 (Hbk.)
978–0–19–969685–7 (Pbk.)

Printed and bound in Great Britain by
CPI Group (UK) Ltd, Croydon, CR0 4YY

PREFACE AND ACKNOWLEDGEMENTS

The anthropology of law is concerned with the nature of law as a social form. This project is more analytically focused than much of the scholarship generally classed as 'legal anthropology', which includes studies of courts, government, power, domination and resistance, and different types of social norms. These are broadly legal topics, but such studies have not often addressed the nature of law itself. Law is a distinct social form: it may, at times, seem elusive, but the proliferation of law in the modern world, the social ends that it is supposed to achieve, and the widespread faith in the ideal of the 'rule of law', provide ample reasons for studying it. We fight wars in the name of democracy and justice, but what assumptions lie behind our reification of the legal?

This book encourages the anthropologist to take law seriously as a subject for study. It is also intended for the legal scholar concerned with either the theoretical or the empirical study of law. It demonstrates the potential of using empirical case studies, both historical and contemporary, to reflect upon the nature of law, exemplifying the benefits of including unfamiliar—sometimes marginal and peripheral—examples for comparison. This is distinct from the goal of exploring the functions of law in society, a project that characterizes much of what is termed 'socio-legal' or 'law and society' scholarship. Exploring the nature of law may include consideration of its functions and relations with other social forms, but the goal is to understand what it is, not just what it does.

A great variety of case studies is discussed in the book and comparisons amongst them can test and refine our understanding of the nature of law. This is central to the anthropological project. While many are small-scale and marginal, they include examples from the great legal systems of the Hindu, Islamic, Chinese, and Roman worlds, and some of the debates that surround them. These are complex topics and the reader can refer to any number of good introductions, written by specialists, for further details. But any scholar concerned with the nature of law should have at least some knowledge of these great legal systems. It is too easy for both theoretical and comparative work to be over-reliant on examples drawn from the familiar western realm; and the Anglo-American common law is distinct among them. If this book encourages scholars in both law and anthropology to read and consider comparatively the work of legal historians, orientalist scholars, and religious specialists, alongside the contributions of legal anthropologists, then it will have achieved at least a part of its purpose.

The themes and arguments of this book have, to a large extent, been inspired by the thought and writings of Paul Dresch, at the University of Oxford, and the seminars and discussions of the Oxford legalism project. Here, Judith Scheele, Hannah Skoda, Patrick Lantschner, Tom Lambert, John Sabapathy, and Alice Taylor, among others, presented many of the examples and ideas that have found their way into this work. Several of the book's themes were also the subject of seminars on my *Law in Society* course, where Masters students from both law and anthropology subjected them to perceptive questions and stimulating debate.

I would, in particular, like to thank Denis Galligan, William Twining, Morgan Clarke, Don Davis, Georgy Kantor, and Neil Armstrong for providing careful and constructive criticism of several draft chapters. Judith Scheele, above all, has been generous with her time and advice, providing distractions from the task of writing when they were needed, and encouragement when the law seemed to offer more potential for confusion than clarity.

Over the past decade I have been lucky enough to hold a position at the Max Planck Institute for Social Anthropology in Halle, where Franz and Keebet von Benda-Beckmann directed the Legal Pluralism Project Group; although they may not agree with of all its arguments, this book owes much to their encouragement and support. At the Centre for Socio-Legal Studies of the University of Oxford, Denis Galligan created a stimulating research environment and inspired an anthropologist to engage seriously with legal theory. I hope they will be content to count this book as part of their legacies.

The University of Oxford is generous in its provision of sabbatical leave, without which this project would have been impossible, and the Faculty of Law has provided valuable research support. I am also grateful to Marina Kurkchiyan for allowing the sabbatical to be a real one, to Eva Pirie and

Matilde Gawronski for correcting textual errors, to Paul Craig for encouraging me to write the book in the first place, and to Alex Flach and Natasha Flemming at OUP, who have been helpful throughout.

CONTENTS

I

INTRODUCTION

What can anthropology bring to the study of law? What questions can it answer and what aspects of law can it illuminate?

Anthropology is an empirically-grounded discipline. Its material is observed in the real world, typically through long-term, focused participant observation. The anthropologist studies social forms as they exist in all their variety, including ideas as well as physical activities, and what may be regarded as archaic or marginal. The exploration of law can thus include the work of scholars in far-flung corners of medieval Europe or on the grasslands of Tibet, as well as the regulation of international finance and the legal claims of human rights activists.

Laws are intangible phenomena and the ideas expressed or symbolized by them are as important as the ways in which they regulate behaviour. The social forms we commonly think of as 'law' do not constitute a straightforward category, however. Law is idealized as the 'rule of law', held up as an international standard, and promoted in the name of democracy, good governance, and nation-building. But is it always clear what is understood by these claims and what 'law' might mean for those amongst whom its 'rule' is promoted? What does it even mean to identify law in different parts of the world? As notorious jurisprudential debates about the nature of law indicate, neat definitions are elusive. Anthropologists can address the concept of law by examining comparatively the empirical phenomena to which we properly apply the term. Without seeking precise definitions, we can look for connections and commonalities amongst them, as well as differences, inconsistencies, and contradictions. We are not seeking to perfect a philosophically refined model: we promise less than the legal theorist, but our accounts should be richer, more detailed, and more nuanced.

What can this project bring to anthropology? Why should anthropologists ask about the nature of law? The object is not to provide answers to irresolvable issues of definition, but to raise a set of questions into the nature of law, an approach that focuses on legal thought and form, as well as function. This is a particular line of inquiry within the broader field of legal anthropology. Asking about legalistic thought draws attention to texts as well as processes, and philosophy as well as government; it means examining codes, ideas, and forms of reasoning. Exploring legalism, as a way of thinking about and organizing the world, means examining law as rules, categories, and argument; and it means examining what law promises, not just what it does.

In this chapter I outline the nature of that project and the ways in which it relates to other types of scholarship, in both law and anthropology.

SOCIAL ANTHROPOLOGY

Social anthropologists study social forms, that is institutions, patterns of behaviour, and social relations, the ideas that underpin them, and the symbols that give them meaning. Identifying what is socially or culturally distinct is often easier when the material is unfamiliar and anthropologists have often sought out what seems different or remote for their studies. However, careful observation can lead to insights into aspects of our own societies. How well do we understand what it is like to find oneself in a magistrate's court, for example? How does a Baptist community in the United States regard the state's legal system? Why do businessmen engaged in international trade adopt legal forms without obvious means of enforcement?

The anthropologist investigates the experiences and practices that characterize these social realms and the ways in which people within them understand themselves and their roles in the world. The task is to describe and explain how people make sense of who they are, of what they do and what is around them, and the models, assumptions, and explanations that guide their actions. For example, what might seem like a mere misfortune to us might be regarded by the Zande of east Africa as evidence of hostility or witchcraft (Evans-Pritchard 1962: 226–27). The fight that ends in a death is not a case of murder for the Tibetan nomads, but retaliation for an earlier death, demanding not punishment but revenge or payment of blood money (Pirie 2005).

Human behaviour is distinctive in having a dimension of 'meaningfulness' (Ryan 1970: 16). As the anthropologists Dresch and James (2000: 4) describe, the social scientist tries to trace the thought or meaning 'underlying the assumptions of a period, a cultural climate, a shared tradition'. Social anthropologists, they explain, study societies as moral systems, not as natural systems, that is as composed of human associations based upon moral judgements and values (Evans-Pritchard 1962: 26). They are interested in what makes behaviour meaningful, seeking patterns, not scientific laws, to interpret rather than to explain. The task of the anthropologist is, then, to delve into the understandings and assumptions that shape social practices. Among the pastoralists of eastern Tibet, for example, what state officials dismiss as violence or backwardness might be regarded locally as anger, something that is justified, or even compulsory, and which only makes sense in the context of local relations of loyalty and tribal organization; equally, the success of the mediator may relate to and reinforce his status as a reincarnate lama (Pirie 2012).

As Wittgenstein argued, social behaviour is to be understood as rule-following, not as causally regular behaviour (Ryan 1970: 128). We could say that the anthropologist is interested in the rules (of all sorts) that guide the way people act. These may, however, remain implicit and the task of understanding social life is not straightforward. It would be wrong to assume that it can be too systematic:

as an anthropologist one tries to make intelligible, to oneself and others, forms of human life. These are complex ... by definition no one account is adequate; yet they possess a certain objectivity despite this, for, at the least, there is a choreographed circulation of words, images, things made, formulae or interactions, which [appear] in a particular setting and inform the lives of the people living there. (Dresch and James 2000: 7)

We must not look for social forms or rules that are too neat and straightforward, or for precise and over-simplified analytical explanations. If social life is messy and contradictory, as it often is, our analysis must be nuanced, allowing for caveats and exceptions; we can seek objective patterns and continuities, but must also allow for exceptions and change.

The sociologist, economist, and political scientist may look for more objective and definite links between ethnic violence and economic conditions, say, which require the use of precise and predetermined categories for measurement. Surveys, samples, and carefully delineated questions and measures mark their work.[1] Such methods may be employed by the anthropologist, too, but as adjuncts to ethnographic fieldwork methods. As Merry (1990: 5) remarks, research into 'legal consciousness' conducted through large-scale surveys tends to flatten out the way people understand and use the law, assuming that each individual has an overall stance towards law as a thing, rather than a series of interpretations of different facets of law. Ethnographic methods, by contrast, reveal complexity and contradictions. The anthropologist typically spends long periods in one field-site in order to look behind practices, to discover attitudes and assumptions, 'listening for the unsaid, looking for the visually unmarked, sensing the unrepresented, seeking for connections among parts of the obvious which remain locally unstated' (Dresch and James 2000: 23).

Law as an anthropological subject

As anthropologists we cannot take either the nature or the presence of law for granted. We must always question the categories of analysis that we can appropriately employ to describe what our subjects do and how they think about legal phenomena. Indeed, in many parts of the world the label 'law' is not the right one to use: the people we are studying do not have or create law and do not possess a category that maps neatly onto our concept of law. Even close to home, we know that French and German concepts, with their distinctions between *la loi* and *le droit* or *das Gesetz* and *das Recht*, do not correspond precisely to the English notion of law. Scholars of ancient Greece have long debated whether and in what circumstances *nomos* can be translated as 'law' (Gagarin 2005); and this is not a new problem. There were no exact equivalents between the terms used by the Ancient Greeks (*nomos, dikaion*) and Romans (*ius, lex*) and medieval writers used the Latin terms imprecisely (Brand 2012: 59–64; Kantor 2012: 66–70). Law is a category of the English-speaking world, although its history

---

[1] In contrast to my work among the pastoralists of eastern Tibet I could, for example, mention illuminating studies by economist Andrew Fischer (2004, 2008, 2009).

lies in more ancient languages, and we must not assume that it reflects a human universal. Other terms may be needed for description and analysis.

Laws do not emerge with the same features the world over; nor do they aspire to the same ideals; indeed, many communities seem to do perfectly well without anything that could be classed as the rule of law or a legal system. Anthropology, through its use of detailed case studies and careful comparisons, can clarify the concepts we use to make sense of these different forms, exploring what is culturally specific about them, discovering differences across social, geographical, and cultural divides, and highlighting the historical influences that have shaped a particular image of law. Debates over the ambit and definition of law have been far from conclusive, several scholars even advocating that we abandon the term, whether for analysis or as a means to define the field of study; but we can still ask about what law is. Scholars across disciplinary divides persist in using the term, and the idea of the rule of law is widely accepted as a political ideal in the twenty-first century. Meanwhile, indigenous groups make legal claims for the protection of property, culture, and rights.

Exploring the nature of law inevitably means starting with a category of the modern, English-speaking world. Here, law has come to be firmly associated with the nation state, but we cannot assume that other people must or should organize their lives in similar ways; we must take care not to construe the rest of the world, including our own legal history, in the same terms. This is a danger that faces politicians, policy-makers, and the public at large, as well as scholars of law, but it is the latter who have the resources to address these problems directly. Max Weber, for example, defined law in terms of the actual determinants of human conduct (1968: 312). As the examples of later chapters in this book indicate, however, legal codes from early medieval Europe, as well as examples from Tibet and village constitutions in north Africa, yield examples of what look like legal codes with no certain impact on either judges' decisions or daily life. Wormald (1999), a legal historian working on the early Middle Ages, describes legal codes drawn up for or maintained by Germanic and Anglo-Saxon rulers, which seem to have had no practical purpose, either as judicial instruments or as guides for conduct amongst a largely non-literate population. Working on documents from tribal Yemen, anthropologist Paul Dresch (2006) found a series of pacts and agreements which set out, in 'legalistic' terms, a series of complex agreements and relationships amongst the tribesmen. These could hardly be described as anything other than legal rules, taking the forms of conditional statements and stipulating when men could claim help and compensation from one another, among other things, but without any body politic or central authority to enforce the rules (Dresch 2006: 295). Here we have examples of laws, or what look like laws, which should surely make us question the assumption, commonly made by legal scholars, that law needs to be guaranteed or enforced by a ruler and can usefully be identified and assessed in terms of its practical application.

The idea that legal rules and categories define social wrongs, determine their consequences, and resolve conflict remains strong, despite the fact that jurists, as well as anthropologists, have remarked that some societies seem to do very well without law when settling disputes (Markby 1905: 21; Salmond 1920: 13; Evans-Pritchard 1940: 162). During my own fieldwork in a Ladakhi village it quickly became apparent that the villagers felt no need to refer to any rules to address disputes or discipline those guilty of aberrant behaviour. I found a set of community values, connected to the micro-political organization of the village and a fear of the consequences of overt conflict or antagonism, supported by a strong sense of civic morality, which shaped their responses to conflict. Rather than regarding a dispute in terms of a clash of rights, the villagers saw it as a tear in the fabric of the community, which must be mended with the payment of fines and a ceremonial process of reconciliation (Pirie 2007b: ch 4). A fellow anthropologist, conducting fieldwork in a nearby village, once asked me whether I had been able to record any village 'laws' governing sexual offences. She had observed a tragic case of what she described as 'rape', in which the girl had died in childbirth, but the man had merely had to pay a fine to the girl's household and to fund a purification ritual in the village (Gutschow 2004: 410–26).[2]

---

[2] Gutschow comments on the ability of the father to work side-by-side with his daughter's aggressor in later years. For the villagers it was essential that community relations were maintained.

It became clear during my research that there were no local rules or laws dealing with such 'offences'. A fight, or even a case of 'rape', would be regarded primarily as the cause of problematic relations between two households, rather than an event involving an 'offender', 'victim', or 'rapist'; the Ladakhi villagers felt no need to employ general categories or abstract rules in order to resolve these problems (Pirie 2002: 253–56).

Legal scholars have emphasized institutions (Raz 1970), morality (Fuller 1964; Finnis 1980), and rules (Hart 1994) in order to define what they take to be law. But anthropologists can often produce counter-examples. Legal codes may be drafted by religious scholars with no certain political authority; Davis (2010) discusses the ancient Hindu texts as forming an intellectual system more than a governmental one, rather like the jurists' law of ancient Rome. Meanwhile, the Hindu idea that the ruler should nevertheless punish wayward behaviour was adopted by Buddhist scholars, but simultaneously regarded as contravening the principles of Buddhist morality (Zimmerman 2006). The English common law is not an obviously rule-based system (Simpson 1987). If these are examples of law, on the basis of what features are we saying so? If not their institutional basis, is it their form as explicit and generalizing rules; if not their moral basis, is it their intellectual status; if not as explicit rules, is it as a form of reasoning? 'Philosophy', says Waldron (1995: 635) 'proceeds by making familiar facts seem strange to us'. The same can be said about anthropology. Case studies do not just provide information about the world but can force us to question our assumptions about it.

What, then, does it mean for an anthropologist to study law? Does what Monaghan and Just (2000: 2) call the 'descriptive richness that comes out of the specific encounters anthropologists have with particular peoples and places' simply yield too many variants to render law useful as an analytic category?

Law as a polythetic category

Wendy James (2003: 55) suggests that even philosophical analysis:

should not be founded on pure metaphysical speculation transcending any particular starting point but should operate critically from the present upon the whole range of ways in which we can discover that humanity has thought.

As Allen (2000: 245) says, more simply, the task of social anthropology is 'to come to terms with the whole range of socio-cultural forms about which we can know'. We should not reify a concept like 'law', assuming we are talking about a single entity amenable to precise definition, but we can use empirical examples to reflect upon the nature of law, and seek out connections and commonalities, looking beyond familiar western examples. We need to problematize our notion of 'law' without losing sight of it, its meanings and implications, and the contexts in which they appear.

To adopt a concept from Wittgenstein's later philosophy, we can regard law as a category of phenomena that display no more than a 'family resemblance' to one another. As he explains, 'we see a complicated network of similarities overlapping and criss-crossing: sometimes overall similarities, sometimes similarities of detail' (1958: 32). But there need be no single identifying or defining feature; it may be impossible to build a single model in order to explain what law is. If we think that 'law' must have a precise definition or we misunderstand the complexity of the phenomena that the category encompasses, we make mistakes about what it is and assume that it works in a certain way; we may ask the wrong questions—about origins, institutions, or functions; or we may deny that social phenomena are law in a way that does not make sense. If we are to be true to our own concept, and to the language rules that govern its application, we must recognize and explore this diversity.

There are, nevertheless, right and wrong ways to apply any particular term and to analyse it. The rules and definitions for the use of a concept do not need to be very precise (Wittgenstein 1958: 39–40); if a category, such as law, is abstract, then the rules are complex, and metaphorical usage may increase this complexity, but they must be explored if we are to understand and analyse its nature. How, then, is this exploration to be done? We are after more than a discussion of how the term 'law' is used in everyday language. Rodney Needham (1975) adopted the term 'polythetic classification' to capture Wittgenstein's notion of family resemblance and to discuss the challenges it presents for the anthropologist. 'It is the recognition ... of a class composed by sporadic resemblances', he says, that is needed for the study of jural institutions, as much as for the study of human capacities (1975: 352). Comparison provides a particular challenge. What is needed 'is not a convenient technique for cutting down the number of variables, but a means of accommodating as many as possible' (1975: 362). The possibility of borderline cases is always present.

In the case of law, then, the task is to look for recurrent features amongst the class of phenomena that bear a family resemblance one to another, but without assuming we can identify a set of common or essential features. Marginal and peripheral examples can be considered, to test the boundaries of that class and to highlight what may turn out to be surprisingly contingent features—the state, legal institutions, and enforceable norms, for example. We also need to explore recurrent themes and connections, highlighting features that can easily be overlooked if we confine ourselves to familiar examples—the work of scholars, a mistrust of legalism, the borrowing of legal forms. Only by casting our gaze widely over the class of phenomena we commonly and properly call law, can we see the relevant connections and contrasts, and overturn the assumptions that are too easily made if we seek simple definitions. In this way we can be true to our own concept, imprecise and multi-faceted though it may be.

The object is to find paradigms and analytical concepts that will capture what is distinctive about law, without unduly restricting the examples we can consider. In the following chapter I discuss a wide range of what ordinary language would label as 'laws'. It becomes evident that no single idea, whether expressed in terms of institutions, functions, ideals, or form captures what is distinctive about them and neatly distinguishes this class from non-legal examples. Nevertheless, it is form rather than function, rules more than commands, and legalism rather than conflict resolution that most usefully seems to distinguish law from other social phenomena.

Law in legal anthropology

Law and society scholarship has traditionally been less concerned with what law is than with what it does (Silbey 2005: 324). In his Introduction to the *Law and Society Reader*, Abel (1995) declared that social scientists examine everything about law except the rules: they study its institutions, structures, processes, behaviour, personnel, and culture. However, this would be to ignore an important class of social phenomena. Rules are as much a part of social life as the rest, not just in their effects and power, but in what they express. Legal rules and categories specify the way society ought to be; at their most basic, they are a public expression of moral order. In this section I review the principal themes that have emerged in legal anthropology and suggest that the field would benefit from a more concentrated focus on legal rules, along with legalistic thought, argument, and texts.[3]

Many of the earliest studies by legal anthropologists concerned conflict resolution, mediation and adjudication, and the work of judges and mediators (Moore 2001). Comaroff and Roberts' (1981) distinction between the rule-governed and processual paradigms as ways of understanding legal processes has, for example, been influential on both anthropologists and other scholars (Tamanaha 2001: 50). Ethnographic work on the experience and use of state courts and laws in westernized countries followed similar studies in non-western societies, as I describe further in chapter two. The experiences of indigenous people in both national and international courts continue to attract attention (Freeman and Napier 2009), as do court processes in other areas.[4] As Snyder (1981: 145) points out, however, this scholarship tends to displace law, along with substantive concepts and rules, as the subject of study, subordinating it to the analysis of procedures, strategies, and processes. Law may or may not play a part within them; but this makes it even more relevant to ask when it does and how. What is distinctly legal about legal argument? How do people employ it, why, and with what effects?

The regulation of society and maintenance of order has been another important theme in the development of legal anthropology. Outstanding was Moore's (1973) depiction of the semi-autonomous social field, which was the starting point for an influential line of scholarship on legal pluralism, which I discuss further in chapter two. The idea of grounding empirical study in social norms still has purchase: Moore (2005), for example, states that legal

---

[3] This is not a review of legal anthropology, but an overview of its themes. The work I cite here is, therefore, illustrative rather than comprehensive.

[4] Studies in Islamic areas, for example, include Hirsch (1998), Bowen (2003), Stiles (2009), and von Benda-Beckmann (2009), along with those discussed in chapter four.

anthropology should include enquiries into enforceable rules and norms, and Donovan (2007) characterizes law as one of a number of norms of social regulation, as do certain empirically-minded legal theorists (Tamanaha 2001; Twining 2009). But what is distinctive about law as a form of regulation and basis for order? As Moore (2005: 1) recognizes, state law is not the only source of organized social order, and continuing debates over legal pluralism illustrate the difficulty in identifying the legal amongst them. Tamanaha (2001: ch 8), among others, argues that we should recognize and study a great variety of sources of social order, effectively abandoning law as a defining analytical category.

Leaving issues of definition to one side, explicit calls have been made for the analysis of law in the context of history and power relations, notably by Starr and Collier (1989). Nader (1997, 2002: ch 3) has argued forcefully that law should be studied as a controlling process. Much of this work has concerned colonialism and post-colonial dynamics (Merry 2003; Darian-Smith 2007: xii); imperialism, whether explicit or implicit (Mattei and Nader 2008); and law as an aspect of government or state regulation and control (Mertz and Goodale 2012: 78). The issues of imperialism, and what Darian-Smith (2007: xiii) calls the shifting, refractory, and disintegrating relations of power, are broad and important topics that can, and do, attract considerable scholarly attention and investigation. But the anthropologist needs to do more than recognize the fact that law is often implicated within them: what, if anything, is distinctive about the role that it does and can play, and about the exercise of power when it takes legal form? For Nader, law 'legitimates the take' (2005: 199) and for Benda-Beckmann et al. (2009: 2–3) it creates, produces, and enforces meanings of concepts such as 'justice', 'authority', and 'rights'. But, as the latter recognize, there may also be contention over who has the power and authority to generate law. How, then, does law come to define these concepts and to play its legitimating role? Analytically, we need to disaggregate law from power, if we are better to understand the connections between them.

The anthropological literature also encompasses important studies of the ways in which law can be employed as a means to resist power or engage with political processes. Many of these concern colonial or quasi-colonial situations and, as I discuss in chapter eight, there is a large, and related, literature on human rights and transitional justice. Alongside anthropological studies of laws and legal categories that fail to do justice to indigenous social forms, then, are those that describe how they provide resources for people to argue for their 'rights'. This is particularly true in the case of human rights, but even under colonial regimes, it was possible for some people 'to appropriate imperial legality in order to reconstitute themselves as civilized beings' (Merry 2003: 578). A wealth of historical examples, discussed in later chapters, from the ancient Greeks to E.P. Thompson's study of eighteenth-century England, demonstrate that law has never merely been a tool of the powerful, nor indeed one of resistance, but both at the same time. As Moore (2001: 103–06) points out, the paradigm of domination and resistance is too simplistic to capture all that is involved in these dynamics. We need to ask what it is about law that means it can be used to both exercise and resist power; how does it come to be turned back against those who would employ it to dominate and control?

Similar dynamics are apparent in international settings, which have also been the subject of anthropological study, as I discuss further in chapter eight. Mertz and Goodale (2012: 87–88) refer to the legal complexity of the modern world, which results from the intersection of local, national, and international laws, and call for the 'integrative study of law across cultures', one that is 'adequate to the complex world it seeks to understand'. But how is this to be done? Some anthropologists have urged the study of legal (or normative) pluralism in international law. Merry (2006a: 108) suggests a focus on knowledge practices, and that the use of ethnographic methods can illuminate the impacts of international law. But we need to go beyond the practices of small spaces to address what she describes as 'the systems of meaning that shape international actions and their historical and structural origins' (2006a: 106). If law creates or shapes international relations across different cultures, we need to ask how it does so, and about the systems of meaning it draws upon or embodies.

Studies of legal language offer inspiration here. A number of anthropologists have suggested that laws are practices or techniques of knowledge, and that these are, above all, grounded in its language (Mertz 1994; Mundy 2002: xxiv). Law has technologies for producing truth and defining identity; legal forms, concepts, and practices take on a force of their own, made explicit in writing and documents, and producing a form of truth, which can provide the basis for political and ethical reflection or intervention (Riles 2004; Merry 2006a: 108). As Greenhouse (2008: 82) observes, the production of legal truth is a matter of rendering the specific as general. These are important insights, on which this book seeks to build. As other anthropologists have noted, laws create distinct categories of phenomena, particularly types or attributes of persons and property, and they serve to define relations between states and individuals (Coombe 1998; Mundy 2002; Pottage and Mundy 2004). In this way, laws constitute society, they do not merely regulate or control it. More than that, law provides a language for expressing what is right and just. It is by encapsulating values that transcend power and politics that it can serve both to legitimate power and to resist or control it.

The anthropology of law can do more than contribute to the understanding of local dynamics, contexts, and indigenous claims, or conversely wider issues of power, domination, and resistance; and it can do more than recognize the fact of pluralism. By attending to its language and exploring the significance and attraction of what is distinctly legalistic, we can begin to answer questions about the multiple roles law plays in a complex world and what is distinctive about it as a social form.

LEGALISM

Within these dynamics and empirical examples, I suggest, a certain style of thought and argument characterizes what we might regard as distinctly legal forms and processes. Legalism, as a way of describing and prescribing human conduct in terms of categories, generalizations, and rules, is a recurrent, albeit not universal, social form. It is apparent, for example, in the legal categories discussed by Strathern (2004) in her study of personhood in Papua New Guinea. She notes the abstract and general nature of law, contrasting this with the particularistic and relational in the lived reality to which it is applied. The result, she suggests, is that laws tend to 'flatten out' reality. Many anthropologists have noted the tensions that arise when law meets life (Santos 1987). Conley (2008), for example, notes that law demands and produces coherent and consistent forms of personal identity, while individuals' own sense of self may be more fragmentary and inconsistent. This could be regarded as an essential characteristic of law: legal rules and categories describe the world in terms of general, often abstract, concepts— vendor and purchaser, husband and wife, resident and immigrant. It simplifies, specifies, categorizes, and clarifies, but it also constitutes social phenomena and relationships. Legal categories imply social obligations, they reflect moral assumptions and set up the possibility for new, often complex, relationships, such as marriages and mortgages.

This legalism is not the same as the implicit rules for conduct that are exemplified in behavioural regularities. It involves the explicit formulation of rules and categories; and these set standards for behaviour and provide discursive resources that can be used for justification and argument about right and wrong. Although some rules may be enforced, law is about more than regulation: legalistic thought classifies and organizes, providing a basis for a type of argument that legal philosophers call 'practical reasoning'.

Legalism characterizes many forms of rule-based organization, not all of which we would call 'law'. We are more likely to apply the term 'law' to rules and categories that claim to create order and promote justice. There is an idealistic element in many forms of law, illustrated by numerous examples in later chapters. Unlike the rules of rowing or cricket, laws tend to stand apart from practice, with a certain autonomy from their context, evoking an order that outlasts the particular moment (Dresch 2012: 15). But this moral or religious commitment, as it often is, can also lead to a mistrust of legalism and criticism of the legal form. A tension between the two recurs, and is exemplified in the studies discussed in subsequent chapters.

The concept of legalism, I would suggest, helps us to identify common threads amongst the phenomena within the more general and contested category of law. It also allows us to think beyond the model of state law without letting our analytical categories expand to encompass all forms of normative and social order. And we need to look beyond the state, as well as back in history, to take account of the full range of social forms that can be called laws.

Law and history

In all these cases a clear understanding of what might differentiate the legal or legalistic from the non-legal can sharpen the analysis and bring into focus the continuities, as well as the discontinuities, across social forms and practices, geographical distance, and time. It is useful, for example, to recognize that legal technologies and language are not just recent or western phenomena. There is much to be gained by delving into legal history: laws have had international reach for millennia and the legal landscape has often been complex. Historical, as much as contemporary, examples can help us question the paradigm of state law, which equates law with sovereignty, assumes a world divided neatly into jurisdictions, and presents law as the foundation of regularity and order. There were laws and legal phenomena before the rise of the nation state, that is ways of thinking about and organizing societies that are still visible in texts—both legal codes and writing about law. This includes realms of legal activity associated with religion, especially in the Islamic world, or claiming ancient historical origins, notably the English common law. An anthropology of law that employs a comparative historical perspective can suggest new paradigms and possibilities for analysis: the appeal of the legal form, the idealistic elements—the ways in which law tends to invoke a higher order—the practical efficacy of law without enforcement, and legal borrowing.

Textual laws have rarely been at the heart of anthropological studies, and social scientists have almost never brought them into their comparisons. As Abel (1995) noted, they have tended to avoid rules and texts altogether. This may be inevitable when the subject is a non-literate society, but large parts of the Chinese, Indic, and Islamic, not to mention the Christian, worlds have created, used, and reproduced legal texts for centuries, ranging from esoteric religious tracts to village constitutions, all important in different ways to those that made or used them. Later in the book I draw upon a number of fine analyses of legalistic texts and thought undertaken by historians and orientalist scholars. Such laws constitute an important set of resources through which people make sense of their worlds, and for the anthropologist they provide rich material with which to explore the nature of law.

LEGAL THEORY

If the anthropologist is to explore the nature of law, to what extent is this project different from that of the analytical philosopher?[5] Lacey (2000: 18–19) suggests that the contributions of sociology and philosophy to the task of theorizing the law are not obviously very different, and that what distinguishes the former is not so much its methodology as a general commitment to understanding law as a social phenomenon. As Galligan puts it, legal theory seeks to investigate a general framework of legal thought, including both common and essential features of legal systems (2010: 978); however, 'legal theory, while philosophical in method, still has as its subject a social phenomenon, created and practised for social ends', so it must have at least a footing in social reality (2010: 991).

The academic field of legal theory or jurisprudence is characterized by debates and divisions, as much over the nature of the project as over the detail of the resulting theories. There are those based upon empirical examples, while others take the form of abstract conceptual analysis; some theories aim to describe, others to build an ideal model; but a number of distinctions can usefully be drawn amongst them.

Firstly, there are theorists who recognize that law is essentially an ordinary language concept. As Lamond (2001: 38) says, law is a concept through which we understand aspects of our own and others' societies:

A philosophical account of the nature of law involves an attempt to draw out from these phenomena a systematic and structured conception... identifying its key features and the particular roles which it plays within social life. This account is quite self-consciously an exploration of *our* understanding of law, anchored in our experience of the legal systems we inhabit.

This is essentially the approach adopted by 'positivist' theorists Hart and Raz, albeit not so explicitly. In his Preface to *The*

---

[5] Legal theory is now the term normally used for what used to be called jurisprudence. A distinction can be made between legal theory and philosophy, the latter being a narrower field, while the former can encompass theory from other disciplines, such as sociology or political science (Galligan 2010: 977).

Concept of Law (1994: vi), for example, Hart describes his book as 'an essay in descriptive sociology', involving inquiry into the meanings of words and standard uses of relevant expressions. The book is simultaneously, he says, a work of analytical jurisprudence, clarifying the general framework of legal thought. The implication is that description of usage is the foundation for philosophical analysis. Raz (1998) also emphasizes the ordinary-language analysis of concepts. He draws a distinction between having a concept, in the sense of knowing how to use the word (like 'law') correctly, and having a thorough knowledge of the thing it is a concept of (that it, understanding what law is). To be able to explain what law is, then, means demonstrating the connections between law and other phenomena (1998: 256–57). This distinction mirrors that between what Wittgenstein calls language games, knowing how to use a concept appropriately, and the task of explaining or shedding light upon its nature. The former must be the starting point for any anthropological (or other) analysis of law, although the aim is to elucidate a concept that can properly be applied cross-culturally.[6]

Other theorists may not be so explicit about the assumptions they make, but their accounts are inevitably based upon core elements of law found in the familiar realms of western legal systems. As Finnis (1980: 4) notes in his review of legal philosophy, most theorists build upon what they assert to be common conceptions or understandings. Even the author of more normative theory, Ronald Dworkin (1986: 92), appeals to a 'pre-interpretive identification' of the domain of law, in this case legal practices and institutions. This has to be so: any analysis must start with ordinary language concepts.

---

[6] As Raz points out elsewhere (1996: 5; 2009: 36), to understand other societies we must master their concepts, but we must also be able to relate them to our own, and this means possessing concepts that can be applied across the divide between us and them. He is surprisingly dismissive of the value of ordinary language philosophy, however: 'by and large as long as in one's deliberations on the nature of law and its central institutions one uses language without mistake there is little that the philosophy of language can do to advance one's understanding' (1998: 254). This may be true, but it is not always so easy to use language without mistake. Many anthropologists have over-extended the use of the term 'law' in a way that confuses categories of phenomena that ought to be kept analytically distinct. As Raz (2009: 24), himself, says, people can make mistakes about concepts.

The project of description and analysis undertaken by Hart and Raz, among others, can, however, be contrasted with more normative projects. Dworkin, for example, asserts that law is an 'interpretive concept', 'our law consists in the best justification of our legal practices as a whole...it consists in the narrative story that makes of these practices the best they can be' (1986: vii). As he says, his account 'asks a judge deciding a common law case...to think of himself as an author in the chain of common law' (1986: 238). This is a normative account, asking not about what law is as a social form, but how it ought to be, as the practice of judges in the common law world. Finnis (1980) also regards the task of the legal philosopher as evaluative in a moral sense, not just descriptive: 'no theorist can give a theoretical description and analysis of social facts without also participating in the work of evaluation, of understanding what is really good for human persons, and what is really required by practical reasonableness' (1980: 3). The purpose of legal theory is, then, 'to assist the practical reflections of those concerned to act' (1980: 18). As Waldron says neatly, 'a natural lawyer regards the concept of law as a sort of moral aspiration and not merely a descriptive concept of social science' (1990: 35).[7] As Galligan puts it (2007: 37), Dworkin and Finnis, along with Rawls (1971) and Habermas (1996), share the aim of understanding law, but add the further aim of positioning law in a moral context, of wishing to relate it to the wider principles and purposes of human association. This is not the anthropological project.

One way of conceptualizing the difference in these approaches is by reference to the distinction, found in many European languages, between *la loi* and *le droit*, or *das Gesetz* and *das Recht*. *Le droit*, like *das Recht*, carries the sense of 'right' or 'just', that is law in the sense of human right. Simply as a philosophical or semantic matter, however, law is not a normative concept like justice: there may be different ideas among people of what is just—disagreements about the social justice of redistributive taxation, for example—but to describe something as just is to

---

[7] Waldron's project is often explicitly normative, for example his construction of an ideal model of legislation (1995), yet it is always rooted firmly in empirical and historical examples.

ascribe a moral quality to it: the idea of immoral justice is an oxymoron. The same cannot be said for law: it makes perfect sense to criticize a law—a provision for detention without charge, for example, or a new taxation measure—as being unjust or contrary to moral principles. As Hart puts it, a narrower conception of law, one that regards it as essentially moral, would exclude abhorrent laws, but 'would lead us to exclude certain rules even though they exhibit all the other complex character- istics of law'. This would split, in a confusing way, our effort to understand both the development and potentialities of law (1994: 209–10). Law frequently promises justice or claims moral or other authority—as Raz (2009: 1–4) says, 'legal discourse is moral discourse', it claims to have reconciled power and morality—but this aspiration is an empirical matter, an aspect of the laws or the claims of the law-makers that can be observed as social forms.

Thirdly, theorists vary in the extent to which they refer to and employ empirical examples: Lacey (2000: 19) maintains that we cannot understand law as a sphere of meaning independently of the socio-historical context in which it exists. By contrast, analysis of the philosophical foundations of law, concerned primarily with the moral coherence of particular doctrines, represents law as founded—actually or ideally—on a metaphysics (Lacey 2000: 21). Her own work considers the history of philosophical ideas about legal personality in the context of the historical development of the criminal law, in order to contribute to a contemporary theo- retical debate on corporate criminal liability. This requires paying close attention to the interaction of legal conceptions and social factors (2000: 38). Historians can also use their material to critique legal theory, for example, the model of legal authority accord- ing to which legislation, as a means of political domination, is authoritative. Jansen (2010: 138) discusses examples ranging from the Roman world up to the commercial codes of the twentieth century in order to question the idea that the authority of private law is essentially based upon a legislator's political will.

Tamanaha (2001) and Twining (2009) are notable among legal theorists for embracing a range of empirical examples, extending far beyond the western world and including many studies by anthropologists. The result, however, is that their subject matter, like the concept of legal pluralism, expands to encompass an extensive range of phenomena, raising the classic issue of where we stop talking of law and start describing social life (Merry 1988: 878–79). Tamanaha is explicit in his conclusion that we should abandon law as a defining category and concentrate, instead, on normative pluralism. In this book I take a different view, arguing that we can consider a wide range of empirical examples without letting go of the concept of law. I return to these debates when considering legal pluralism in chapter two.

Other legal theorists, by contrast, largely ignore empirical studies. Hart did not consider anthropological examples, for instance, even in his discussion of primary rules in 'simple societies'. His rule-centred account has even been criticized on the basis that it does not fit the reality of the English common law. As Simpson puts it, the common law is not so much a system of rules as a system of customary law, that is, a body of traditional ideas received by experts (2011: 361–62). Postema (2002) uses seventeenth-century jurisprudence in a similar way, to critique Hart's, along with other positivists', accounts. He describes the common law as 'a practice of common, practical reasoning', more than a set of norms, prescriptions or propositions of law (2002: 602). Honoré (1977), too, examines 'real laws', that is, examples of UK legislation and common law doctrine, to critique Hart's account of rules.

Finally, much legal theory seeks out the essential or common features of law (Galligan 2010: 978). Recognizing the inde-terminacy of our ordinary language concept, Hart denies the possibility of coming up with anything so precise as a definition of 'law', but says that the diverse range of cases to which we apply the term 'law' can be linked, even if only indirectly, to a central case (1994: 81, 199). It is possible, he suggests, to isolate and characterize a central set of elements, building upon the paradigmatic case of a 'municipal legal system', at the heart of which is the idea of a rule (1994: 16–17, 80). This leads him to a model of law characterized by a structure of primary rules of obligation and secondary rules of definition, which determine how we can recognize, interpret, and change the primary rules. Raz also places the 'typical case' at the heart of his analysis, albeit recognizing that its general traits may not be found in all exam-ples (1975: 150). He is cautious about how definitively a concept like law can be explained (1998: 266): theoretical explanations, he says, are incomplete; they try to reduce the vagueness in a concept as we find it in the more chaotic and fluctuating social life of the linguistic community, but this can only be limited, or the explanation will not be true to the concept explained. 'A correct account of the nature of law will be more or less vague in the same way as the concept of law is vague' (1998: 272).

Finnis is more positive about the possibility of the central case:

one's descriptive explanation of the central case should be as conceptually rich and complex as is required to answer all appropriate questions about those central cases. And then one's account of the other instances can trace the network of similarities and differences, the analogies and disanalogies, for example, of form, function or content, between them and the central cases. In this way, one uncovers the 'principle or rationale' on which the general term ('constitution', 'feud', 'law'...) is extended from the central to the more or less borderline cases, from its focal to its secondary meanings (1980: 11).

Aristotle's idea of 'focal meaning', he says, corresponds to Weber's 'ideal-type' or 'conceptual construct' (Gedankenbild) (1980: 9).

The idea that there can be a single central case to which all others are more or less peripheral, must be treated with caution, however. How are we to decide what is properly regarded as central or common for the purpose of building a theory? As Lamond asks, is it not more plausible to suggest that different instances of law are connected partly through overlapping features and that they display nothing more than a family resemblance to our own practice, so that the search for 'essential' features is a will-o'-the-wisp? (2001: 37). Weber's ideal type is somewhat different from the central case. He allowed that a great many ideal models could be constructed, each claiming to represent a single concept, and an ideal type is not an ethical imperative or a model of what 'ought' to exist; it is, rather, an 'objectively possible' model (1949: 91–92).

An ideal type may suggest connections and patterns that help to explain empirical examples and they are often useful in description. However, Weber did not expect such models to mirror the world exactly (1949: 90). Finnis proposes that the central case of law must involve an assessment of what is important and significant and that this is to be assessed by asking what is considered

as such by those whose concerns, decisions, and activities create
or constitute the subject matter (1980: 12). But how are we to
assess importance and significance in the case of foreign examples?
The danger is that we impose a model rooted in the values
of one particular culture onto a term that we need to use for
cross-cultural comparison. They should not be used like a car-
penter's templates, as Parkin (2000: 92) puts it, to copy precise
outlines onto new material; a model should, rather, describe
an arc of actions, movements, words, and sentiments, none of
which is likely to be exactly reproduced.[8]

Raz, for example, bases his account on the 'common conception
of law prevalent in our society' that it is 'normative, institutionalized and coercive' (1970: 3, 216). Elsewhere he suggests that 'a court
in a country with law but which does not think of it as such
will be concerned to decide cases in accordance with the rules of
the system, which are in fact rules of law' (1998: 280).[9] Looking
beyond western examples, however, it quickly becomes apparent that this emphasis on institutions does not capture what we
think of as ancient Indian or even Islamic law, let alone numerous more local examples. An ideal type needs to be used by way
of analogy or example; it is illustrative, not determinative, and
empirical research can often nuance the model suggested by an
ideal type, or even be the basis for a wholly new one.

The anthropological project can, therefore, be regarded as a form
of legal theorizing, but a particular one: it takes as its starting point
the ordinary language concept; it is based upon consideration of
empirical examples; it aims to describe, rather than to idealize; and
it finds and employs suitable concepts and ideas in order to identify and describe overlapping features, without assuming that any
are essential or that it is possible to construct a central case. If we
take into account the empirical work of historians, classicists, and
orientalists, as well as anthropologists, and their studies of what

[8] In this light we must also be cautious about Galligan's (2007: 6) recommen-
dation that we take analytical jurisprudence as a starting point for analysing law
in society. This risks imposing a paradigmatic model of law on empirical data to
which it may not appropriately be applied.

[9] In later writing his characterization of this conception is rather more
nuanced. He still places institutions at the forefront of his description, but he also
recognizes that 'law confronts its subjects as a system of reasons' (2009: 8).

they refer to as 'law', as I do throughout the later chapters of this book, we find overlapping features; but these are matters of form more than function; they point to legalism, more than to institutions or regulation. Legalism is a type of thought, rather than a mechanism for enacting the commands of a ruler, resolving disputes, or promoting regular and predictable behaviour. Laws may do all of these things, in particular cases, but it is a distinctive type of thought that, I suggest, creates a sense of resemblance amongst different examples.

Legal theory can shed light upon this type of thought. Theorists have, over the centuries, had an impact upon what we think law is, indirectly shaping our ordinary language use of the concept. As Lamond (2001: 37) says, the particular form that law takes in our culture is to some degree the product of our beliefs about it and our attitudes toward it. Lacey (2000: 18) suggests that sociologists must 'learn the rules' of legal theory, at least to some extent, if they are to understand law as a social phenomenon. This, she says, includes such matters as the distinct normativity of law, its method of reasoning, and its relatively autonomous character (2000: 39). Anthropologist Annelise Riles (2004) also argues that we should make the character and work of legal theory a subject of ethnographic study. The examples discussed in subsequent chapters bear out the importance of these features: it becomes apparent that we must take seriously norms and doctrines that inspire commitment, not limiting ourselves to practices of conflict resolution, and that law has a distinct style of reasoning; there is also a recurrent sense that law is autonomous, set apart from the undifferentiated realm of social norms. The insights of legal theorists can help the anthropologist to reflect upon the ambit and distinctive nature of legalistic thought.

AN ANTHROPOLOGY OF LAW

For all that the concept of law is broad and indeterminate, made up of examples bearing little more than a family resemblance to one another, and despite the fact that it cannot be translated exactly into many other languages, as a concept it is important. An anthropology of law must examine law as a social form, along with the assumptions and ideas that give it meaning. This means taking seriously the whole range of social phenomena we can properly label as law, in all their variety and inconsistency, while seeking out the patterns, commonalities, and connections amongst them. The task is to describe rather than prescribe, seeking common features and the concepts that will capture them in the most straightforward way. Like some legal philosophers, then, we describe in order to analyse, but the anthropologist's project is generally broader, taking into account what is different and unfamiliar. We produce accounts that are less philosophically tidy, but detailed and nuanced, and these, in turn, enrich the empirical material available to philosophers of law.

We must avoid the assumptions, commonly made by those who confine their attention to familiar examples, that law is a determinant of conduct, that it needs the guarantee of a state or ruler, that it comprises institutions or processes of conflict resolution. The anthropologist must start with the ways in which the concept is used in ordinary language, but seek marginal and peripheral examples to test its boundaries and highlight overlooked features, connections, and absences. Equally, we must not let the concept expand to encompass all forms of normative and social order, court processes and conflict resolution, thereby losing all analytical purchase.

It is useful, I would suggest, to focus more closely on the legal amidst the broad range of topics now studied by legal anthropologists. This means examining texts as well as social practices, form as well as function. It also means looking to the great legal systems for examples of sophisticated legal thought. Taking seriously the nature of law, and the range of examples to which we properly apply the term, leads to a focus on legal thought and the use of generalizing rules and abstract categories, that is legalism. The following chapters of this book discuss empirical studies by historians, classicists, and orientalists, as well as anthropologists, in order to illustrate how this can be done.

In chapter two I consider themes in the literature on legal anthropology. They question the claims commonly made on behalf of state law that it guarantees social order. However, they also illustrate the dangers of allowing the concept to over-expand. In chapter three I discuss the possibility of considering law as meaning and the apparent alternative of considering law as an aspect of power, and their limitations. The apparent dichotomy between the two, calls for a different approach. I then turn to examples of archaic legal codes to introduce another way of thinking about law, codes that invoke order and invite commitment in and of themselves. This sets the scene for the remainder of the book. In chapters four and five I move to the great legal systems of the Hindu, Roman, Islamic, and Chinese worlds, using case studies by historians and orientalists to consider the scholarly and intellectual nature of law. In chapter six, which might be regarded as the heart of the book, I turn to legalism, that is, to the type of thought that employs general rules and abstract categories, and the distinctive nature of the legal reasoning that this produces. As well as considering developments in post-Roman Europe, chapters six and seven move to more marginal and small-scale societies, discussing examples of village and tribal codes, often produced on the peripheries of the great legal systems, and their connections with different forms of community. Chapter eight turns to relations between rulers, states, and the law, discussing human rights and international laws.

Throughout the book comparisons are drawn widely across geography and time, highlighting common themes and tensions, and illustrating the different forms that laws can take. Alongside the recurrent, albeit far from universal, tendency to think, argue, prescribe, and describe the world in legalistic ways, an element of idealism, the evocation of divinity or promise of justice, recurs within the examples. This, in turn, often provokes mistrust of the legal form, and a tension between what might be called legalism and idealism seems to mark many of the social forms we think of as law. These are the themes to which I return in the conclusion.

2

ORDER, DISPUTES, AND LEGAL PLURALISM

The maintenance of order and resolution of disputes have been recurrent themes for legal anthropologists. They have asked how societies maintain order without the apparatus of a legal system, courts, and even governments, successfully questioning common assumptions about the necessity for and functions of law. However, there has been a tendency within this scholarship to allow the concept of law to expand beyond its normal usage, drawing our attention away from what is distinctive about legal, as opposed to other forms of social organization and conflict resolution. In this chapter I examine these issues in some detail, along with some of the social and political implications of allowing the concept of law to over-extend.

LAW AND SOCIAL ORDER

Malinowski, widely regarded as one of the pioneers of ethnographic methodology and, hence, of modern social anthropology, was among the first to demonstrate that centralized government and laws are not necessary to the functioning of a well-ordered society. His short book on law, *Crime and Custom in Savage Society* (1926), describes the 'mutual obligations and duties' that structure the fishing activities of the Trobriand islanders of the South Pacific. A well developed system of obligations, he says, creates 'law, order and definite privileges', which function in the absence of authority, government, and punishments (1926: 21). In the following decades numerous anthropological studies of small-scale, relatively egalitarian societies without rulers decisively undermined the idea, promoted by rulers and their apologists from Justinian and Hobbes to contemporary governments, that social order is only conceivable in the context of some form of centralized government. Often conducted amongst the stateless societies of Africa, such studies also questioned the assumption that conflict and violence inevitably represent a breakdown in social order.

In a classic of legal anthropology, *Order and Dispute* (1979), Simon Roberts reviews this scholarship and demonstrates the variety not just in the social structures and processes that constitute social order but also in attitudes to peace, violence, and disorder found in different societies around the world.[1] As Roberts points out, some societies explain conflict and disorder in terms of cosmological disturbance or activities in the realm of the spirits, while in other cases it is accepted as being inherent in their social structures; in some societies the slightest conflict is regarded as a dangerous matter, while in others, typically the feuding societies of east Africa and the Middle East, a certain type of violence is admired and encouraged; even in the West conflict lies near the heart of our legal system, 'for the adversary process is sublimated combat' (Barkun 1968: 36).

Famous among studies of feuding is Evans-Pritchard's (1940) *The Nuer*, influential in the development of social anthropology. In this work he describes relations among the tribes of Southern Sudan, including their segmentary lineage structures whereby the members of a tribe claimed descent from a common ancestor, but divided into smaller segments, descended from closer forebears. Their feuding followed a logic of group loyalty, which obliged members of one segment to combine to take revenge for the aggression of another. The result was a political system that formed a sort of equilibrium between opposed tendencies towards fission and fusion; 'the blood feud may be regarded as a structural movement between political segments by which the form of the Nuer political system...is maintained' (1940: 158). As Roberts puts it, such studies undermine 'a long-standing assumption that order is only conceivable if there are strong men in positions of authority ready to tell others what to do' (1983: 10).[2] 'It is not the fault of anthropologists', he remarks, 'if the lessons

---

[1] He argues that a certain minimum level of regularity and predictability is surely necessary for a society to exist; on the other hand, without any form of conflict or tension, as Georg Simmel long ago pointed out, 'an absolutely centripetal and harmonious group...not only is empirically unreal, it could show no real life process' ([1908] 1955: 15).

[2] Even some anthropologists, such as Pospisil (1958), essentially adopted this position. Roberts elsewhere undertakes a thorough and critical assessment of Pospisil's work and its place within the anthropology of law (2005: 7–11).

of these studies, clear as they are, have yet to be absorbed by some legal and political theorists' (1983: 5).

The idea that law is something that needs to be imposed upon society can be traced back to the work of Hobbes in the seventeenth century. His *Leviathan* (of 1651) famously posits the need for a 'common power' or commonwealth, that is a government, in order to make law and thereby produce justice, equity, modesty, mercy, and property relations (1909: ch 17). In his later *Dialogue* he argues forcefully that law can only originate in a sovereign, against earlier theorists such as Coke and Blackstone who maintained that law originated in ancient tradition or morality (Hobbes 1971). It was this view of law as 'the commands of the sovereign' that was promoted by legal theorist, John Austin, in the mid-nineteenth century, and followed by Hans Kelsen with considerable influence on subsequent legal theory, until largely undermined by H.L.A. Hart in 1961. Meanwhile, even if not unchallenged, this view has captured the imagination of legal scholars and political scientists, not to mention politicians and policy-makers, who may, of course, have their own reasons for promoting the idea that government and guaranteed law is essential to the smooth running of modern society.

Behind this model of society is the idea that human beings are by nature asocial and inclined to a state of conflict (Hobbes's 'Warre') unless controlled and socialized by government. Anthropological examples have challenged this basic idea. Strathern (1985), for example, mounts an explicit critique of the idea that law is essentially a matter of social control (1985: 111).[3] This model, she suggests, is often taken for granted in our ideas about the social functions of law. As she puts it, the 'self-description of law...upholds the notion that order is the proper state of society, and society itself is imposed upon individuals who are by natural propensity asocial beings' (1985: 115). The corollary of this assumption is that the outcome of judicial or other conflict resolution processes is taken to be the reimposition of order and exercise of control (1985: 112–16). Law, on this model, is needed by society in

---

[3] Hobbes's legacy is apparent in the works of her referents (Black 1976; Burman and Harrell-Bond 1979).

order to regulate disorderly behaviour, while violence is read as indicating the breakdown of social order.

To counter these assumptions Strathern (1985) describes the conflictual social relations and public processes of conflict resolution undertaken by the Hageners, one of the many distinct groups that inhabit the island of Papua New Guinea. As she presents their ideas and practices, 'dispute settlement procedures comprise a special type of social activity... but they do not mark themselves off as regulating or overriding behaviour considered in some sense anti-social or non-social in nature' (1985: 118). Among the Hageners, relations between groups necessarily involve elements of conflict and different groups normally have opposed interests, so that it is not always possible to resolve conflict. Certain forms of violence are thus taken to be part of the normal flow of social relations, rather than representing a break-down of order. Dispute settlement is, rather, 'a form of public, collective activity which mobilises support and contributes towards a definition of inter-group relations predicated on reciprocity' (1985: 124).

Strathern is explicit about the anthropological project and the dangers of imposing familiar models, without reflection, upon other societies:

> while we may use problems of our own to explore those of other peoples, it often turns out a totemic illusion to 'discover' those problems within the symbolic and ideational systems of those we study.... [for example] when we juxtapose the formal law of our society against the informal legal procedures of other societies, and thus discover a realm of social control which apparently operates according to principles and ideas not dissimilar to extra-judicial processes in our own (1985: 116–17).

Simon Harrison (1993), also drawing upon fieldwork in Papua New Guinea, explicitly calls into question the model constructed by anthropologist Marshall Sahlins (1968, 1972), ultimately derived from Hobbes, that conflicts are due to the absence of centralized power. The Avatip, as Harrison describes, 'have a long history of belligerence against their neighbours', formerly practising competitive headhunting. Their male initiation cult, even decades after the ending of these practices, 'is elaborately preoccupied with warmaking and with fostering aggression in men' (1993: 27). An ability to kill has to be imparted by magic and ritual and turns men into a dangerous menace to all other people, including their own families. However, this type of violence is not considered to be pathological, rather it is a necessary achievement for young men. He suggests that such violence is regarded as important for the Avatip in order to achieve a ritual hierarchy and a political identity for their community, free from the normative claims of outsiders (1989: 595). As he describes it, and not dissimilar to the Hageners, there is an assumption of peaceful sociality; a web of relations links communities with indissoluble ties of kinship and clanship, which need to be overcome by warfare. The problem for the Avatip is how to limit this sociality, rather than how to achieve it. Violence and its effects are still a problem, 'a threat to their physical existence but not apparently to their conceptions of the social' (1989: 584).

Lest these latter examples, which should make us question functional models of law, seem peripheral, we can turn to the most populous nation on earth, China. Stephens's (1992) study of court use in the early twentieth century contains a reflection on the different ideas about order, conflict, and dispute resolution within indigenous Chinese society, which differ radically from those of the western world. He found 'fundamental divergences in the theoretical and philosophical concepts of the nature and purposes of the processes of dispute resolution and the maintenance of order in society' (1992: 4). Chinese ideas, as he characterizes them, contrast with the western view of order as a deliberate achievement of society, brought about, managed, and controlled in predetermined forms according to the conscious will of a transcendent power. The Chinese have an idea that harmony, the antithesis of chaos, arises naturally in a hierarchical universe. While, then, western court proceedings involve adjudication between opposing claims, presented in terms of rights and duties, with the aim being the active enforcement of individual rights, Chinese processes are conceived in terms of instruction and punishment. The aim is to maintain the cohesion of the group, which the nation's subjects ought to pursue individually, by settling their disputes amongst themselves. It is, therefore, appropriate to discipline those who bring their disputes to the courts. According to Chinese theoretical ideas, as he describes them, honesty and morals should guide human conduct and individuals need to be disciplined if they act inappropriately, given their place in the overall hierarchy.

As Bourgon (2011: 173) also asserts, concepts of liberty and rights have no equivalent in the Chinese tradition, which is, rather, centred on ties of subordination. Stephens is not, here, considering China's elaborate, imperial, penal codes, which I describe in chapter five; it is not that China had no laws. His focus is, rather, on court procedures, which do not seek to balance rights and duties according to predetermined codes and rules of obligation (1992: 4–5).[4]

Such examples raise questions which challenge theoretical models of law centred upon its functions. Most obviously, this includes the 'positivist' theories of Austin and Kelsen, but also later work, including that of Raz, with a functionalist emphasis on judicial institutions. If it is not necessary, and not seen to be necessary, for social order to be imposed through law, then on what basis can we assume that institutions are necessary sources of law? Is it right to regard the existence of duty-imposing rules as of the essence, as Hart suggests (1994: ch 5)? Should we, rather question the legislators' claims that laws are necessary and appropriate for the control of deviant behaviour in modern society?

Law as social order

In the introduction I suggested that law and legalistic thought can be expressive, evoking a moral world as much as providing rules to be imposed. Within legal anthropology an implicitly functionalist model has, however, enjoyed a long history. Malinowski's conclusion from his study of Trobriand society was that if a functioning system of mutual obligations and duties does not need to be imposed upon society through a body of rules enforced by an independent authority, then law must be found in other comparable obligations. Instead of questioning the role and function of law, he extended his definition of what law is. The minimum definition of law as 'the body of rules enforced by an authority independent of personal ties', is too narrow, he says, because there may be other compulsory obligations in society. The sorts of rules and obligations he describes as 'legal' involve what we might call economic sanctions

---

[4] Stephens's study has been criticized for suggesting that China had no law (Dicks 1995; Nader 2009: 63), disregarding his account of disciplinary order (as to which see Hurlock's (1993) approving comments). However, both this criticism and Stephens's disregard of the penal codes tacitly assume that law, to be law, must be evident in the resolution of conflict and court processes.

and social pressure to reciprocate. Law, he says, consists of any 'rules conceived and acted upon as binding obligations' (1926: 15). Later, he defines 'civil law' as, 'the positive law governing all tribal life [which] consists of a body of binding obligations, regarded as right by one party and acknowledged as a duty by the other, kept in force by a specific mechanism of reciprocity and publicly inherent in the structure of society' (1926: 58).

In the opening chapter of his book Malinowski explains that one of his aims is to contradict the assumptions, then common, that primitive people 'slavishly' and 'blindly' follow their customs. His object is to demonstrate that there is some binding mechanism among the Trobriand islanders, backed up by real motives, interests, and complex sentiments (1926: 12). He is clearly concerned to attribute rationality and a legal order to the islanders and their society, and thereby to undermine the stereotype of irrational savages. It is not surprising that Malinowski should have identified the maintenance of social order and the existence of binding social norms as the essence of law. As Chanock (1985: 219) asserts, it was from the British tradition of jurisprudence, which conflated questions of law and order, that legal anthropologists derived their ideas about what law was and what it did; Malinowski, himself, declared that 'law ought to be defined by function and not by form' (1934: lxiii).

This attitude was also encouraged by the current sociological tradition. As Roberts (1983: 3) puts it, the straightforward functionalist character of Malinowski's writing, like that of many of his contemporaries, involved a view of order which owed much to Durkheim. Social life was seen as a matter of compliance with rules: normal behaviour was rule-governed behaviour. In *The Division of Labour in* Society, first published in 1893, Durkheim had described law as 'the visible symbol of social solidarity' or as 'a mirror of social life' (1984: 24–25). The role of law was to ensure respect for beliefs, traditions, and collective practices (1984: 42). The implication was that in a society without centralized government social solidarity was provided by social norms, and these constituted its law.[5] Although Durkheim's writings on

---

[5] In his later writings Durkheim gives a more subtle account of the intertwining of the legal, moral, and political aspects of society, and the nature and role of the

law are scattered, the view that traces law back to shared social norms, as opposed to the institutions of government, came to have a powerful influence on legal and political anthropology, and continues to do so today. When combined with the view that social order must be achieved through the imposition of law, it leads naturally to the idea that every society must have its own law, discoverable by the anthropologist in its social norms and the processes by which conflict is resolved. Moore (2005: 1), for example, one of the most important legal anthropologists of the late twentieth century, defines law as 'the source of organized social order' or the 'processes of establishing order'. The sociologist John Griffiths (2006) similarly asserts that social control is the proper subject of study of a sociology of law. This would attribute law or 'law-like activities', in some shape or form, to any society.

But why should legal anthropologists attribute law to all the societies they study? Surely we should be able to distinguish different types of social norms and obligations and separate out what is law-like or legalistic, without labelling them all as 'law'.

Law as conflict resolution

A similar tendency for anthropologists to extend the category of law is found in the works of those who turned their attention to conflict resolution. Notable amongst these are Max Gluckman's detailed studies on the Barotse of what is now Zambia, then under British colonial rule. His ethnographic accounts, most importantly *The Judicial Process amongst the Barotse* (1955), describe the court processes of the Lozi, the models their judges were working with, how they took into account contextual factors, and the place of events and participants within the wider flow of social life. This provides a rich account of dispute resolution and its role within the social order, but it is apparent that the Lozi rarely appealed to law or laws, in the form of explicitly stated rules. The proceedings he describes were characterized more by notions of right and justice. Mirroring Lozi linguistic usage, Gluckman explains that he uses the word 'law' to describe the whole reservoir

state. The emphasis shifts to law as an expression of ideals, something that has moral meaning, as a repository of aspirations (Cotterrell 1999: 16).

of rules upon which the judges draw for their decisions, including regulations, orders, customs, traditional usages, matters, and habits (1955: 164). It is apparent, however, that the Lozi operated with a notion of justice and fairness, that is, law in the sense of *le droit*, more than by applying explicit rules, law in the sense of *les lois*.

The 1950s to 1980s saw numerous studies of conflict resolution, which are all revealing, in their own ways, of the societies they describe (Moore 2001). Gulliver (1963), for example, draws a useful distinction between adjudication and mediation,[6] and Keebet von Benda-Beckmann's (1981) study of 'forum-shopping' employed a useful phrase to describe the strategic way in which individuals in many situations can, and do, choose between different court and judicial processes. As Comaroff and Roberts (1981) remark, however, the writings of these scholars mostly approach conflict resolution as a social process, and focus on the negotiation of individual rights and interests, rather than on law-dominated judicial activities. Anthropological attention has subsequently turned to the experience and use of state laws and courts (Merry 1986, 1990; Harrington and Merry 1988; Greenhouse et al. 1994), including the experiences of indigenous people (Sierra 1995; Speed and Collier 2000; Richland 2008). The focus has often been on litigants' interests and strategies and struggles over property (Moore 2005: 3), but what does this focus on the individual tell us about the law, itself? What is it that they have to contend with when they face the law?

Like many other anthropologists, rather than concluding that disputes may be resolved without recourse to laws, Gluckman suggested that the notion of law encompasses all that is achieved by such processes and the resources they draw upon. Such studies give the impression that the legal realm can be generally identified by reference to practices of conflict resolution. But is it necessary, or useful, to describe all process of conflict resolution as 'legal'? Evans-Pritchard (1940: 162) was equivocal about applying the term to Nuer mediation processes, whereby the parties to a feud would submit to mediation by a 'leopard-skin

---

[6] As Roberts (1983: 17) says, anthropological examples challenge the thesis of Maine (1883: 170), widely held by others, that there may be a general shift from arbitration to adjudication.

chief' and eventually might accept appropriate compensation as a termination of hostilities.⁷ As Greenhouse (1986: 29) describes, the 'case method' was thought to be the most feasible means of discovering the rules, both literally and figuratively, that govern a population. However, the achievement of this method, she says, is primarily its detached display of problematic social relations in cultural contexts, and anthropologists have tended to obscure important distinctions between rules and other normative formulations (1986: 30–31).

Two examples, drawn from my own fieldwork in Tibet, illustrate the importance of maintaining these distinctions. In the Ladakhi village already mentioned, I found that the villagers were strongly inclined to deal with all disputes as internal matters. Even what we might call a suspected murder in a neighbouring village was kept from the attentions of the police, not to mention the serious case of rape, referred to in the previous chapter. It was apparent that the villagers' practices of conflict resolution needed to be analysed by reference to their ideas about anger and an aversion to explicit antagonism, which could be related to their social structures, including the complex relations between households, strategies for maintaining relations of equality, and methods for distancing all manner of outsiders from certain village affairs. Ultimately, it was the village meeting that was responsible for resolving all disputes. There were no explicit rules and nothing referable to any external authority; it was as if they were jealously guarding the authority of the village meeting to resolve their own disputes. A sense of 'us', our community, as a sacred whole lay behind these ideas; the village remained autonomous of any model of order that might be imposed through law, even internally-generated laws (Pirie 2007b).

These attitudes could be contrasted with the ideas about violence, conflict, and order that I observed at the other end of the Tibetan plateau, amongst the feuding tribes of Amdo (2005). The Amdo Tibetans' social structures and processes of feuding and mediation have much in common with those described by Evans-Pritchard

⁷ He suggests that the term 'law' could be used to refer to 'a moral obligation to settle disputes by conventional methods' (1940: 168), but also, and rightly in my view, declares that 'in a strict sense Nuer have no law' (1940: 162).

(1940) amongst the Nuer. They admire violence, if it is in response to aggression, although there are conflicting norms of restraint which are brought to bear on those who must get angry. I have elsewhere described their elaborate processes of mediation, and the principles and expectations they involve, including payment of blood money (Pirie 2005; 2007a). The nomads accept the authority of an external mediator, inevitably brought in to resolve difficult disputes, who might be a reincarnate *lama* in the most intractable cases, but resolution is utterly dependent on agreement. Either party may walk away at any time. Again, there is nothing here that could be called 'law' (*la loi*), rather than principles of justice (*le droit*). The absence of law, I have suggested, seems to preserve the autonomy of each party involved.

Law, in the sense of explicitly stated norms, is absent in each of these societies—save to the extent that they are now subject to the state regimes of India and China, respectively. Both societies form part of the wider Tibet ethnographic region, however, in which literacy and a highly intellectual religion were, and are, greatly revered; there were centralizing governments—before the region was divided between India and China; many communities had resident, literate scholars, in the form of astrologers and medical practitioners, as well as monks; and there was an idea of law, *trims*, which could be used to refer to custom, but also to legal codes and writings about law. Nevertheless, within both of the communities I studied there seemed to be a positive antipathy towards legalistic modes of thought. Exploring this important facet of Tibetan social life depends upon distinguishing law from other forms of social process.

This is not the only part of the world in which a resistance to the use of law for the resolution of conflict has been noted; indeed, in medieval Europe it was made explicit. In an article entitled 'Law and Love', Michael Clanchy (1983) describes a persistent line in medieval thought that opposed two ways of settling disputes. An early twelfth-century compilation of English laws (*Leges Henrici Primi*) declares that 'agreement prevails over law and love over judgment' (*pactum legem vincit et amor iudicium*). Such ideas were reflected in the out-of-court settlements, disapproved of but sanctioned by the courts, and the 'lovedays' specifically set aside for reconciling disputants (1983: 50). A contrasting tradition, traceable to the Roman *Corpus Iuris Civilis*, regarded law as reducible to a code of rules and order as something that had to be imposed from above. Clanchy illustrates these contrasting traditions by describing the ideologies and images surrounding two thirteenth-century monarchs, Emperor Frederick II of Italy and Louis IX of France. In the first case the ruler was presented as an infallible adjudicator, handing down coercive judgments in accordance with law, 'written down in books, expounded by professors... and applied by a hierarchy of judges' (1983: 54). In the second case justice was dispensed by the monarch, responding to direct petitions while seated under an oak tree at Vincennes, exemplifying the idea that love prevails over law.

The 'love' that was set against the law, Clanchy explains, referred to a bond of affection, established by public undertakings before witnesses, upheld by social pressure, and characterized by the link between lord and vassal. The idea was, he says, that love alone brings freedom and security; in the stateless societies of the early Middle Ages it was seen as being more powerful than law, over which it prevailed (1983: 48). With the reforms of Henry II, in the late twelfth century, and the establishment of the King's Courts—generally regarded as the birth of the English common law—compromise between two parties after issue of a writ came to be seen as an insult to the king, albeit that reconciliation continued, often sanctioned by the courts. 'Pessimistically interpreted', Clanchy says, 'Henry II's reforms had the long-term effect of weakening and straining the bonds of affection existing in feudal lordship and kindred loyalties and putting nothing adequate in their place' (1983: 62). Law was explicitly recognized as only one of the means of resolving disputes, and the growth of the common law in England, with its new and powerful institutions, was mistrusted by many as a means of authoritative social control. It is an important distinction: not all societies want, or need, law for the settlement of disputes. Legalistic forms of argument, on the one hand, and practices of mediation, on the other, are distinct types of social process; law and conflict resolution may or may not coincide in any particular case.[8]

---

[8] At the same time, legal processes may not have social harmony as their object, as Strathern's (1985) study indicates. Davis (2010: 116) also points out

Ethnographic and historical studies can, in such ways, shed light not just on the functions and limitations of formal, centralized legal systems, but also on ideas about law and its role in society, including the differences between using law and other forms of conflict resolution. Some ethnographic studies have, unfortunately, tended to blur the distinctions between law and other social norms, and legalistic and other social processes; in this way they mask much that is of interest about legalism as a type of thought and argument. This is a tendency that has continued with the study of 'legal pluralism'.

LEGAL PLURALISM

In an influential article, 'Law and Social Change: the Semi-Autonomous Social Field as an Appropriate Subject of Study', Sally Falk Moore (1973) famously highlighted the different forms of social order that may coexist in one society. Her article draws a parallel between the Chagga of Mount Kilimanjaro and their experiences under colonial rule, and the garment traders of New York, whose activities are governed by informal, extra-legal norms. In the case of the Chagga she describes how the persistence of traditional, historical social norms effectively perverted the intent of colonial laws, in particular when it came to property relations. In the case of the garment traders, she describes their network of complex and effective social norms, which likewise subverted the intent of the union's legally-binding rules. This study is important for its vivid demonstration of how informal patterns of normative order can effectively regulate aspects of social life, even within the heart of one of the most developed western societies. It is not, however, that the garment traders lived in a type of bubble, insulated from the effects of the state laws. Rather, the legal framework, and the possibility that someone could invoke it and appeal to its enforcement agencies, shaped the context in which informal norms were developed and played out.

that the jurisprudence of the Hindu legal process, *vyavahara*, (described further in chapter four) does not involve a notion that its goal is communal or social harmony or that a negotiated dispute settlement is preferable to clear victory and knowledge of what is good.

As a call to question the efficacy of state law in maintaining social order, this piece is unquestionably compelling. Even legal scholars have, somewhat belatedly, been taking seriously the non-state norms that effectively regulate relationships within the modern US, for example, cattle ranchers in California (Ellickson 1991).[9] This has led Galligan (2007: ch 6) to advocate the concept of 'social spheres', a rather neater phrase than Moore's 'semi-autonomous social field', as a useful focus for the study of these dynamics.

Moore's article had a more immediate and profound effect on legal anthropology. Referring to this study, John Griffiths (1986) made a strong case for the study of 'legal pluralism'. The term had already been used by Franz von Benda-Beckmann (1970), among others, but Griffiths' article, published in a journal of the same name, argued for its more widespread use, in order to identify and describe the subject matter of empirical legal studies. Moore had not, herself, used the concept; nor had she applied the term 'law' to the informal norms she was describing, rather— and somewhat awkwardly—using the term 'reglementation'. Nevertheless, Griffiths boldly declared that what Moore had been describing was a case of legal pluralism, that is, the coexistence of two or more legal systems in one society. The implication was that scholars should study non-state norms as a form of law.[10]

There followed numerous studies that adopted the approach Griffiths had advocated, examining 'the dialectic, mutually constitutive relation between state law and other normative orders' (Merry 1988: 880). It also led to more theoretical articles advocating a programme of research into the interaction between different configurations of plural legal orders, not just state law and other types of law recognized by it—such as religious and international or, in some cases, 'customary' law—but also between informal legal orders and others. There was an explicit academic agenda behind much of this, to draw scholars' attention to the

[9] This study, like that of Black (1976) is, however, based upon the assumption that order is a matter of social control based upon a system of rules and sanctions. It leads Ellickson to suggest that legal scholars can and should develop a taxonomy for such rules and norms.

[10] Griffiths (2006) has subsequently changed his view.

existence and importance of forms of non-state ordering; it was a 'self-conscious movement' to critique the 'legal centralism' said to dominate legal scholarship (Roberts 2005: 3). Conventional jurisprudence was characterized, not entirely unfairly, as being preoccupied with state law and having an ideological quality that privileged and reflected 'the moral and political claims of the nation state'. This disguised the failure of state and colonial legal systems to dominate their societies and hindered good empirical legal scholarship by deflecting scholarly attention from a wider range of legal orders. As de Sousa Santos (2002: 385) puts it, beyond state law, distinctive in being 'the only self-reflexive legal form, that is the only legal form that thinks of itself as law', lies 'a great variety of legal orders circulating in society'. Teubner (1992: 1443) refers to the 'suppressed discourses' of non-state law. The legal pluralists, that is, insisted on extending the term 'law' to a disparate range of normative orders.[11]

It seems that the idea appeals to legal scholars as an attractive banner under which to study non-state forms of law, and that this now extends to those concerned with 'globalization' and 'transnational law' (von Benda-Beckmann 2002; Merry 2006a). De Sousa Santos (2002: 92), for example, considers that the debate now concerns 'suprastate, global legal orders coexisting in the world system with both state and infrastate legal orders'. Menski (2006: 19, 600) advocates legal pluralism as a means to understand global legal diversity and calls for the 'liberal inclusion of all potential claimants under the umbrella of "law"'. Twining (2009: 363–63) argues that in order to take non-state law seriously we need to consider forms of law that include supra-state law, non-state law, and various forms of 'soft law', albeit that he recognizes the difficulty of extending the concept of law to encompass all these phenomena. The most explicit advocate of 'global legal pluralism', Paul Berman, argues that pluralism provides a framework for understanding a hybrid world where normative assertions of multiple entities compete for primacy, and he argues for a 'cosmopolitan, pluralist jurisprudence' where all positions are equivalently embraced (2012: 18). We need, he

---

[11] I am indebted to Roberts (2005) for his concise and illuminating summary of the legal pluralism project.

argues, a more capacious definition of law so that we do not miss the hugely important influence of normative communities that, even without state sanction, can and do assert alternative normative universes, enforce order in certain spheres, and exert a strong hold on those who deem themselves bound by their judgments (2012: 326).

But why should legal, or any other scholars, feel the need to attach the label of 'law' to something in order to be able to take it seriously as an object of study? Denis Galligan's concept of 'social spheres', as an area of investigation, like Sally Falk Moore's 'semi-autonomous social fields' would seem to draw our attention just as well to arenas in which non-state normative orders operate. To put it more bluntly, what is the nature of such non-state 'law', how is it to be identified and what are its characteristics? Franz and Keebet von Benda-Beckmann (2006: 12–13), strong promoters of the legal pluralism agenda, have defined law as 'the summary indication of those objectified cognitive and normative conceptions for which validity for a certain social formation is authoritatively asserted.' 'Law', they continue, 'is a generic term that comprises a variety of social phenomena (concepts, rules, principles, procedures, regulations of different sorts, relationships, decisions) at different levels of social organization.' At the very least, this is extremely wide, and it is hard to see how it could be employed in a way that sheds light on the nature of law.

The agenda of the legal pluralists has given rise to considerable critical comment, much of it cogent and persuasive (Tamanaha 1993; Fuller 1994; Roberts 1998; 2005). As a research programme it is surely too general to be particularly useful: the coexistence of plural legal or normative orders is a universal fact of the modern world, so the concept points to nothing distinctive (Fuller 1994: 10). It is the implicit broadening of the concept of law, however, and the lack of any satisfactory attempt to define its consequent ambit, that has attracted the strongest and most cogent criticism. Merry (1988: 878–79) had already sounded a note of caution in an article largely supportive of the project: 'where do we stop speaking of law and find ourselves simply describing social life?' Of course, there need not be any hard and fast way of distinguishing law from other forms of normative order. Indeed, given the nature of the ordinary language concept, it would be a mistake to try to construct one; there may always be borderline cases. But we do need a sense of a border. If not, the concept of law simply dissolves into the notion of social order and the norms, of all sorts, that provide it with shape and meaning.

Among the convincing critiques of the concept of legal pluralism and its proponents, Roberts (2005) says that the extension of the term to 'negotiated orders' is unwarranted, given the specialized and differentiated character of our concept of law. The result is a loss of analytic purchase. We are liable both to fail to identify the distinguishing features of 'law', properly so called, and also, as Fuller (1994: 10) points out, to attribute negotiated orders with the characteristics of law-centred models. To characterize the understandings and practices of stateless societies as legal orders and embrace all normative universes as equivalent, does not tell us much of what we might want to know about them.

Law and government

Roberts develops his critique of legal pluralism by suggesting that our 'native' concept, or what he elsewhere refers to as 'the cultural assemblage we have come to call "law"' (2005: 1), is intrinsically linked to notions of government and centralized political control. He suggests that:

our sense, in the West, of what law 'is' is bound up with, and has been created through, state law's association with a particular history: early on a complex relationship with the Judaeo-Christian religious tradition; later the emergence of secular government in Europe; later still, the management of colonial expansion....Law is a concomitant of centralising processes, processes that, at a certain point, resulted in the formation of the nation state. (2005: 12–13)

More shortly, law was 'called into being by the attempt to govern' (2005: 13). The paradigms of the legislator and the judge, he says, have 'been dominant in England for a long time'; 'In the modern period Austin articulated much of it, notably the element of command...; Maine filled in the rest a bit later, particularly through his shift in focus to the judge,...there was general agreement that law developed as an instrument of rule in the context of kingship and matured with the process of state formation' (2005: 2). Roberts places Hart's (1961) theory of law in the same lineage, a successor to 'Maine's confident delineation under which "law" begins to "emerge" when those in power cease making decisions on an ad hoc basis and begin pronouncing the same judgements in similar situations' (2005: 11).

Although this model of law was the product of a particular trajectory of state formation, Roberts does not regard the associated ideology of law as being tied to that of the state: it remained a variant of an overall configuration, which appeared 'wherever the aspiration to "govern"—to be in power—became a serious and sustained project' (2005: 13). Our concept of law reflects a political configuration, then: an attempt to employ a particular mode of decision-making, that of command, followed by the discursive formulation of an ideological justification for the leader's authority, the articulation of normative propositions, the attempt to achieve compliance with such rules, and the provision of adjudicative agencies (2005:14). 'Law is centralist in its very nature' (2005: 17).

This is a powerful and persuasive argument, which gains considerable support from the fact that a government-centred model has been promoted by many legal scholars. It is also implicit in the work of many sociologists of law, writing in a tradition that has its roots in Weber's model of law as the achievement of a leader. Cotterrell, for example, stresses the imaginative and constitutive power of law to influence the meaning of basic categories that colour and define social relations (1998: 177). However, he goes on to identify law by reference to political authority: law 'is given discursive coherence and unity only because its intellectual insecurity, its permanent cognitive openness, is stabilised by political fiat' (1998: 181).

As I have argued elsewhere (2010), however, and seek to do throughout subsequent chapters in this book, it is not, in fact, so difficult to think of law without government. Anthropological and historical examples from around the world, and often from long back in history, should persuade us that we properly apply the term 'law' to codes and rules that have an intellectual life independent of any project of government. Another sense of what law is, apparent when we give any sustained thought to Islamic or Hindu law, for example, has survived or developed alongside the attempts by legal theorists to attach it to the state. The danger in adopting too restrictive a notion of law is that we ignore such examples, as many legal anthropologists have done, and the light that they can shed upon the nature of law.

Tamanaha's 'non-essentialist' concept

Having initially asserted, like Roberts, that law should be identified with the state, Tamanaha's *General Jurisprudence of Law and Society* (2001) develops what he calls a 'non-essentialist' concept of law. The question 'What is law?' is unavoidable, he says, and what is needed is a 'socio-legal positivism', a 'theoretically sophisticated and empirically informed way to understand law and its relations with society' (2001: 135). However, law has no essence and the approach he proposes 'asks how groups of people talk about law...it examines what they do with law', not dictating what law is (2001: 155). Law is, then, 'whatever people identify and treat through their social practices as "law" (or *droit*, *recht* etc.)'.

Tamanaha is surely right to start with ordinary language. However, there are right and wrong ways of using the concept, which his definition, or lack of definition, does not help to tease out. His analysis stops with the very wide and diverse ordinary language category, without trying to identify the nature of what lies within that category. To start to say anything interesting about the nature of law we need to identify recurrent features, to analyse the reasons we distinguish informal norms from laws, while allowing the concept to apply to both state and non-state forms. This definition also ceases to be workable at the boundaries of the English-speaking world, as Tamanaha himself recognizes (2001: 203). To say that law is whatever people identify as law, 'or *droit*, *recht* etc.' is to define law implicitly in terms of these concepts; but why chose *droit* and *Recht*, rather than *loi* and *Gesetz*?[12] Moreover, the idea that we can identify law as 'whatever people identify and treat through their social practices as "law"' is problematic. What, in any particular case, are the social, as opposed to the linguistic, practices surrounding law? What counts as treating something as 'law'? These are, surely, exactly the questions we want to ask when we analyse the nature of law.

---

[12] The same objection can be made to Teubner's account (1992: 1452).

Tamanaha continues by suggesting that our analysis should not be limited to what can definitively be regarded as law, but should start with a typology of social orders—the unarticulated substrate, shared norms and rules, self-interest, instrumentalist behaviour, love and sympathy, coercion and so on—and continue with a typology of kinds of law—state, customary, religious, international, indigenous, natural (2001: ch 8). A similar approach is now also advocated by John Griffiths (2006).[13] This is effectively to abandon law as an analytical category.

The patent difficulties in definition do not, however, mean that we cannot seek more precise concepts, such as 'legalism', with which to distinguish the phenomena to which we apply the label of law, and to differentiate amongst our subjects of inquiry. The fact that we have different concepts, those of 'norm' and 'rule', and the fact that we make distinctions between a 'legal order' and a 'social' or 'negotiated order', indicates that we think of law as something distinct from other norms and forms of order. To turn back to the empirical examples, is the term 'informal norms' not a better way of describing the practices of New York's garment traders? They, themselves, must have distinguished these norms from the laws that could attract the attention of the state's enforcement agencies. It is implausible that they should have considered and described them both as 'laws', and Moore does not suggest that they did. If a distinction resonates with those we study, then we should not ignore it.

If we start with the way in which people talk about law, as Tamanaha suggests, we also need to take seriously the distinctions people make—between law and love, or law and social norms—and to tease out the significance of those distinctions. The law contrasted with love in the Middle Ages was associated with a form of rule-based adjudication, but this does not mean relying on the possibility of enforcement to distinguish law. In this book I suggest that the creation and use of explicit rules

[13] Twining (2009) also urges a general jurisprudence that takes into account a diverse range of forms of normative order, arguing that law is 'concerned with the ordering of relations between agents or persons' (2002: 4). His important work can be regarded as an attempt to bring empirical studies into dialogue with legal philosophy. While wholly supporting the enterprise, I do not agree that this is the best way to do it.

and categories, and a type of associated reasoning, distinguishes legalistic from other social forms, and this legalism can account for the fact that scholars regularly talk of Hindu or Islamic law, for example, which have rarely been associated with centralizing governments.

LAW AND THE COLONIAL ENCOUNTER

It matters for an understanding of the nature of law that we start with a proper sense of the boundaries around the category. However, there are also practical reasons for attending seriously to our concept of law and not allowing its ambit to extend unduly. These are illustrated most clearly in studies of the role played by law in colonial contexts and the discovery, or 'invention', of 'indigenous' and 'customary' law. Such concepts continue to have practical effects when nation states seek to recognize the customary laws of minority groups, or when indigenous groups claim legal recognition.

Both Chanock (1985) and Cohn (1989) describe the search for, and ultimately the invention of, 'customary law' as part of the British colonial encounter in Africa and India, respectively. Within a long and complex history in each case, the policy of indirect rule came to require that indigenous law be discovered, written down, and made available for implementation. The assumption was that 'native law' could be recorded as a set of rules about how social life should be ordered, and then applied by local magistrates in the settlement of disputes. Lawyers, says Chanock (1985: 220), had a mission to use law to aid development; anthropologists had assured them that customary legal systems were 'there' and they aimed to assist in the integration and modernization of the legal system of the new states. However, in many cases they misunderstood the nature of their own common law system, assuming that it involved the straightforward application of rules and precedents, rather than their adaptation to fit new situations, and this affected the ways in which they envisaged the operation of 'customary law' (1985: 238). The colonial project, therefore, combined several assumptions, based upon the role played, or thought to be played, by law in Britain: that law was central and essential to the maintenance of social order, that the application of law was the way to resolve disputes and, crucially, that any form of law could properly be expressed as a set of written rules.

Chanock describes the way in which 'legalisation led to a freezing of rural status and stratification, henceforth defined and not negotiated', with the result that 'custom was transformed from a way of representing and manipulating the world into a set of government rules' (1985: 47). His study is also important for the emphasis it lays upon the role played by indigenous leaders, particularly after independence, in maintaining the structures of 'customary law'. As he says, 'Africans were the active users, not the passive recipients, of the new form [of law], creating a customary law to deal with their new situation' (1985: 237).[14]

Cohn (1989) describes a rather different situation on the Indian subcontinent, which had a long tradition of legal scholarship. He traces the British colonialists' attempts 'to create a system of rule congruent with Indian interests' (1989: 136), which went through different stages over the course of the colonial period and was affected by the understandings and ideas of the individuals placed in charge of the project. All seem to have appreciated the fundamental differences between the English common law and the legal traditions of Hindu and Muslim India, but they made assumptions about the legal texts they found, typically that they were codes on the basis of which legal specialists could provide authoritative decisions. Hindu usages were regarded as having been fixed from time immemorial, such that the earliest texts, in particular the Code of Manu, were regarded as the most authoritative. The author of the Code was thus regarded as a legislator and law-giver. But had these laws ever been applied by judges or courts in the resolution of disputes? Were they even regarded as obligatory rules or practical guides for daily behaviour? As Cohn describes, one administrator seems to have regarded his project as akin to Justinian's codification of Roman law, motivated by a comparable desire to give the natives 'security for the due administration of justice' (1989: 145), while his successors made idealistic attempts to restore pre-Islamic law

---

[14] As Fallers (1969: 3) puts it, customary law is not so much a kind of law as a legal situation which develops in imperial or quasi-imperial contexts, in which the dominant legal systems recognize and support the local 'law' of politically subordinate communities.

for the benefit of the Hindus. Ultimately, the colonists imported a model of English law through the establishment of the court system: given the differences amongst the source materials, the judges developed a system of precedent that essentially reproduced a form of the common law in India.

Meanwhile in Malaysia, under Dutch colonial rule, the jurists found *adat* and transformed it into customary law. According to Geertz (1983: 208), *adat* is 'a form of legal sensibility' which, during the colonial period, came to be transformed into *adatrecht*, that is, 'customary law'. This meant that it came to be regarded as 'a set of traditional rules traditionally applied to traditional problems', which needed to be researched, recorded, sorted, and—backed by the power of the colonial state—administered. As Geertz comments caustically, the notion of custom, when employed by anthropologists, reduces thought to habit, while in the hands of legal historians (and jurists) it reduces thought to practice.

In all of these cases a concept of law derived from one cultural context was (unwittingly) imposed on another, in which it did not match local understandings and organization. A model derived from the English common law, or Dutch jurisprudence, or even Justinian's codification, was imposed upon local texts, ideas, practices, and authority structures, along with the assumption that law must be central to the regulation of social life in the interests of the maintenance of order. Individuals may have doubted the wisdom of this project, but colonial policy demanded a system of rule-based government along with a laudable attempt to respect local customs and practices.[15] Although most anthropologists would justifiably claim the ability not to make the mistakes of the colonialists, we can see in the colonial agenda the practical equivalent to their approach. If every society must have some sort of 'law' as the basis for its social order and if 'customary law', in practice, regulates social life, then is it not logical to seek to discover, record, and enforce this 'law'?

---

[15] Scholars have made similar observations about other colonial encounters, for example Schacht (1964: ch 14) on Anglo-Muhammadan law and le Droit Musulman Algérien; Read (1972) and Vincent (1989) on east Africa; and Hooker (1978: 23) and Huxley (2001) on Burma.

A parallel, and equally problematic endeavour, often motivated by similarly laudable aims, can be seen in attempts by legal anthropologists to support and promote the 'indigenous' or 'customary' laws of minority people. In doing so they are often supporting the claims of such people that their own 'laws' should be recognized in national and international contexts. Of course, the claim to autonomy is more powerful when phrased in terms of indigenous 'law' than 'customs' or 'traditional' ways—of using land, for example—implying equivalence with the state's legal provisions. Anthropologists have studied legal claims to recognition by Canadian aboriginal people (Cassell 2009) and Botswana Bushmen (Sapignoli 2009), while Techera (2009) and Wheatley (2009) both discuss the international provisions concerning indigenous rights, making idealistic appeals for the greater recognition of customary and indigenous law. Considering Africa, Chanock (1985: 221) describes how the former world of the legal anthropologist, 'the "customary" systems of "tribes" and "regions", appear[s] as the embattled legal world of the peasant struggling with the twin oppressions of capitalist change and the new state'. 'Customary law' is thus serving new 'tribes' as a method of legitimation. It is part of 'an ideology of traditionalism', defining practices that are special to groups and helping people to legitimate new demands (1985: 238). This is, however, to put it at its most benevolent. Chanock is cynical about the wider implications of such moves:

[T]he colonisation of Africa by western legal forms and institutions continues under the aegis of the growing legal profession... This process... is partly being legitimated by its presentation as a development of a customary law which is essentially African, a recapturing of a pre-colonial dynamic. Yet... if it is 'custom' that is wanted, in the sense of a system which uses living principles in flexible and popular disputing processes, one could have this without the oppressive and authoritarian legalism of the neo-traditional customary law.... masquerading as stemming from African communities, it pre-empts their more fruitful participation in this area of national life. (1985: 238–39)

It is the state, itself, with apparently unimpeachable motives, that is encouraging the recognition of customary and indigenous law in other cases. The Constitution of the Republic of South Africa, drawn up in 1996, requires that 'the courts must apply customary law when that law is applicable' (s. 211(3)). But what this customary law is and how it is to be identified, proved, and implemented is not spelled out. Both scholars and judges have, of course, been making strenuous efforts to render this provision effective, trying to elucidate the nature of this 'law', on the one hand, and implementing it on the other. Thus Weeks (2009), in a doctoral thesis based upon several months of ethnographic field-work, does her best to describe and analyse what could be referred to as the 'customary law(s) of succession' among the Swati of South Africa. Perhaps not surprisingly, she finds little that can be stated in law-like terms, that is, as a set of rules and proposi-tions that could be applied by a court (2009: ch 7). Rather, she describes a set of roles, practices, expectations, structures of au-thority, practices of dispute settlement, and economic constraints, all of which contribute to shape practices of succession. This type of 'law', she says, is 'negotiable as an expression of identity' (2009: 353).[16] Her thesis also charts the ways in which the con-stitutional and other courts have tried to apply this provision, bending over backwards to render it effective, while also tying themselves in legal knots. Early cases, for example, decided that the constitutional provisions encompassed both 'official' customary law, recognized in statute, and 'living' customary law. The latter, it was said, is an independent source of norms within the legal system.[17] However, problems quickly appeared when it became necessary to determine how such law was to be ascertained from practice and usage, and how best to give effect to its changing and developing nature. How, in particular, was this flexibility to be balanced against the values of legal certainty, uniformity, and respect for vested rights demanded by the constitution? Albeit with the best of intentions, this interpretation of the constitu-tional provisions requires the application of the term 'law' to social practices that cannot properly be described as such.

---

[16] It is interesting that she still holds to the label 'customary law' to describe her subject matter, clearly not wishing to suggest that the constitutional provision is an empty one.

[17] 'Living law' was a term used by Ehrlich (1936: 493) and adopted by many subsequent scholars to describe law in practice, including customs and usages.

On the face of it, the recognition of indigenous law in a nation state that comprises a heterogeneous population, some of whose interests had been cynically ignored for decades, is surely right. Who could quarrel with the respect this constitutional provision obviously grants to the minority populations? To recognize their law must be to recognize their dignity and autonomy. But it doesn't work in practice. Like the African tribes' struggle for legitimacy, such legislation is sought or enacted for symbolic purposes, with aspirational but impractical aims. It also has the more problematic effect of drawing our attention away from the real nature of the social practices that might be found within the communities in question. It effaces the rationalities of negotiated orders, which involve a different orientation to the normative repertoire, different forms of decision-making, and different relations of power and trust (Roberts 2005: 23). Indeed, Weeks, herself, found that people seldom spoke of 'law', rather of 'their ways' or 'what we think is best for us' (2009: 300). Property ownership and possession were constantly changing, 'complex and apparently indefinable forms' (2009: 297). To gloss all of this as 'law' is to deny that indigenous interests and traditions must be recognized on their own terms.

For my purposes, the point is that the unwarranted expansion of the term 'law' to other types of normative order does not just have academic significance. Indeed, the danger that good ethnographers will fail properly to distinguish between different types of norms is small. As legal pluralists themselves reasonably point out, they are perfectly well able to distinguish between different types of social phenomena and to make appropriate distinctions amongst the examples they subsume under the category of 'law'. Problems are encountered when the term 'law' is taken up and used in its extended sense, generally as 'customary' or 'indigenous law', in practical and political contexts.

This tendency to over-expand the ambit of the concept of law stems from an assumption that law can be defined in terms of its functions and discovered everywhere in the world. It is an assumption that can, in turn, be traced back to the justification for the state's control over law. This diverts our attention from other examples of law, while the emphasis on functions masks the fact that law can have meaning, that is social significance, without ever being imposed or applied. It is to this aspect of law that I turn in the next chapter.

3

LEGAL THOUGHT: MEANING AND POWER

In the 1960s Barkun, a political scientist, undertook a sustained comparison between ethnographic and international forms of law, drawing heavily on anthropological examples. His description of what law is builds upon the idea that it imposes 'a character-istic picture of reality' upon its subjects; ideas have consequences and the law compels us to look at the world in particular ways (1968: 75–77). As he puts it, law is a model, 'a representation, a sophisticated and highly developed form of metaphor' (1968: 87); facts are organized and made meaningful through the categories of law, and 'legal concepts are the concepts within a jural community that define community structure. They allow the establishment of relationships'. Rules, thus, provide a kind of symbolic grammar out of which reality may be constructed (1968: 92).[1]

Law can work symbolically, that is, by providing categories through which people and social relationships may be described and represented. Even amongst familiar forms of law this becomes clear if we consider that legal categories define the ways in which people may hold and use property, in the form of freehold, lease-hold, licence, easement, or reversion—under English law; they define and specify contractual relationships, instances of tortious liability, the nature of trusts, crimes, corporate personality, and so on. This may seem obvious and technical to any lawyer, but the implications have not often been fully considered by socio-legal scholars. Law does far more than provide rules for conduct: it establishes a whole set of categories and relationships that define interactions between people, property, and other social entities. These are also categories and relationships in terms of which people can think about, describe, and evaluate the world. Definitions of crimes, ideas about duties of care, fiduciary

---

[1] His wider project is problematic, however, proposing a structural comparative study of law (1968: 33).

relationships, and constructive trusts express a form of social morality. They make provision for the ways in which people can and should relate to one another. Law provides a model for how society can be.

In this chapter I tease out some of the implications of this, and contrast the approach taken by anthropologists who concentrate on law as an element in wider power relations.

LEGAL CATEGORIES AND JUDICIAL PROCESSES

Recognizing law as a 'technique of knowledge', a number of anthropologists have analysed the significance of legal language, either explicitly or implicitly. In the study of judicial processes, in particular, both anthropologists and other scholars have explained the power of legal language by emphasizing the fact that law establishes conventions and provides categories into which ordinary facts must be fitted (Mertz 1994; Coutin and Yngvesson 2008).[2] Thus, Conley and O'Barr (1990), in a study of lower court use in the US, describe the ways in which judicial institutions are selective in hearing, reporting, and preserving voices.

Through this process of selection, legal institutions shape both the questions they address and the answers they provide....Professional legal discourse finds its raw materials, indeed its very reason for being, in the everyday discourse of disputes...But the law selects among [the voices of litigants], silencing some and transforming others to conform to legal categories and conventions. (1990: 168)

The conventional legal view, they say, 'is that when the law speaks authoritatively, it does not adopt the actual voices of its constituents or practitioners, but uses a voice of its own which is separate, distinct and neutral' (1990: 169) and their own case studies bear this out. Bourdieu similarly notes the predominance of passive and impersonal constructions in French courts, producing a rhetoric of impersonality and neutrality, along with recourse to fixed formulae, which allow little room for individual variation (1987: 820). In modern Lebanon, Clarke (2012: 108) describes a

---

[2] The literature is extensive and notable studies include O'Barr (1982), Hirsch (1998), Philips (1998), Mertz (2007), and Richland (2008).

shari'a judge who switches between a 'brotherly' mode of engagement with the petitioners and the use of 'dry' and 'harsh' language
after the court session opens, when he deals with them 'as a judge'.

In a study of litigants' experiences in the lower courts of the
US, conducted in the 1980s, Merry suggests that:

> law works in the world not just by the imposition of rules and punish-
> ments but also by its capacity to construct authoritative images of social
> relationships and actions, images which are symbolically powerful. Law
> provides a set of categories and frameworks through which the world
> is interpreted. (1990: 8–9)

More generally, the law 'encompasses the ability to determine
the thinkable and the unthinkable, the natural and the cultural
ways of doing things'. Legal discourse, Merry says, is a discourse
of property and rights, of the protection of the self and one's
goods, of entitlement, facts, and truth. Folk understandings of
legal relations may not be detailed and precise, but they involve
notions of contract, property, decision-making based upon rational
discussion, and the presentation of evidence in order to determine
the 'truth' (1990: 112ff).

Interestingly, she finds that in the lower US courts it is the
plaintiffs, having turned to the law, who try to frame their problems
in legalistic terms, couching their descriptions of events and character in terms of the categories and remedies of the law (1990: 10).
Attempting to persuade the court officials to take them seriously,
they present private problems concerning spouses, lovers, children, neighbours, and landlords by squeezing them into the legal
categories of 'assault', 'harassment', 'breach of contract', 'truancy',
and so on (1990: 13, 98). It is the lawyers and court officials, including the judges, who often try to dissuade them from launching
or pursuing a legal case, encouraging them to take advantage of
mediation or other social services, and framing their complaints
in more general, moral, or therapeutic terms in order to do so.
Thus, a teenager could be a 'criminal', 'an irresponsible kid', or
'an acting-out adolescent', depending on the context (1990: 130ff).

As Conley and O'Barr (1990: 168) describe, when a dispute
enters the legal system and becomes a 'case', its expression is
transformed. Lawyers listen to the participants' stories and decide
which ones or parts of them to include within the bounds of the
case. The lawyers reformulate their clients' accounts to conform

to the requirements of the legal categories applicable to the particular case, as well as to the general conventions of legal discourse. In the higher courts, too, in London (and doubtless elsewhere) lawyers are well aware that a legal case may not go to the heart of what their lay clients regard as the core problem.[3] Judges, even here, may try to persuade parties to a legal case to settle out of court, steering them towards a practical solution, and it is not unknown for a bad-tempered judge to denigrate a case as a 'squabble'. But conversely, the legal case may be part of an ongoing series of commercially-oriented manoeuvres through which the client is seeking to gain a strategic advantage over another party, strategies of which the lawyer, himself, may hardly be aware. The law provides a specialized set of language and arguments, which may only partly relate to the commercial or moral realities of the clients' world.

As the legal sociologist Roger Cotterrell recognizes, 'law constitutes social life to a significant degree by influencing the meaning of basic categories (such as property, ownership, contract, trust, responsibility, guilt and personality) that colour or define social relations' (1998: 177). It is not only the law that frames problems in distinctive ways: as Mather and Yngvesson (1980/81) emphasize, problems may also be transformed during mediation processes, as events are framed in a way that is conducive to settlement. There are many ways of presenting or transforming problems, but legalistic framing is distinct amongst them. As Chris Fuller (1994: 11) puts it, 'all judicial processes, to a greater or lesser extent, are characterized by distinctive and often powerfully self-validating systems of thought whose analysis and interpretation ought to be central to legal anthropology'. Nor is this peculiar to the legal systems of the west. In the Islamic world, Powers (2002: 165) describes a property dispute in Fez from around 1400: 'as the case passed through the apparatus of justice, its underlying socioeconomic and emotional basis was transformed into a question of textual analysis, that is, to the relationship between law and language'.

---

[3] I am drawing here on my experience of legal practice as a Chancery barrister at the London Bar.

If this distinctive, and often transformative, capacity of law is not understood it can lead to criticism of the ways in which laws relate to other social forms and categories. De Sousa Santos (1987) has famously characterized law as a map, but emphasizes the 'distortion of reality' and 'organized misreadings of territories' that it produces. As Pottage and Mundy (2004: 2) point out, an untheorized assumption that legal rules correspond to natural or social facts, including the distinction between persons and things, underpins a number of anthropological critiques of legal constraints. We need only think of intellectual property to appreciate the transformative power of legal categories: by creating a framework for the regulation of patents and allowing an 'owner' to restrict and license use by others, the law effectively creates property where there was none before.

LAW AS A SYSTEM OF MEANING

Law, then, creates the rules and categories in terms of which problems can be recast in order to make them more amenable to adjudication; it can also create new (legal) relationships outside the courtroom. Legal categories provide a means of understanding, not just manipulating, the world. In an important article, *Fact and Law in Comparative Perspective*, anthropologist Clifford Geertz (1983) advocates bringing an 'interpretive' or 'hermeneutic' approach to the study of law. Law, he suggests, provides categories and rules that may be imposed upon facts, but also through which they may be represented. The potentially problematic nature of this relationship was recognized long ago by the ancient Greeks, he says, in their 'grand opposure of nature and convention' (1983: 171).[4] It is a relationship that legal systems, themselves, present in a particular way, as the application of general precepts ('if–then' rules) to concrete facts, resulting in a decision ('as–therefore'): in the common law system the court's task is first to ascertain the facts, what *is*, then to apply the law, what *should*

---

[4] This opposition, between *physis*, the natural world, and *nomos*, the human world, has had a significant impact on the subsequent history of legal thought (Kelley 1990).

be, in order to reach a judgment, what *must be*. The process of judgment and 'the institutions of law translate between a language of imagination and one of decision and form thereby a determinate sense of justice'. This is what he terms a 'legal sensibility' (1983: 174–75).

The dichotomy between fact and norm that this model suggests is too stark, however: as Geertz recognizes, 'the legal representation of fact is normative from the start' (1983: 174). Law is just one of the ways through which facts can be represented and, therefore, known, and through which they gain meaning. Law provides an example of the wider issue of representation, also addressed by science, art, religion, ethics, ideology, history, and other meaning-making intellectual exercises. Our social world is full of schemes that provide facts and events, not to mention people and groups, with meaning, and through which we perceive it and decide how to act. As such, and to use one of Geertz's most memorable phrases, law is 'part of a distinct manner of imagining the real' (1983: 173). His argument is that law should be studied hermeneutically, as a system of meaning; a focus on the concepts and ideas at the heart of a legal system, its 'legal sensibilities', will tell us much about the social world and culture of its participants. In his own case studies he uses the examples of *dharma*, *haqq*, and *adat*, central legal concepts in the Indic, Islamic, and Indonesian worlds, respectively, to do just this.

Geertz thus confirms the capacity of law to create meaning, not just to reflect shared social norms. It is:

a mode of giving particular sense to particular things in particular places (things that happen, things that fail to, things that might be), such that these noble, sinister, or merely expedient appliances take particular form and have particular impact. Meaning, in short, not machinery. (1983: 232)

Or, more firmly, 'law, rather than a mere technical add-on to a morally (or immorally) finished society, is ... an active part of it'; law provides 'visions of community not echoes of it' (1983: 218). In this way Geertz rightly, in my opinion, sets his ideas about law against those that assume laws represent or emerge from shared social norms. When norms are shared they need not be made explicit as law. As I found in the remote villages of Ladakh, for example, the irrigation systems, on which all agriculture was dependent, were too important to be open to question (Pirie 2007b). People could tell me what they did, how the water rotation system worked, but it did not need to be spelt out in the form of laws. Their explicitly articulated customs, on the other hand—and even here I do not regard them as 'laws'—concerned matters ranging from the division of property among family members to the ways in which they organized their festivals: differences of opinion were inevitable, given the social structures, and the explicit articulation of 'our customs' established a village standard. Law, like the customs in this case, is more than a mere reflection of shared norms.

As I have already noted and discussed elsewhere (2010: 219) Geertz's approach hardly sheds light upon what is distinctive about law over the other social forms that endow the world with meaning, however; Geertz, himself, mentions religion, art, ideology, science, history, ethics, and commonsense, in this regard (1983: 230). His approach does not take us very far in understanding what might be thought of as distinctly legal forms.[5] As Roberts (2005: 8) puts it critically, 'law becomes lost in cosmology and symbolism'. However, although he is not concerned to distinguish the ways in which law confers meaning from the ways in which other schemes do, Geertz does hint at what is distinctive about law and legalistic thinking. As he says, law 'describes the world and what goes on in it in explicitly judgmatical terms'; and juristic techniques are 'an organised effort to make the description correct' (1983: 174). He illustrates these points with a vivid example of legalistic organization in a Balinese village, where rules about the conduct of village affairs were carefully spelt out on palm leaves. He describes a case in which one man's refusal to take his turn as one of the local council chiefs had terrible consequences, leading him to lose his land, his social status, and his political and religious rights, and ultimately to becominge an

---

[5] Geertz, himself, is equivocal about how to apply the label 'law': 'whether the adjudicative styles [discussed in the case studies]...are properly to be called "law" or not...is of minor importance; though I, myself, would want to do so. What matters is that their imaginative power not be obscured' (1983: 215). It is clearly not crucial to his project to take a firm view on the nature and distinctive character of law over other schemes of meaning.

outcast. This was despite the intervention of the king, exalted in numerous other respects, who was not considered by the village council to have any authority in the matter: village rules and the consequences of the man's contumacy were not negotiable. Geertz reflects upon this story by saying that 'what seems to run through the whole case ... is a general view that the things of this world, and human beings among them, are arranged into categories, some hierarchic, some coordinate, but all clear-cut, in which matters out-of-category disturb the entire structure and must be either corrected or effaced' (1983: 180).

The villagers had rules and categories concerning the segmentation of domains of authority and the definition of fault as one of public etiquette; standing apart from the facts of the particular case, they had an authority, in themselves, which could produce disastrous results. The villagers employed legalistic categories and rules, that is, which had to be respected and whose authority transcended that of the king. It is this legalism, or what Geertz refers to as 'juristic techniques', that gave the village laws their force and allowed them to be used to make definitive judgments.

Meaning in legal theory

The imaginative power of law has not gone unnoticed by legal theorists. Some of their writings are well known although they hardly improve, I suggest, on the work of the anthropologists. Legal scholar Robert Cover (1983/84), for example, analyses legal rules as a part of our 'normative universe', the world of right and wrong. Law, he says, is 'a resource in signification' that, like other norms, makes certain types of activity possible. Thus, we can only refuse sacraments, desecrate religious feasts, or pay taxes if there are religious and fiscal rules that establish sacraments, feasts, and taxes in the first place, along with the norms of behaviour that relate to them. Moreover, the meaningful activity that this makes possible goes much further than simple acts of obedience or refusal: laws, like other norms, enable us to submit, rejoice, struggle, pervert, mock, disgrace, humiliate, and dignify, as well as resist or comply. Of course, these points apply to all sorts of norms, not just the legal, but among the possibilities for action provided by laws and norms, it is useful to be reminded that they allow us to lead unprincipled, disrespectful, and ironic, as well as compliant or disobedient lives. Cover, like Geertz, stresses the imaginative quality of law and the interpreted nature of social forms: 'The sense that we make of our normative world', he says, 'is not exhausted when we specify the patterns of demands upon us' (1983/84: 8).[6]

A different approach to law as a system of meaning is taken by the legal scholars Niklas Luhmann and Gunther Teubner. Luhmann insists that law is a system of communication, that it frames forms (sentences) in the medium of meaning with the help of communication (2004: 70–74). We should regard it as an autopoietic, self-distinguishing system, he says, characterized by 'operative closure'; it creates its own meanings and definitions, which are not directly mapped onto the real world. Like Geertz and Cover, Luhmann thus emphasizes the capacity of law to create meaning and the function of law, he says, is to stabilize normative expectations, allowing us to expect or predict what will meet with social approval (2004: 148).

Luhmann's explanation of how law achieves these ends involves a binary code legal/illegal (2004: ch 4). This can account for most matters of contract and tort, as well as criminal provisions: the positive value (legal) is applied if a fact conforms to the norms of the system (2004: 183). The implication is that law sets normative standards—fulfilling contracts, not committing torts, complying with taxation requirements, and the duties imposed by property relations and equity, and so on—conditional legal statements then determine what will be legal or illegal in the context of these standards (2004: 198). Clearly it is this feature of law that enables judicial decisions to be made. But does Luhmann's theory, extensively elaborated though it is, amount to any more than the fact that it allows for definite answers and adjudication? More importantly, does the insistence on a binary code not mask

---

[6] He goes on to draw a distinction between 'world creating' norms, found in a common body of precepts attracting general commitment and 'world maintaining' norms, those that are imposed upon us, implicitly by a ruler, and he identifies law with the latter: 'the precepts we call law are marked off by social control over their provenance, their mode of articulation, and their effects' (1983/84: 17). The attempt to distinguish between legal and other sorts of norms thus leads him to identify law as that which is backed by political authority.

the subtleties and creative possibilities of legal systems? The law is asked to do far more than adjudicate on the validity of, or compliance with, contracts, or on the commission of torts. As Tamanaha (2001: 176–79) says, law enables, performs, confers status, defines, legitimates, confers power, symbolizes, and more. English law allows someone a choice of whether to repudiate or affirm a contract, whether to seek damages or specific performance; it gives judges discretion in many cases; it requires people to come to court with 'clean hands'—denying a remedy to someone trying to profit from his own wrong; it sets out the steps a company must take before it can buy its own shares; it provides a complicated set of rules and principles to determine how the assets of an insolvent company should be shared between the secured and unsecured creditors, and who falls into which category; it allows people to become vendors, mortgagors, guarantors, and trustees and sometimes imposes these relations upon them—in the case of a constructive trust. This is all within a western system: Islamic law, with its categories of forbidden, disapproved of, neutral, approved of, and compulsory, produces yet another range of complexity. To describe all this as a binary code hardly begins to do justice to what law is and does; it says no more than that law promises definite answers, and in cases of judicial discretion the law does not even do that.[7]

Teubner (1989) builds on Luhmann's theory of autopoiesis, taking it to something of an extreme.[8] 'The legal discourse is closed . . . and produces its own construction of reality' (1989: 745); it amounts to 'the autonomous construction of legal models of reality under the impression of environmental perturbations' (1989: 740). We must surely question the dichotomy this sets up

[7] A similarly impoverished view of law as a system of rules that define the licit and illicit, that prohibit, censor, and demand obedience is offered by Foucault (1976: 107–20). Law (*le droit*), he says, is a system of transgressions and prohibitions, which function through laws (*la loi*). Foucault's main interest is in the way in which this 'juridico-discursive' representation of power masks other techniques of normalization and control that go beyond the state and its apparatus. Like Luhmann, he ignores the positive, enabling, and constitutive possibilities of law identified by Geertz and Cover.

[8] Teubner explains that he is writing in the tradition of Berger and Luckmann (1966), whose book entitled *The Social Construction of Reality* had a tremendous influence on sociologists, although its principal idea can hardly have surprised anthropologists.

between legal and other types of knowledge. Laws provide categories and relationships but these still have to be applied to real life
events if we are to orient our behaviour, as we do, towards the
law; and those events can be put in evidence in the courtroom
through documents and witnesses. The court has to work with
ordinary language descriptions of things and events, which it does
through selection, presentation, and the application of categories,
which hardly seems to be captured by the notion of 'environmental
perturbations'. As Galligan (2007: 42) points out, 'there is no real or
significant difficulty in converting economic, moral, and political
issues into legal language and doctrine'.[9] Teubner's theory lacks the
richness and clarity that comes from detailed empirical examples
and hardly takes us further in elucidating the nature of law or
distinguishing it from other systems of meaning.[10]

For all that these scholars emphasize meaning, the issue of
the law's authority hovers in the background to their accounts.
Cover defines law in terms of the norms that are imposed upon
us, implicitly by a ruler. Luhmann and Teubner reject the notion
of a powerful law-maker, but are left with what they see as a
paradox, Luhmann's (1988) 'unanswerable question': namely
what makes it right for a judge to give a definitive answer to a
legal question; and the vision of an authoritative judge is also
present in Teubner's account (1989: 750). Luhmann's question is
too limiting, however. We should not look for a single account
of authority, whether in institutions, legislation, judicial decisions, or previous practice. An anthropologist must approach
both law and its authority as factual matters, social forms to be
studied empirically, in all their variety. What should interest us

---

[9] As Murphy (2004: 121) points out, the law creates a framework for
decision-making; but it also has to deal with pre-legal claims, questions, and assertions, for example when recognition is demanded for 'culture'. The legal recognition
of listed buildings, World Heritage sites, 'historic' objects, and 'original details', for
example, are the state's response to an agenda set outside the law.

[10] His article illustrates the ways in which German courts have recognized and
dealt with ideas and models from the other social sciences, including economics, sociology, policy, and psychiatry. Such ideas are inevitably refashioned when
they are considered by lawyers and judges: a court can, of course, only hear
certain sorts of evidence, in a manner largely determined by its own rules, both
substantive and procedural.

is the claims to authority that law makes for itself, and the different bases on which people do, in fact, attribute it with authority. We need to ask why people want their activities to be governed, at least ostensibly, by law. The idea that law provides meaning is radically impoverished if we assume that behind it must stand an authoritative judge.

LAW AND POWER

De Sousa Santos (1987) has called law a 'map of misreading', which distorts reality. Merry (1990) emphasizes the paradox of the litigants who seek to escape from their private worlds by invoking the law, and find themselves caught up in and constrained by the state's legal framework. Conley and O'Barr identify the power of the court to select and transform the material presented by litigants, emphasizing the problem of the litigants' 'missing voices' and lamenting the way in which the courts ignore everyday discourse and concerns (1990: 168–70). Asking why the legal community is not more concerned to understand the thought of the litigants is to miss the point, however: the role of the legal professionals is to present a case in a way that the court can hear.

There is a tendency on the part of anthropologists to be diverted into the easy paradigms of power and domination in this way, thereby reducing law to a matter of social control or governmental power, and obscuring its capacity to provide a meaningful map or model for the world. Starr and Collier, for example, in the Introduction to their edited volume, *History and Power in the Study of Law* (1989), urge anthropologists to carry out historically-grounded analyses, taking into account the wider power relations surrounding law and legal systems: we should ask questions about competition for power and privilege, and obstacles to achieving it, they say. Implicitly criticizing the limitations of the fine-grained analysis of meaning, as well as those scholars who pay close attention to processes of dispute resolution, they demand that we should regard law as something that legitimates particular ideologies and 'asymmetrical power relations'; 'legal orders incorporate inequality' (1989:6–7). Work on legal language has analysed it as a technique employed within the creation and manipulation of power relations: it is an instrument for the imposition of hegemony (Mertz 1994: 447), or 'the symbolic representation of interests of particular groups, especially groups in power' (Starr and Collier 1989: 24).

It is true that among the early anthropologists some ethnographers tended to portray societies as static, leaving to one side the power relations, including the historical effects of wars, colonization, and their incorporation into new nation states. They were more interested in the underlying social structures and cultural forms than dynamics, either new or historic, brought about by wider political forces. But Starr and Collier are doing more than remind us to take such empirical factors into account. Although they assert that legal systems are cultural systems (1989: 11), the significance of regarding law as an aspect of culture, they say, lies in the fact that people treat legal orders as appropriate vehicles for asserting, creating, and contesting such things as national identities (1989: 11). We should focus on 'the enabling aspects of law'; how people and groups use legal rules to accomplish particular ends (1989: 12).[11]

Starr and Collier do not explicitly distinguish their project from Geertz's interpretative approach, but some of the contributions to their volume are critical of his work. Moore (1989: 278), for example, argues that:

'linguistic' or 'literary' analyses of the conceptual elements in a legal order do not take one very far in understanding what people actually do on the ground or why they do it at particular times and places. I agree with Geertz that it is essential to know in what terms people think about basic moral and legal issues. Yet however elegantly such ideas may be described, presenting the 'traditional' categories of legal discussion without the context of discourse offers statements without speakers, ideas without their occasions, concepts outside history.

Yngvesson elsewhere (1989: 1690) suggests that, 'While interpretivist accounts of legal culture illuminate the diversity of law by focusing on local production of meaning, they are less attentive to the centrality of power in the meaning-making process;

---

[11] Influential sociologist Susan Silbey (2005: 358–59) also characterizes law as a particular way of organizing meaning and force and maintains that the critical sociological project is to explain the durability and ideological power of law.

questions of how the kind of interpretation produced is shaped by actors who are endowed with particular social characteristics are unexplored'. In a similar criticism levelled at Teubner, Tamanaha (2001: 191) says that reducing law to communication, as autopoiesis does, eliminates raw physical violence from within law. Even Fuller (1994:11) remarks that 'Geertz's approach is...idealistic; after all, the law is about repression just as much as imagination'.

Law is obviously bound up in power relations in many ways: it might be the product of class and social hierarchies, as Yngvesson points out; its application or invocation is affected by the social context, as Moore emphasizes; and law might itself represent a form of power, Fuller's 'powerfully self-validating systems of thought'.[12] But how do we explain what is distinctive about law as a social form, including its capacity to exert hegemonic power? An important strand of legal anthropology answers these questions by emphasizing legal language as a technique of knowledge (Mertz 1994; Mertz and Goodale 2012: 86). Bourdieu (1987), for example, recognizes that what is special about law is its language, its 'universalizing attitude'. Law, he says, 'claims to produce a specific form of judgement, completely distinct from the often wavering intuitions of the ordinary sense of fairness, because it is based upon rigorous deduction from a body of internally coherent rules' (1987: 820). It transforms 'irreconcilable conflicts of personal interests into rule-bound exchanges of rational arguments between equal individuals' (1987: 830–31). As he recognizes, law and legalistic argument produce a particular form of reasoning. Law produces 'the quintessential form of the symbolic power of naming that creates the things named, and creates social groups in particular' (1987: 838). Bourdieu interprets this as an exercise in power, both by the legal profession, which comes to exercise a monopoly over legal knowledge, and by the judiciary, whose power to ratify 'reproduces and heightens the immanent historical power which the authority and authorization of naming reinforces or liberates' (1987: 840). This is related to the class backgrounds of the legal professionals and their links with those who hold political power (1987: 841–53). In this

[12] Von Benda-Beckmann et al. (2009) further illustrate the dynamics of law and power that might be the subject of anthropological attention.

account, important insights into the nature of legal reasoning
and its ability to universalize and produce rational, rule-bound
argument become lost within a wider and more predictable analysis of struggles over meaning and the reproduction of political
power and social status.[13] Similarly, accounts of court processes
often emphasize the 'violence' that legal categories, including
those of human rights, do to social relations and understandings,
especially on the part of indigenous people. As Jean-Klein and
Riles (2005: 185) point out, there is a danger that such scholarship foregoes ethnographic engagement and description for
pre-figured analyses and slogan-making.

What Bourdieu's account does, implicitly, recognize is that
the analysis of law as meaning must precede the analysis of law
as an instrument of power. Examining the colonial encounter
in India, for example, Cohn (1989) is able to explain the transformation of the Code of Manu into a form of law applied by
the courts by analysing the assumptions about law inherent in
colonial attitudes: erroneous assumptions about the common
law, an idealistic vision of Justinian's project, and an unexamined
vision of the neutrality of case law and precedent. But is this all
we should examine? Do insights into the hierarchies of power
and the activities of an elite exhaust the interest and significance
of law for the anthropologist?

Peter Just (1992), in a masterful review article, suggests that
an opposition seems to emerge in these works between the 'hegemonic' and 'hermeneutic' approaches to law. It is a tension, as
he describes it, between the fine-grained analysis of meaning—
involving ever subtler examination of the ontological and epistemological categories of meaning in which the discourse of law
is based—and an analysis that moves 'outward into the grand
historical machinations of class and cash, power and privilege'
(1992: 375–76):

Are we to see law and the behavior it produces, however broadly
defined, as a cognitive system, a system of meanings, an expression
of culture produced from the inside out? Or are we to view them

[13] E. P. Thompson makes similar, subtly critical comments about Marxist
analyses that over-emphasize the 'class-bound and mystifying features of the law'
(1975: 259–61).

as products of history, themselves an arena of contestation for class, gender, ethnicity, an expression of society produced from the outside in? (1992: 387)

And must we choose, he asks, between the two? This is, of course, a tension that may apply to the study of more than just law: scientific knowledge, the notion of an elite artistic form, or a system of etiquette may also be understood as products of and resources within class and power struggles (Bourdieu 1984). But a hegemonic approach, as Just says, risks reducing them to the teleologies of class and losing sight of what goes on in people's hearts and heads.[14]

The Balinese case discussed by Geertz is interesting, not because the laws supported the interests of a village elite, but because the villagers felt compelled to expel a villager for whose plight they nevertheless had sympathy, and because even the king had to respect the authority of their rules. Law can constrain power as well as enabling it, and laws can express meaning and morality as well as acting against them. The questions we should ask concern what it is about law that enables it to do these things. If the presence and power of rulers, judges, and other enforcement agencies do not explain this capacity and cannot, as a result, properly distinguish law from other schemes of meaning, then what can?

CODIFIED LAWS

The apparent dichotomy between meaning and power as subjects of analysis for the legal anthropologist seems to lead to a dead end. But this might be linked to the tendency to look at what law does, rather than what it is. Work on legal language points to the distinct techniques of the law itself—the rules, categories, and forms of reasoning through which meaning is constructed and, indeed, through which power is exercised. We need, I suggest, to seek out further examples that can illustrate the distinctive thought, or language, of the law—its legalism—in order

---

[14] Elsewhere (2007b), I have discussed the shortcomings of this type of approach, as particularly exemplified by Nader (1990) in her work on 'harmony ideology'.

to understand the capacity of law to both create meaning and work as an instrument of oppression. Law and power need to be disaggregated, better to analyse the complex relations between them. This means, maybe surprisingly, moving away from the judicial process, from what we might regard as law in practice, and to do what anthropologists have long eschewed, that is to look at law on the books.

In the remainder of this chapter I consider a number of legal texts created around the world—writ on parchment or carved on stone. They demonstrate that law is not always, or only, an instrument of the powerful, and they also include examples of law without any obvious or direct instrumental value. This prompts questions about the nature of law, which must be answered by starting not with its functions but with its form. We can usefully bear in mind Hart's (1994) account of law as a system of rules. As later examples suggest, not all law consists of rules, but the legal codes considered here provide examples with which we can usefully address the question of how to understand law as a system of meaning, rather than letting it dissolve into dynamics of power and control. Equally, they shed light on those aspects of legalism that make it attractive to states and rulers.

An example from medieval Iceland, discussed in detail by Miller (1990), is a good place to start, and sheds some light on the attraction that the legal form might hold in and of itself. Until around 1262 Iceland was, as he describes, a society without a coercive state apparatus; it had only a weak sense of lordship, yet at the same time it had a highly developed legal system, with courts and elaborate rules of procedure, and equally complex rules of substantive law (1990: 5).[15] Miller emphasizes the Icelanders' obsession with rule articulation and categorization: the surviving collections of laws, known as Grágás and dated to around 1260—although law had been committed to writing in the early twelfth century—are remarkable for their length and extraordinary detail, containing some 700 densely printed pages of non-duplicated provisions (1990: 43). They contain rules about physical harm and compensation, but also

[15] The population was probably less than 100,000 during this period (1990: 16).

concern marriage contracts, sales of goods, repayment of loans, pledging of land and livestock, and rights in driftage; they attempt to regulate virtually every facet of farm management, from employment contracts to the separation of and accounting for hay blown into a neighbour's field; some provisions even establish liability for the failure to exploit hay production at maximum levels (1990: 223). Many of these laws seem to have been abstracted from specific cases, rather than deduced from abstract principle.

As Miller describes, legal expertise flourished in Iceland, with numerous men counted as being 'skilled in law' and the appointment of a Lawspeaker, whose duty it was to recite the laws at regular intervals, and with whom young men were sent to train. A reputation in law was a reputation that induced respect. Law also loomed large in the imagination and life of more than just the chieftain class: even pauper children found the subject matter for plays in lawsuits, while servants from neighbouring farms would get together to hold mock courts (1990: 226–27). We can only guess, says Miller (1990: 228), at how Icelanders understood their will to make law. Some provisions of the law codes seem to be more in the nature of a meditation on rules, without any certain relation to practice; some appear as nothing more than the satisfaction of a juristic and aesthetic urge toward systematization and conceptual order. Others do, however, seem to have been intended to constrain the vagaries of practice: 'people felt that law promoted order, not just the systemic order derived from the assignment of things to a place in a legal and social structure, but actual peace' (1990: 229). As he says:

if a law was respected simply because it was law, then elevating a hypothetical practice or one practice of many actual competing practices to the status of legal rule could confer on the desired behavior a certain legitimacy and positive value in relation to competing behaviors, thus making the rule in some small way self-enforcing, even those rules whose origin and motivation may have been jural elegance rather than the regulation of practice. (1990: 229)

The Icelanders did, it seems, try hard to ensure that their actions were legal, preferring to have law on their side rather than against them. There was, then, a body of respected rules, which were distinguishable from other norms of behaviour: the Icelanders' law was not embedded in the norms of kinship and marriage, nor those of production and exchange. Law stood apart, with a life of its own (1990: 256).

The complexity and specificity of the Icelandic laws that Miller describes are features that have been noted of other law codes. The code of Hammurabi in Mesopotamia (created in around 1770BC), the Twelve Tables of the early Roman republic (from around 450BC), and Germanic codes in early medieval Europe, all contained long lists of penalties and the monetary compensation to be made after the infliction of injuries (Whitman 1996). The earliest Greek inscriptions on stone and bronze, some dating back to the seventh century BC, contain lists of penalties and specify the duties of officials responsible for dealing with misdemeanours (Thomas 2005). Surviving fragments of laws from imperial Tibet—of the sixth to ninth centuries—likewise provide lists of compensation payments due after hunting accidents or attack by dogs (Richardson 1989, 1990); and punitive tariffs are found in all the codes and *dhammathats* of Buddhist South-East Asia (Huxley 1997: 322).

Many of these laws, including those inscribed on stone slabs at Gortyn, in Crete, are famous for their detail and complexity (Thomas 2005: 48). As Whitman (1996: 49) points out, the Germanic codes go into baroque, and somewhat unreal, detail in their description of penalties: there are so many kinds of compensation that it is hard to believe that each codifies an actual precedent. The forms of compensation specified in the Tibetan documents largely depended upon the social status of the victim, while both Hammurabi and the Twelve Tables refer to rank and status. Laws of compensation were obviously a means by which social status was explicitly, if hypothetically, marked. But the legal form, it seems, has an attraction of its own. Miller's comments on the jural elegance of the rules is echoed in Whitman's (1996) discussion of the apparently systematic aims of many early law codes. Reviewing a number of examples, he notes a prevalence of concerns with mutilation and price-setting. Composition tables, that is lists of compensation payments, recur, along with a more general concern with price, which includes provisions for other matters, such as commodities and wages (1996: 51–53). A similar concern with systematization and tariffs can be found in the law codes of traditional Tibet, where the Annals of the empire record that the king made a census and law book (in AD654–55) and, later, measured and marked out fields and other territories (Bacot et al. 1940). Huxley (2012: 239–40) talks of the Burmese Buddhists' predilection for packaging normative information into numbered lists.

Whitman notes the apparent aim of such codes to 'order the law': the extraordinarily elaborate Germanic codes, in particular, seem clearly systematizing in spirit (1996: 74–75). It appears as if the creation of laws of punishment and compensation is an act that generates order in the same way that the creation of standards of measurement does. The use of money equivalents to do this remains a puzzle for Whitman, and he asks why it is that humans should ever regard weighed metal as the equivalent of anything (1996: 82). But it may be that money, including obsolete coins, simply provides a measure, or scale, against which other things can be set. Charlemagne's monetary system continued to be used in Europe long after the relevant coins had ceased to circulate (Graeber 2011: 47–48). As Dresch (2012: 13) suggests, specifying monetary compensation is a way of asserting equivalence—despite other differences, every person's life or limb is the same—and it can, of course, also define difference.

Consideration of these codes should, as Whitman demonstrates, convince us not to read law codes in too functional a way, either as reflecting or reinforcing custom and practice, or as a means of regulation or dispute settlement, or indeed as a method used by rulers to arrogate to themselves a monopoly over the use of force. They may be one or other of these things, in any particular case, but their relationship with these more functional aims seems mostly to be contingent. Societies and rulers generally have other means of reinforcing custom, settling disputes, and asserting power. Rules and categories can provide definition to social life, while the legal form can promise system and order, in and of itself. The significance of the laws must be assessed in terms of what they express, as much as in what they achieve in directly practical terms, and it is apparent from the Icelandic example that law can inspire commitment, setting standards to which people aspire, as well as rules to be imposed upon them.

Are these codes truly examples of law, we might ask. Can the Mesopotamian or Cretan codes really be considered as falling within the same category as the legal systems of the modern world, and the activities of judges and law-makers, or even the villagers' laws in Bali? What could they be, however, if not laws or legal codes? The scholars writing on ancient Greece, like those analysing the 'laws' of imperial Tibet, or medieval Iceland, and Europe, seem to have had little trouble in describing them as such. The fact that we struggle to find another appropriate term indicates that they embody something of what we naturally think of as 'law'. If that term is appropriate, then on what basis is this so? It must be to do with the form of these texts as rules, with purportedly uniform application to different classes of case, classes that are specified by the use of abstract terms and categories. They are legalistic in form. This suggests that we need to approach and identify law not as something essentially functional or institutional, or caught up in relations of power and domination, but rather as something expressive, something that provides meaning and creates order in and of itself.

These are the ideas that I exemplify in the following chapters. I consider many different examples of law, examining their formal and legalistic features, but also analysing their capacity to be expressive and meaningful, as much as practical and constraining. In chapters four and five I consider the legal thought exemplified by the great legal systems of the world, their forms of reasoning and jurisprudence. Complex legal systems, like the Hindu and Chinese, and even the historical development of the common law in the Anglo-Saxon world, have rarely been considered by anthropologists, and chronologically they invite consideration as a prelude to more recent examples. Moreover, as the examples of simple legal codes in this chapter demonstrate, the law tends to complexity and any attempt to describe the nature of law must take this into account.

4

LAW AS AN INTELLECTUAL SYSTEM

The scholarly activities of lawyers, jurists, and judges were central to the great legal traditions of India, Rome, and the Islamic world, which are the subject of this chapter, as well as to the English common law, which I discuss in the next. These laws were the products of intellectual activity as much as social forms with practical aims or instruments of government and power. Indeed, the laws were, at times, able to constrain the activities of rulers, as well as to facilitate them; but they also provided a framework of principles, categories, and rules, through which people could make sense of their social relations and disputes, and each had a profound and lasting effect on a succession of different societies and polities.

This chapter is not an attempt to describe or characterize any of these traditions as a whole: each is far too diverse and extensive, in almost all respects, to make much generalization a feasible and instructive endeavour. Rather, the object is to illustrate the importance that intellectual scholarship and argument has had in developing forms of law. Case studies drawn from each system demonstrate what law can be, the forms that it can take, and the roles it might play in a wider social context.[1]

LAW IN THE HINDU WORLD

Sanskrit texts containing legal rules, principles, and ideas date back several centuries before the common era. The tradition found in these texts is said to be based upon the ancient Vedas, largely ritual texts, none of which is extant. As Lingat (1973: 8) describes, the Vedas are thought to represent eternal truths, forming a kind of code with infinite prescriptions of which only the Supreme Being can have perfect knowledge, but which have been revealed to the chosen few and written up in the received

[1] There are, of course, other legal systems that could usefully be considered in this regard, notably the Jewish.

sacred texts. The oldest texts in this tradition are the *dharmasūtras*, some of which relate back to the sixth century BC. They primarily concern the conduct of rituals, although they also contain rules defining social relationships and regulating the activities of daily life. It is the rather more extensive, and later, *dharmaśāstra* literature that contains more rules of a juridical character, the most famous of which is the *Manusmrti*, popularly known as the 'Laws of Manu', created before AD200.

The dharmaśāstra texts lay down the duties relating to caste (Lingat 1973: 73). Dharmaśāstra means, literally, 'science of the *dharma*' and the whole Hindu law tradition, it is said, can be regarded as ultimately concerned with the issue of dharma, what it is and how people are supposed to know and do it (Davis 2010: 16). Dharma has been characterized as 'the privileges, duties and obligations of a man, his standard of conduct as a member of the Aryan community, as a member of one of the castes and as a person in a particular stage of life' (Kāne 1930: vol. 1, p. 3).[2] It is primarily a matter of duty, therefore, and comprises more than law. As Lingat puts it (1973: x), Hindu law is based upon a notion of duty, rather than coercion, which extends beyond the domain of law, without encompassing it entirely.

The dharmaśāstras, themselves, contain rules of religious and ritual, as well as practical, importance, setting out the requirements necessary to maintain the cosmic and moral order (Lingat 1973: 135–36). They are presumed to teach the eternal and immutable dharma contained in the Vedas, to enable members of society to harmonize their existence with the universal order, that is the ideal, moral, and eternal order of the universe represented by the concept of dharma (Larivière 1987: 465). Nevertheless, they contain precepts of a juridical character, typically reading like a list of rules specifying what people may or should do: they elaborate duties connected to household and ancestral rites, to the making of gifts, the doing of penance, legal proceedings, and the duties of kingship; they make provisions for such mundane matters as eating, bathing, being a student, marriage, sex, contracts, sales, partnerships, wages, boundaries, life-cycle rites, the

---

[2] The meanings and significance of the notion of dharma are complex and, not surprisingly, the subject of extensive scholarship (Olivelle 2009).

five daily sacrifices, gifts, funerary rites, and penances. As Lubin (2010: 447–48) puts it, 'the household provides the framework for dharma in general; instead of presenting itself as emanating from the state, Hindu law extrapolates from the smallest social unit'.[3] The provisions of the dharmaśāstras are, in this way, regarded as an extension of vedic ritual principles into the widest possible sphere of human activity and social life.

The king is the ultimate guarantor that dharma is adhered to in his kingdom and the texts make it clear that it is the ruler's own dharma to specify and enforce punitive sanctions, thereby protecting the people in his kingdom and promoting the system of castes and life-stages (Lingat 1973: Pt 2, ch 3). They describe instances of wrongdoing and appropriate sanctions—in relation to debt, for example—and go into great detail over the issue of crimes and punishments. There has been considerable debate and disagreement over the question of the Hindu king's practical power to legislate. The general view seems to be that, even apart from the power to make administrative provisions, which were largely beyond the principles of dharma, the king had some legislative authority. However, he was also bound to sanction and enforce regional custom and convention (Larivière 2004). The texts confirm that existing custom has a claim to validity with which the king is bound not to interfere and, indeed, that the people can dethrone a king who fails to adhere to his own dharma.

In practice, the actual implementation of the guidelines contained in the texts was always localized and fragmentary and it was a British misinterpretation, as described in chapter two, to regard the dharmaśāstra texts as a code on the basis of which judges could make authoritative decisions. As Larivière (2004: 623) says, the texts were not composed as literary templates to be applied to every situation and every dispute without differentiation. They were collections of aphorisms, guidelines, and advice, which could be drawn upon when required to inform and validate a judge's, guru's, or king's opinion. In this way they are concerned with the administration of law, but they are not codes in a modern, western sense.

---

[3] As he points out, this is also a feature of ancient Greek and Jewish laws.

The texts, then, contain practically-oriented rules and specify permissible actions, and these, in turn, define what a righteous believer in the Vedas should do and how. It was the design of the texts to prescribe rules that would guide each member of society so that he might live his life as fully in accordance with dharma as possible (Larivière 1987: 466–47). The purpose of the legal system was not so much to deliver justice as to ensure that the entire populace adhered to the duties and obligations of dharma. The precepts express the requirements necessary to maintain the cosmic and moral order (Lingat 1973: 135, 258). It is the duty of men to profit from this if they want salvation. The law shows the way which one should follow, but it does not impose that way; it is supposed to enable as much as it constrains. As Lubin (2010: 450) comments, it was the distinctive genius of Hindu (and other) religious laws to coordinate state-imposed violence with a regime of self-discipline oriented to invisible realities and self-correction, both nominally under expert religious authority.

Hindu law in practice

Davis (2010: 15) describes the dharmaśāstras as textbooks for the Hindu scholastic tradition of religious jurisprudence, containing a form of legal theory. As has often been noted, evidence of their application and the effects upon local practice of their rules and principles is extremely slim, particularly because of the dominance of Indian societies by, first, Muslim Moghul rulers and then British imperial administrators. Nevertheless, as Olivelle (1993: 27) points out, the influence of the prescriptive rules found in the dharmaśāstra texts on the thought and practice of later generations should not be underestimated and there is evidence from medieval inscriptions of the use of dharmaśāstra in litigation (Derrett 1973: 274).

Davis (2012: 89–94) suggests that the opinions given by Brahmin scholars were analogous to the *responsa* of the Roman jurists described in the next section, part of a culture of request, petition, and inquiry. The problems they dealt with, he says, were most often moral dilemmas or a doubt about the law, rather than a dispute already in progress. He has also studied what he calls the laws of 'intermediate-level corporate groups', including merchants, religious specialists, soldiers, agriculturalists, and pastoralists (Davis 2005). It was these groups, he says, that mediated the theoretical influences of both local customary laws and the elite Brahminical discourse of the dharmaśāstra in order to establish viable (localized) ideologies of law. The dharmaśāstra texts, themselves, allowed a conceptual space for the incorporation of local laws within their own jurisprudence, recognizing the possibility that such groups might elaborate technical or supplementary rules regarding their own legal governance. Specific provisions were envisaged for such things as natural disasters, repairs to physical structures, provisions for orphans, rituals, migrations, guilds, and even for the activities of heretics.

In practice, as Davis describes, the Brahmins were regarded as the caretakers of the dharma tradition and temple inscriptions indicate that they were making judicial decisions for other castes and specifying such matters as appropriate livelihoods, thus determining their social, economic, and other privileges. Others record them imposing criminal penalties on thieves and making marriage rules for their own caste groups, rules which were to be enforced by the king. Epigraphical examples also refer to kings making laws for such groups. Nevertheless, these directives were always presented as being supplemental and technical, not intended to subvert the rules of dharma. Further inscriptions record groups making their own rules relating to temple donations and other religious duties, giving privileges to soldiers and establishing guild rules. The evidence is not extensive but, Davis concludes, such inscriptions indicate that both śāstric vocabulary and conventions were used in the practical context of premodern inscriptions (2005: 114).

The dharmaśāstra rules thus had a unifying effect on patterns of more localized legal thought, principally through the activities and influence of the Brahmins (Davis 2010: 13). As Davis (1999) describes, a collection of records from Kerala provides evidence of the way in which dharmaśāstra was implemented within the local legal system, through the creation of subsidiary texts and legalistic documentary forms by an influential Brahmin family. There was what he describes as a stable, local legal system in the region, albeit one that was largely unwritten and uncodified, and it is apparent through careful analysis of the texts that the dharmaśāstra literature had a significant and important effect upon it. In one local text, for example, the Brahmins set out what they considered to be the most authoritative rules of legal procedure, the content of which had clearly been derived from the provisions of the dharmaśāstras. More particularly, the records illustrate the influence of dharmaśāstra ideas on forms of mortgage, loan contracts, land sale, and tenure. This occurred primarily through the interpretation, rather than direct invocation, of the texts, but the influence is clear (1999: 191). Thus, he says, the 'dharma literature generally may be characterized as a record of customs presented through the idiom of śāstra texts and subsequently propagated by brahmins in various parts of India'. It was through their influence that dharmaśāstra norms were adopted as the legal norms of local communities (1999: 166).

What was Hindu law?

The Hindu tradition contains a body of scholarly texts that set out matters of legal substance, that is rules and directions for daily life, including provisions for sanctions and punishments. However, as Davis suggests, these might be regarded as matters of theology and jurisprudence, as much as substantive law, and their influence on judicial processes was, at most, indirect. Hesitating to label the dharmaśāstras as 'law', Lingat suggests that the dharma represented in these texts eventually developed into law, as the śāstras became the subject of commentaries. The Hindus gradually derived their law, he says, from the notion of duty found in the concept of dharma. He does, however, recognize the authority of the dharmaśāstra texts themselves:

The dharmaśāstras were certainly not codes in the European sense of that word, but their precepts did not lack authority in Hindu eyes. They were authoritative, firstly because of their origins but also, and particularly in the eyes of the judges, because they were the fruit of profound study and, as a result, offered a framework for juridical reasoning. (Lingat 1967: 161)[4]

Some have been more hesitant to describe the dharmaśāstras as legal texts, regarding them as merely 'pious wishes' with no

---

[4] This is my own translation.

political sanctions, or as purely learned commentaries on ancient texts (Das Gupta 1914; Rocher 1984). Larivière, by contrast, regards dharmaśāstra as ultimately based upon custom, that is upon local law. The provisions for legal procedure, in particular, represent the 'law of the land', which thus became a source of dharma (2004: 611–12).

A bolder approach is taken by Olivelle (1993) and Davis (2010), who regard the theological and legal aspects of Hindu thought as inextricably linked. A theology, Davis explains (2010: 3), is the attempt to understand or give meaning to the transcendent significance of acts. The dharmaśāstras are both theology and law, focused on discovering and transmitting the religious significance of ordinary human activities (2010: 23). Characterizing law as 'the theology of daily life', he describes Hindu law as the instrument and rhetoric by which quotidian human acts are placed into a system or structure larger than human life, one that encapsulates assumptions about what we aspire to as human beings, promising the higher-order coordination of human experience (2010: 1). As he describes it, the dharmaśāstra texts form a conceptual framework that appears to operate outside the bounds of time and space. They form a sacred and transcendent system that lies beyond the activities of humans, even wise rulers. The rules of dharma emanated from the sacred Vedas, but their ritual and impersonal authority has been allied with an abstract sense of community and custom to provide an authoritative basis for the law.

In practice, since the dharma is regarded as having been completely revealed in the Vedas, there is no room for novelty in doctrine, institution, or practice (Olivelle 1993: 8). Hindu scholars thus had to work within established conventions to form an elaborate and systematic reflection upon law. At the heart of their scholastic work was a theory of hermeneutics, *mimāmsā*, that is the understanding, interpretation, and transmission of received sacred texts. This formed what Davis (2010: 20) describes as 'a relatively closed intellectual tradition'. 'It is hard to overemphasize', he says, 'the importance of the idea that law is what results from interpretation, rather than being the basis for interpretation'. Law is, in this way, 'a path that is forged through acts of interpreting legal sources'. Moreover, the hermeneutic task is never complete. It is a continuous process by which revelation is remade in the context of ordinary life (Davis 2010: 64–69). The resulting provisions of the dharmaśāstras are legalistic, containing rules that describe, prescribe, and delimit the possibilities and requirements of daily life. They categorize and clarify: the object is the progressive elimination of choice in human actions (Davis 2010: 167).

Davis's approach has not been accepted uncritically by other scholars. However, following Olivelle, Davis makes a convincing case for recognizing the dharmaśāstra texts and tradition as Hindu law, and this is not seriously challenged by his critics. Even on Lubin's (2010) more cautious account, Hindu law was not the product of the state or political institutions. Hindu law, as described in this way, is first and foremost an intellectual system, rather than a governmental or judicial one. It is a system of thought, centred on a hermeneutics, directed towards the truth of dharma. It is also concerned with the individual, as he or she exists within a moral and cosmic order, rather than with the establishment and regulation of a polity.

For the anthropologist, if law can be a theology, imparting meaning to human life and requiring interpretation and exegesis, we must take seriously the thought it contains and the activities that produce it if we are to understand what it is and does. Of course, as Olivelle (1993: 27) points out, proponents of theological schemes seek to control and regulate social mores, and to classify and evaluate institutions, so we need to understand those institutions if we are to understand the origins and historical development of the theological system, as well as the ways in which Brahmins or kings implemented them in practice.[5] It would be a mistake, however, to think too much in terms of control and regulation when asking about the significance of Hindu legal thought.

The colonial period, of course, caused a profound rupture in the Indian legal tradition, as described in chapter two. As Dhavan (1992) explains, the colonial administration and legislation brought about fundamental changes in the legal identity of the family and religious institutions. Some scholars, notably Fuller (1988), trace a continuity between the traditions of Hindu textual interpretation

---

[5] Olivelle is considering the Hindu āśrama system of life-stages, but the idea can equally be applied to political institutions.

and modern judicial reasoning in India's Supreme Court. Judges
have justified their rulings on the constitutional principle of
'freedom of religion' by reference to authoritative Hindu scrip-
tures, while social equality and other modern values are said to be
affirmed by the ancient texts, recoverable by correct interpretation, carried out according to the methods of traditional textual
interpretation (1988: 238–40). As Fuller summarizes it, the judges
present their reasoning as, in part, the recovery of timeless truths
and values already present in the Vedas (1988: 246). Other scholars interpret the references to these texts as little more than
'window dressing': the judges search the texts to support the
view preferred according to current usage or to endorse what
they see as the needs of society (Larivière 1989: 764–67). Davis
(2008: 323) argues that the 'superficial resemblances' between
the interpretive strategies of contemporary judges and those of
traditional pandits are no more than those that exist between all
modes of legal reasoning. Even if all that remains is, however,
an ideological appeal to the legitimating potential of the ancient
texts and principles, this is to recognize the continuing authority
of an essentially scholastic legal tradition.

ROMAN LAW

If Hindu law was what resulted from the interpretive work of
scholars, placing the activities of daily life into a transcendent conceptual framework, or a higher order coordination of human
experience, then it has much in common with Roman law and the
(roughly contemporary) work of the Roman jurists. A simple reference to 'Roman law' will often be taken to indicate the content
of the great Justinianic codifications of the sixth century, which
have formed a legal paradigm for scholars in most of the western
world. These contain the substance of Roman law at the end of its
initial development, but it was the culmination of almost a millennium of legal thought and activity, shaped by legal assemblies,
judges and legal officials, scholars and advocates, emperors and
historians, and largely based upon the writings of the jurists. The
Roman jurists were scholars, rather than judges or advocates—
although they sometimes combined such roles—and when the
emperors finally came to assert control over the legal realm what

they understood to be the existing law was primarily found in juristic opinion. To understand the phenomenon of Roman law in its historical and intellectual context, therefore, their work must be regarded as central.[6]

Throughout most of the Roman Republic, that is up until the middle of the first century BC, what was regarded as the civil law, the *ius civile*, was theoretically the law of the Twelve Tables. This foundational statement of Roman law is said to have been made in response to demands of the plebeians (the commoner class) in 451–50BC, inscribed on tablets and posted in public view.[7] It was the patrician (aristocratic) college of pontiffs, which enjoyed a form of religious authority, that retained the power to interpret the relatively concise rules contained in the Twelve Tables, but in practice legal disputes were heard by magistrates. There were a few instances of legislation, that is explicit laws (*lex*), made during this period, but private law was mainly developed through the praetors' edicts. The urban praetor was a special magistrate, appointed annually to deal exclusively with the administration of justice. By the end of the second century BC the formulary system had developed, whereby the praetor would hear the parties to a legal case and, if he thought there was an issue to be tried, he would grant a *formula*, effectively a statement of the plaintiff's case. This would specify the available remedy, which could be granted by the judge, the *iudex*, when he had considered the facts of the case. Each praetor, on taking up office, would issue an edict in which he set out how he would operate and what formulae he would accept in the following year. Although they were not specially trained, therefore, and did not possess particular legal knowledge, the praetors would effectively determine the forms of action that could be brought, to some extent developing the law.

During the early period judicial processes for private suits formed what Bruce Frier (2010a) describes as a loosely-organized,

---

[6] In this section I draw primarily upon the classic overviews of Roman law provided by Jolowicz (1932), Nicholas (1962), and Crook (1967), as well as the rather more contentious, but sociologically engaged, work by Frier (1985) and Watson (1995).

[7] The actual time of creation and the truth of the later tradition that they had been made in response to demands by the plebeians are far from clear (Watson 1975).

lay-dominated, system of arbitration. As the praetors' remedies and procedures became more complex, however, the work of legal interpretation was effectively taken over by the jurists, private legal scholars. They would advise those unfamiliar with the judicial process on how to draft the formulae needed to initiate a legal case, which became notoriously complicated, or how to present a defence; they could also draft legal documents, such as contracts and wills. Our sources for their activities are limited and most of what we know about the jurists and their work comes from the extracts reproduced in the Theodosian and Justinianic codifications. However, it is clear that the jurists' writings moved from commentaries upon the Twelve Tables to the giving of written opinions (*responsa*), indicating their recognition as legal experts. As Lewis (2000: 38) describes, their advice came to form the basis for public discussion and dialectical debate, which became a central characteristic of Roman law. As their status grew, their opinions were gathered together and eventually they also came to advise the praetor on the formulation of his edict, as well as the judges on the hearing and decision of legal cases.[8]

According to the Roman jurist Pomponius (writing in around AD 150), it was Quintus Mucius Scaevola who was the first of the jurists to arrange the ius civile into categories and his work, which dates from around the beginning of the last century BC, appears to be the first systematic legal treatise. It was still influenced by the content of the Twelve Tables, but it incorporated certain important legal innovations that had been introduced through the praetors' edicts (Frier 1985: 158–60).

It is the first three centuries AD, during the early empire, that is generally known as the 'classical period' of Roman law. The jurists' writings became more extensive and creative, and they became 'the chief instrument of legal development' (Jolowicz 1932: 372). As Frier (2003: 823–24) puts it, they developed law 'on the basis of what they called the art (*ars*) of law-finding, subjecting existing legal rules and institutions to intense and

---

[8] Under the early empire, in around AD 130, the praetor's edict was made permanent, no longer subject to annual review, and their work of developing the law came to an end.

sustained intellectual scrutiny, with the aim of isolating the basic principles that controlled the rules, and then applying these principles in the creation of new law'. As Watson (1995: 82) says, their reasoning attained a very high degree of conceptualization and was 'suffused with an internal legal logic'. They developed what is known as the 'casuistic' method, using individual, often hypothetical, problems to provide both typical examples of the application of a rule or principle, and limiting cases that illustrated their boundaries. Their writings were mostly concerned with particular problems, rather than the formulation of definitions, abstract statements of legal principle, or general rules. Later in the empire there was more of a tendency towards abstraction and rule-making, but the casuistic approach continued (Schulz 1936: ch 4).

Already in the late republic, the jurists had come to be regarded as legal professionals, whose opinions carried weight in court, and their authority was officially recognized when the first emperor, Augustus, conferred the privilege of giving responsa on certain jurists 'in order to increase the authority of law'. Later, in the second century AD, Hadrian confirmed the jurists' authority while Pomponius declared that the ius civile was to be found solely in their interpretations. Nevertheless, the status of these imperial declarations is not entirely clear and, officially, the iudex remained free to make his own assessment of a legal case. It seems that the power and legal authority of the jurists was never fully spelled out or thought through. Nor, indeed, was that of the emperors and it was only under Hadrian that imperial orders, whether laws (*constitutiones*) or opinions (*rescripta*) were declared to have the force of lex.

The development of Roman law in the hands of the jurists maintained, in this way, substantial independence of political interference, emerging as a more or less autonomous discipline, insulated by its own professionalism from direct social pressure (Frier 2003). However, in the later Empire, and after the upheavals caused by its expansion and division into east and west, new bureaucratic structures emerged, including a judicial system in which the iudex controlled the whole legal case and whose authority came to be linked directly to the sovereignty of the emperor (Frier 2010b). After their heyday in the third century AD,

the jurists' authority was finally superseded.[9] With some justification, officials considered that the jurists' law was confusing:
their opinions often differed and their works offered inconsistent interpretations, due to personal disagreements and rivalries,
as much as the thinking of the two distinct 'schools' that had
appeared in the late Republic. In the fifth century Theodosius
ordered a work of codification and under Justinian, in the mid
sixth century, a comprehensive and lasting codification was
undertaken. This was presented as a project to bring law and
order to the empire; the laws were to remain valid for all time
and no further juristic interpretations were to be allowed (Kelley
2002: 288–90). The law effectively became that of the emperor.

Roman law in practice

A picture of Roman law in the last decades of the Roman republic
can be glimpsed through the procedures and arguments of legal
cases, notably the speeches of the advocate Cicero. One of these,
the *pro Caecina*, made in a land dispute and delivered in around
69BC, forms the subject of an illuminating case study by Bruce
Frier (1985). We only have the speech made by Cicero, who was
not a jurist, although he had also received a legal education. It
was a persuasive, quite possibly successful, attempt to convince
the judge to interpret the law—as found in the remedy sought in
the interdict, the claim on which Caecina's case was based—in a
way that seems to be against both principle and common sense.
But it also includes a spirited defence of both the law and the
work of the jurists, and provides material on which Frier bases a
discussion of the status and 'rise' of the Roman jurists.

The case involved a dispute over a farm between two heirs of
an upper-class woman, one being her husband, Caecina, who had
inherited the bulk of her estate, the other a friend and advisor,
Aebutius, who claimed to have purchased the farm in question at
an earlier date. When it became clear that the husband was laying
claim to the farm, Aebutius occupied it in his own name and this,
as Frier comments, may have caused Caecina to resolve to crush
the socially inferior upstart (1985: 20–21). Caecina requested

---

[9] Some historians have stressed the continuing influence of jurists, albeit that
they were absorbed into the imperial bureaucracy (Humfress 2007: ch 3).

Aebutius's agreement to an act of formalized violence, whereby he would enter the farm and 'be led off in the time-honoured way', so as to lay the foundation for a legal action. Having initially agreed to this course of action, however, Aebutius decided to resist, and raised and armed a band of freemen and slaves from the surrounding area who confronted Caecina when he arrived with a group of companions, threatening deadly violence. When Caecina persisted in approaching the farm he and his companions were showered with missiles and retreated in confusion. Caecina then obtained an interdict *de vi hominibus armatis,* to initiate legal proceedings. This was, technically, an action for the restoration of land from which he had been forcibly expelled. He had not, however, been in possession of the land at the time of the confrontation and this meant that his advocate, Cicero, had to employ ingenious and technical legal arguments to enable Caecina to win his case (1985: ch 1).

It is in Cicero's rhetoric concerning the law and its interpretation that much of the interest, for present purposes, lies. Launching into a eulogy for the law, he declares that the ius civile is an independent body of rules and institutions that constitutes 'the bonds of social welfare and life'. It is the sole reliable basis for determining rights to ownership and legal relations, and for protecting these rights against third parties. He describes law as the incorruptible guarantor of such rights, set apart from ordinary political and social life, 'uniform among all and identical for everyone'. The jurists, according to Cicero, stand between the ius civile and the judicial system, as the 'interpreters of law', their authority bound up with that of the ius civile itself, such that an attack on them would amount to an attack on both the leges and iura. The courts, meanwhile, are the most fallible institutions of the law. Judges ought to decide cases in accordance with the jurists' responsa; a judge might decide that a jurist's opinion is wrong, but even a corrupt judge would not dare to decide against the recognized rules of law (Frier 1985: 184–87).

We must, of course, read this speech as a display of advocacy within an adversarial judicial process. It is an attempt to persuade a court to accept a juristic opinion given in support of his client, which Cicero's opponent was presumably trying to dismiss as wrong or irrelevant. However, Cicero must have considered that what he argued would be persuasive to the court, as a depiction of the law and the authority of the jurists. As Frier (1985: 74) comments, there was also a contemporary debate about praetorian justice, the elite regarding it as an extension of the existing social order, while outsiders, like Cicero, regarded the edict as a source of law that ought to be constant and abiding. It is in this context that we must understand Cicero's insistence on the autonomy of law, the first context in which this idea appears to be expressly articulated.[10]

As Frier (2010a: 224–25) describes it, the jurists were, at this point, analysing the rules applied in the Roman courts with 'a wholly unprecedented degree of sophistication'. They were treating legal rules as an intellectual field, to which the dialectical methods of Greek philosophy could be applied in order to isolate the basic underlying concepts.

> For the first time in history a secular legal system was examined as a distinct and coherent body of knowledge: individual legal decisions, rules and statutory enactments were considered objectively and were explained through reference to general principles and truths basic to the legal system as a whole. Law was finally sundered from the elaborate apparatus of case-oriented rhetorical argument and was made over into an abstract body of norms … gradually the participants in the Roman judicial system were persuaded to understand and use law in this way. (Frier 1985: 286–87)

In practice, he suggests, there was a gradual surrender of day-to-day control over private legal norms by the civil government of Rome—praetors, assemblies, and Senate—to the extra-constitutional body of legal experts, the jurists (Frier 1985: 195). Some scholars disagree with the picture that Frier paints of the 'autonomy' of Roman law (Birks 1987).[11] Frier is not, however, alleging complete independence: the jurists' work was closely related to the courts and primarily took the form of

---

[10] Ambivalent attitudes have been noted on the part of the jurists (Frier 1986: 894) and even on the part of Cicero about the jurists (Harries 2006).

[11] Despite pouring scorn on the idea that the legal realm could have been autonomous in any real way, Birks does recognize the influence of legal scholars, even in twentieth-century England, while others accept Frier's depiction of autonomy (Lewis 2000).

discussion about legal cases. His point is that the ius civile came to be regarded by Romans as something that had its own logic and intellectual coherence, representing a benefit and safeguard which transcended the political and potentially corrupt activities of men.[12]

Like Crook (1967: 25–26), Watson sees the prestige and distinction of the law as the basis for the prestige and authority of the jurists. He describes them as a 'law-making elite', and in his book on the subject (1995) returns more than once to the topic of their 'isolationism', that is, to the independence of their thought and objectives from the practical realities of the judicial and political milieu.[13]

Birks (1987), by contrast, attributes both the growth of the substantive law and the rise of the jurists to the needs of judges and litigants. He suggests that the evolution of rationality in the law has its own momentum, driven by a quest for 'legal security'.[14] It was not just that there were few expressly formulated legal rules, but even those that existed were difficult to find and understand, often expressed in obscure and technical language (Frier 1985: 43). People were reliant, therefore, upon the jurists. However, the idea that this must have been a major factor in the rise of the law and legal experts surely assumes too much. As numerous examples in this book indicate, it is not always the

[12] There is some scholarly disagreement over Frier's depiction of the rise of the jurists in the first century BC and its causes. Harries (2006), in particular, depicts them as struggling for status and recognition during this period. Frier cites contemporary social, political, and economic factors, including the expansion of Roman citizenship, the rise of commercial activity and a need for security in the matters of property, succession, and family relations (1985: 257–58), together with strategic action on the part of the jurists, especially Quintus Mucius Scaevola. Watson (1995) traces the causes of the jurists' rise to a much earlier period, linking it to their aristocratic predecessors in the College of Pontiffs. The law and those learned in it acquired a prestige, he says, as part of the growth of high culture.

[13] Although stressing the intellectual sophistication and autonomy of their thought, Frier does not invoke quite the same picture of isolation as Watson, a picture also regarded as rather extreme by others (Pennington 1997; Humfress 2007: 24).

[14] Rather confusingly, in the literature on Roman law the notion of legal security indicates both certainty that right will prevail during legal proceedings and certainty over what the law, itself, is (Schulz 1936: ch 12; Frier 1985: 33, 183).

case that legal certainty brings social benefits or that its absence is perceived as a lack. The medieval men described by Clanchy (1983) were positively suspicious of the certainty of the law and its benefits as a means of resolving disputes. Moreover, anthropological studies indicate that the outcome of a court case, or more informal equivalent, may be relatively predictable, even if it is not based upon a system of legal rules (Benda-Beckmann and Pirie 2007). To attribute the development of laws to a perceived need for legal certainty is to take the claims that law makes for itself too seriously.

This debate over the development of Roman law nevertheless raises interesting issues about legalistic thought. As Frier (1985: 193–94) suggests, one of the great achievements of the Roman jurists lay in the liberation of private law from its stultifying archaic formalism, which they achieved by basing their methods upon a limited set of principles, concepts, forms, and procedures, introducing equitable concepts, such as that of *bona fides*. The fact that a legal case could founder because of a technical mistake in the formula was notorious. Jolowicz (1932: ch 24) equates that formalism with the 'immaturity' of the ius civile, while the decrease in formalism and rigidity, he says, accompanied a move towards abstraction. The more developed and abstract thinking of the later jurists was, thus, legalistic in a different way, a matter of reasoning more than formalism.

As their work progressed, the jurists encountered what Frier calls one of the great paradoxes of autonomous legal thinking (we might say of legalism), that the quest for certainty through jurisprudence may also lead to an increase in the law's complexity and an apparent tolerance of uncertainty. In practice, there was often lack of clarity over what the law was and which legislation was valid (Crook 1967: 32). Modern scholars seem united in their view that the jurists were not, for the most part, interested in systematizing the law and providing it with overall coherence. Watson, for example, emphasizes the proliferation of legal literature, which contained fine and complex distinctions, and concerns with categories and their boundaries, rather than with any overall system. Quintus Mucius Scaevola and Gaius, in his *Institutes* of around 161 AD, were the exceptions, but their legal schemes seem to have had little impact on the writings of other jurists. Cicero was, himself, scathing of the prolixity of the juristic literature, which provided endless examples without any abstract summary. However, his appeal for a well-ordered and systematic whole, with clear definitions and abstract legal rules, seems to have fallen upon deaf ears (Schulz 1936: 49, 65). While it might appear to be the object of law to provide certainty, and the giving of individual responsa might have clarified the law in some areas, overall the result was not a clear and logical system; Roman legalism was often opaque and frequently confusing.[15]

A tension between law and equity thus arises within this type of legalistic thought. Again, it is Cicero, in *pro Caecina*, who emphasizes the importance of the law but also repeatedly appeals to *aequitas*, equity, building what Frier calls a concept of 'internal or immanent fairness', something that mediates between an abstract, general rule and a concrete, specific case (1985: 120). Literal interpretations of the law, Cicero argued, promise nets and snares, leading along a 'narrow and crooked path', inferior to interpretation in terms of the author's sense and the 'cause of fairness'. In this way, as Frier says, Cicero uses the high ground of aequitas and the spirit of the law to launch a series of devastating attacks on his opponent's literal interpretation of the interdict, suggesting that this would sanction the violence carried out by his client, Aebutius, and deny Caecina a remedy for the wrong that had undoubtedly been done to him (Frier 1985: 120–23). Whatever the merits of these rhetorical arguments, the case highlights the tensions between legalism and equity, as principles of legal reasoning that often pull in different directions, tensions that occur widely amongst other examples of law. This is a tension to which I return in later chapters.

What was Roman law?

In the course of a millennium Roman law and judicial practice went through a succession of forms; acts of law-making were undertaken by the legislative bodies of the Republic, including the Twelve Tables and other leges, by republican judicial

---

[15] Nor does it appear to have had much practical effect upon Roman society as a whole: 'its immediate consequence for Roman society is equivocal...The social and economic institutions of the empire do not appear to have altered significantly despite the encouragement of juristic liberalism' (Frier 2003: 824).

officials, principally edicts of the praetors with their specification of the formulae, and by the emperors with their orders and decrees. Most of these forms of law were linked to or based upon judicial practices, and it was the activities of the courts that were the focus of juristic attention. The courts provided the arena in which law was applied, not where it was made, however, and not where we can find it articulated and explained. It was the jurists, whose scholarly work aspired to logical and philosophical coherence, who expounded what the law was. They were the ones who teased out the underlying principles and concepts, the meanings and application of the formulae, and who drew fine distinctions in order to explore the limits of those concepts and principles. Roman law was inseparable from its jurisprudence and that jurisprudence was an essentially academic exercise. To deny the juristic writings the label of 'law' would be tantamount to saying that Roman law was not really law.

To understand what Roman law was as an empirical matter, therefore, we must ask who the scholars were, how they carried out their work, how they related to the advocates, judges, and law-makers, and how their juristic writings were used. Of course the opportunities for doing so are limited by the paucity of sources, but the writings of Frier and Watson concerning the work and influence of the jurists, controversial though they may be in some respects, shed light upon these issues.[16]

We might also ask what the Romans, at various times and places, thought of their law. As Watson suggests, they were not particularly interested in a theory of law-making. Cicero and Gaius each list a variety, and a different variety, of sources of the civil law. For Cicero, law was found in legislation, resolutions of the senate, decided cases, opinions of jurists, edicts of magistrates, custom, and equity; while Gaius lists legislation, enactments of the plebeians, resolutions of the senate, constitutions of the emperors, edicts, and jurists' opinions (Crook 1967: 19). Cicero's insistence on the idea of a supervening morality and his assertion that law was of divine origin, unchanging and based upon

---

[16] We might also, of course, examine other people and processes, including advocates, litigants, judges, and so on, if the material were available, as Humfress (2007) does for a later period.

reasoning, was not typical (Watson 1995). Nor was the idea that law might be founded upon custom, even if much of the early law must have reflected custom and practice; it was not the law of the people.[17] We are not, therefore, left with any very clear sense of what law actually was for the majority of the Romans.

There does seem, however, to have been a sense that law was something that transcended real life. The plebeians' request for an explicit statement of the law was expressed as a demand for certainty and equality before the law, although this is far from what they actually achieved: the Twelve Tables were prepared by the patricians as the law they were willing to share with the plebeians and they excluded matters deemed to be unfit for them, such as religious rituals and priestly offices (Watson 1995: 37–38). The law was, obviously, regarded as something of an ideal, a privilege hitherto only enjoyed by the patricians, which provided certainty and equality in the form of explicit rules.[18] Moreover, it was only to be enjoyed by Roman citizens, as opposed to the non-citizens living under Roman government, who had their own law, the *ius gentium*. Far from being an instrument of government, then, the ius civile was a resource to which citizens and non-citizens had access in different degrees. Later, it was possible for Cicero to claim that law, as the guarantor of private legal rights, was set apart from ordinary political and social life.

As Watson emphasizes (1995: ch 7), the jurists' reasoning was largely self-contained: it had a particular logic, an intellectual life of its own. This intellectual life was not a religious one: by contrast with the Hindu scholars, the Roman jurists were not concerned to provide quotidian acts with specifically religious significance. Roman law could hardly be described as a 'theology of daily life'.[19] Nevertheless, theirs was also a scholarly attempt to interpret ordinary actions according to a higher-order set of

[17] Custom, *consuetudo*, was recognized as authoritative if it was long-standing, but it could only be relied upon by the courts if it had been recognized in the praetor's edict or an imperial rescript (Stein 1999: 26; Ibbetson 2007). This situation was also more complicated in the provinces after 212AD when local customs were recognized in cases involving new Roman citizens (Kantor 2012).

[18] It is possible, of course, that this idealism developed later and has been projected back upon the earlier period, but the point is that it did emerge.

[19] As Harries (2006: ch 8) describes, there was a distinction between civil and priestly law.

logical and legalistic rules and relations. Like the dharmaśāstra scholars, the jurists' work consisted primarily in the activity of interpretation; intellectual process was as important as substance.

In practice, Roman law also provided ways in which people could relate to one another and to their property, providing a framework for legal events and transactions, concerning inheritance, property, contract, slave manumission, coming of age, and so on. However, we must not be over-influenced by the form of the Justinianic codification to regard Roman law, as it existed during the previous millennium, as either forming a coherent system or an instrument of government. It formed a realm of ideas, which were influential on the activities of both rulers and judges but, as with the Hindu dharmaśāstra literature, it was primarily the product of scholarly interpretation.

THE ISLAMIC WORLD

Islamic law is strongly associated with the sense of a divine vision for the world. The *shari'a*, which encompasses more than law, could be said to be preoccupied with the nature of this vision and the individual's duties towards God. It is thought that God's will for mankind has been only partly revealed in the Quran, however, and must go through a human intellectual process before it can form a cohesive legal system for society (Vikør 2005: 1–2). Shari'a is God's right path through life, then, while Islamic legal science seeks to discover what the shari'a consists of. This science, comprising the rules, texts, teachings, practices, and principles that have been formulated on the basis of God's revelation, is known as the *fiqh*; and it is necessarily flawed and open to debate. As Weiss (1998: 22) says, Muslim juristic thought considers that the law has not been sent down from heaven as a finished product and it is something that human jurists must elaborate on the basis of textual sources.[20]

---

[20] In practice, the term shari'a can also be used to refer to the legal rules formulated by individual scholars but, as Weiss (1998: 22) emphasizes, it is important to draw a distinction between shari'a, in general, and shari'a law, as that part (or product of it) that consists of the rules of law and jurisprudence.

What we might call Islamic law, then, is elaborated in the fiqh; this is a body of learning that includes rules for the regulation of numerous matters of daily life, including inheritance, contracts, injuries, and marriage. These stipulations are often moralistic, in particular those concerning the family—and the integrity of the extended family—the preservation of the patriline, an abhorrence of sex outside marriage, property relations, and commercial transactions, which are organized into categories ranging from the prohibited, through the immoral, neutral, and moral, to the compulsory. Islamic law thus encompasses a whole range of norms, legal, moral, and ritual (Hallaq 2009a: 19). Muslim jurists, as Hallaq (2009a: 28) explains, developed an 'all-encompassing interest in human acts' and viewed the shari'a as 'a mandate to regulate all human conduct, from religious and family relations to commerce, crime and much else'. But the shari'a, in general, has also been characterized as a 'societal discourse' (Messick 1993: 3–4) and the law of the Muslim jurists has been described as 'an interpretive and heuristic project', more than simply a body of prescriptive and controlling rules (Hallaq 2009a: 166). The shari'a provides an intellectual super-structure, which positions the law as part of Islam to provide a link between metaphysics and theology, on the one hand, and the social and material world on the other (2009a: 165).

Islamic law had a formative period under the Umayyad and Abbasid caliphates, following the death of the Prophet in 632 and lasting until around 900. A tradition of Islamic justice developed, which the Abbasids, in particular, attempted to turn into the law of the state. Following the collapse of these early Islamic polities, however, the law was primarily developed by scholars who remained remote from political power and their scholarship developed into four distinct schools of law (Schacht 1964: 3–4).[21] Already in the

---

[21] The Hanafi school, well represented in Iraq and Syria, spread to India and central Asia and was favoured by the Ottomans. The Maliki school spread westwards from Medina and Egypt over practically the whole of north Africa and into central and west Africa. The Shafi'i are more scattered but predominate in east Africa, as well as south-east Asia. The Hanabali school, revived by the puritanical Wahhabis in the eighteenth century, is officially recognized in Saudi Arabia (Schacht 1964: ch 9). The Shi'a formed a separate movement during the first century of Islam, but although the intellectual basis of their scholarship is fundamentally distinct in many ways, their doctrines of Islamic law do not differ

eighth and ninth centuries the literature of commentary was proliferating and the *hadith* texts, the record of the teaching and activities of the Prophet, were formed into great compilations. Their recognition as a source of law led to the production of glosses and commentaries, which ensured what Weiss (1998: 15) calls the literary quality of Islamic law. By around 900 a consensus had arisen that all essential legal questions had been settled and that no further independent reasoning would be allowed; all future juristic activity would be confined to the explanation, application, and interpretation of the doctrine, as it had been laid down once and for all. Islamic law thus acquired an intellectualist and scholastic exterior (Schacht 1964: 70–71, 203).

Rather as in the Hindu world, the subsequent work of Islamic jurists primarily involved interpretation on the basis of analogy. The limited licence allowed for interpretation did not prevent legal development, but there is some debate over its extent and manner. Some writers emphasize its scholarly and intellectual nature (Schacht 1964; Weiss 1998): it was the task of the scholars to identify and understand the foundational texts and discover the legislative intent behind them, using theories of language in order to do so.[22] This meant that the exposition of law was transformed into a largely exegetical enterprise, which demanded advanced hermeneutical skills and the tools of Arabic philology, lexicography, morphology, syntax, and stylistics. The scholars' work could thus involve generalization, systematization, and the generation of legal maxims, but textualism retained its supremacy (Weiss 1998: ch 3). The foundational texts and intentions behind them remained at the heart of legal scholarship.[23]

from those of the Sunni schools more widely than those differ from one another (Schacht 1964: 16).

[22] Scholars had to be faithful to God's rules and the notion of equity was rejected, on the ground that it went beyond the divinely ordained foundational texts (Schacht 1964: 203–04; Weiss 1998: 86). However, they could resort to legal devices and fictions, rather like the Roman jurists, in order to avoid the undesirable effects of a literal application of the law. As Schacht (1964: 79–80) points out, legal fictions were used in Roman law to provide a legal framework for new practices, while in Islamic law it was to circumvent positive enactments.

[23] Paradoxically, the oral transmission of doctrine remained the ideal, as more reliable (Messick 1993). A similar insistence on the superior authority of lines

Others, notably Hallaq (1994, 2009b), insist upon the role played by the practices of jurists and judges in developing doctrine. He emphasizes, in particular, the role of the *mufti*s, private legal scholars who provided guidance for individual petitioners on legal problems by granting opinions, known as *fatwa*s. These included advice given to individuals and judges on the conduct of court cases, and the grant of fatwas has been described as analogous to the giving of responsa by Roman jurists (Messick 1993: 140).[24] Some of the fatwas were gathered together in authoritative collections, which then came to be regarded as a source of legal doctrine (Hallaq 1994). Moreover, as Powers (2001: 191) describes, through careful inductive study of the foundational texts Muslim jurists identified five underlying purposes of the law, the preservation of religion, life, offspring, property, and rationality, constituting what Weiss calls 'the Islamic social vision', which could be invoked to derive new rules.

There are, then, different views of the nature of legal change, and whether it was intellectual and scholarly, or more practically-influenced. What is less contested is the intellectual hierarchy that put the jurist above the mufti, who was himself above the *qadi* (judge). As Gleave (2010: 15) explains, there is an increasing level of involvement in the particulars of the practical world as one moves down the hierarchy. The scholar jurist deals in universals and has the highest authority. The scholars' textual approach was firmly grounded in a rich legacy of reflection and argumentation: their authority was declaratory, rather than legislative. Meanwhile there was ambivalence, even 'stigma', surrounding the judgeship (Messick 1993: 143–44).

Islamic legal scholarship was also not monolithic: the schools referred to different texts and their distinctive styles of reasoning came to be endowed with their own authority. A tension thus arose between the requirements of stability and authority on the one hand, and what Messick calls 'interpretive dynamism' on the other, which gave many of the texts a quality of 'openness'. He describes the jurisprudence of one of the foundational Shafi'i

---

of oral transmission within a literate culture was also found in ancient Greece (Thomas 2005) and the Tibetan world.

[24] Messick also notes parallel institutions within medieval Jewish law.

manuals, for example, as 'an unstable mix of the settled and the contested' (1993: 34–35). Despite the theoretical limitations on interpretation, the corpus of legal literature expanded over the centuries; interpretation was at the heart of Islamic legal scholarship, as it had been at the heart of the dharmaśāstra texts and the activities of the Roman jurists.

Islamic law in practice

Islamic law was developed by the jurists in the context of a polity, and it was their law that Muslim governments were supposed to apply and enforce (Weiss 1998: 114). Their activities produced practical laws, not just an idealized body of reflection.[25] The authority of the legal scholars was, however, linked to their personal piety and they formed what Weiss (1998: 7) has described as a grassroots spiritual leadership, independent of the caliphate and its political regime. It was, moreover, regarded as being part of the purpose of juristic thought to delimit the rights of God carefully, so as to deny the government any pretext for encroachment on the rights of private persons. As Powers (2001: 191) confirms, Islamic law places severe limits on the power of the state: a polity is needed to secure the Islamic social order, but the idea is that that order is best realized by a government that knows the limits of its authority.

Of course, theory and practice are very different things and the history of the Islamic world demonstrates that rulers regularly sought to assert control over legal scholarship and authority, often by co-opting scholars, as well as qadis, into their structures of government. As Hodgson (1974: 105) puts it, the shari'a played a major role in all Islamic empires and the prevailing religious scholars, the *ulama*, tended to accept a *modus vivendi* with the de facto military rulers.[26] Close links with the scholars, the 'heirs of

[25] In fact a good deal of customary practice and norms was also incorporated into Islamic law and influenced the work of the judges, particularly in the realms of crime and punishment (Weiss 1998: ch 11; Peters 2003, 2005).

[26] In the states of Mongol heritage the ulama found themselves somewhat subordinated within a military state, while in the Safavid empire the shi'i ulama were for a time subordinated, but gradually worked themselves free, in the end forging an alliance on their own terms. In the Moghul empire of India the ulama were brought under control by Akhbar, while under the Ottomans

the Prophet', and their institutions as the locus of religious and moral authority could, of course, provide rulers with legitimacy. The Ottomans, in particular, sought to bring the law within the realm of state control, initially through the founding and funding of large and influential *madrasas*, shari'a educational institutions, judicial practices were centralized and brought within the governmental bureaucracy, and the shari'a, as a body of substantive law, was supplemented by the decrees and edicts of the sultan and eventually incorporated into a civil code (Messick 1993: ch 3; Hallaq 2009a: ch 6).

It was, however, the qadis and the muftis who were the principal conduits through which Islamic law flowed into the course of everyday life. As Schacht (1964: 203) says, the aim of Islamic law is to provide concrete and material standards, not rules for the clarification of the play of contending interests or the determination of disputes. The issue of a fatwa was a moment when the law was made real and its concepts, rules, and doctrines were brought to bear upon the facts of actual dispute (Powers 2002: 231). There is a considerable literature on the work of qadis and muftis, including both historical and contemporary accounts, often using a combination of court records, fatwas, other historical documents, and ethnographic research from different parts of the region.[27]

Analysing collections of fatwas from the Maghrib, Powers (2002) found that in the fourteenth and fifteenth centuries the Maliki muftis were able to operate creatively within the theoretical constraints of a rigid system of law.[28] A slander case, for example, illustrates the legal reasoning deployed by a mufti who was concerned not just with the production of justice but also with a potential rift in the local community (Powers 2002: ch 5). The case concerned an inheritance dispute from around 1439,

---

the alliance between ulama and amirs was maintained on a relatively equal basis (Hodgson 1974).

[27] There are, for example, companion volumes edited by Masud, Messick, and Powers (1996) on muftis and legal interpretation and by Masud, Peters, and Powers (2006) on qadis and the administration of justice.

[28] He examines six cases, concerning paternity, fornication, water rights, family endowments, slander of the Prophet, and disinheritance of children.

during the course of which a heated argument arose between a father and son on the one hand, and a *sharif* on the other. The sharif are descendants of the Prophet Muhammad and in the course of the argument the father and son uttered words that arguably violated the sacred honour of the Prophet, an offence for which the penalty was death by stoning. The chief qadi of the city referred the case to a distinguished mufti and his fatwa forms the subject of Powers's analysis. The fatwa contains a close analysis of the words uttered and their significance, the difficult epistemological issue of establishing descent from the Prophet, the substance of the legal doctrine relating to punishment, and its application to the case in hand. He employed 'subtle linguistic argument' and ultimately exploited a procedural loophole in order to achieve an equitable result, which recommended punishment short of the death penalty.

As Powers (2002: 203) says, the fatwa was an occasion for thought and argument that took the form of a literary performance, articulating the norms and values that defined what it meant for the society to be Islamic. In order to do so, the mufti drew upon his extensive knowledge of the Islamic literary tradition to select pertinent verses of the Quran, sayings of the Prophet, and statements of authoritative jurists; it was a performance in which he established his own point of view through the voices of earlier Muslim authorities. It was also designed to have maximum impact upon his audience, a community divided into extremist groups, between which he attempted to find a middle-ground. The mufti considered that the dispute had divided the residents of the city into two factions, who were tending towards two reprehensibly extreme positions, arguing for the death penalty on the one hand, and absolution from any form of punishment on the other. This rift also needs to be understood, Powers says, in the context of broader religious and political changes in the region, whereby Sharifism was being integrated into Maghribi society (2002: 204–05).

Powers comments that while the mufti was seeking a position that was balanced, objective, and dispassionate, his opinion achieved a distinctly non-legal result. It exemplified the tension between legalism and equity, that is between the application of abstract and general legal doctrine, and the production of justice in the particular case, which characterizes any legal intervention in a practical dispute. This is exemplified, even more strongly, in the first of Powers's case studies, a paternity dispute in which the qadi sought to use legal doctrine to achieve what he evidently considered to be an equitable result (2002: ch 1). The language of muftis was generally more formalistic than that of the qadis, employing abstract and impersonal categories to describe the parties to a case and their legal relations, while the qadis' reasoning was often directed towards the restoration of social equilibrium and the promotion of equity, but the tension between legalism and equity evidently recurs within both. On the whole, the interplay between legal and cultural norms created a discursive space in which men who were learned in the law could practise their skills of legal interpretation, drawing upon a vast repertoire of hermeneutical methods and rhetorical strategies (2002: 164–65).

There was, as Powers puts it, a hierarchy of specialized religious knowledge within which both the qadi and the mufti acted: the opinion of the mufti conferred religious legitimacy on the judgment of the qadi, but the mufti's opinion was not binding and required the powers of the qadi and the ruler for execution (2002: 88–90). The mufti was not without authority, however: his ideal qualities included self-reliance, generosity, and humility, and the closer a jurist came to the ideal of perfection the greater his authority (2002: 60). Turning to another part of the Islamic world, Yemen, Messick found idioms expressing the intellectual pre-eminence of the muftis dating back to twelfth-century texts. Indeed, they are sometimes described as scholars with final authority (Messick 1986: 108). As jurists and as moral beings, Messick says, they distanced themselves from the moral ambivalence surrounding the work of the courts, which could be marred by corruption, coercion, and error (1993: 103). Their status was maintained into the late twentieth century, and Messick's studies contrast the traditional mufti, still using an old-fashioned carved wooden pen and giving fatwas in his private rooms on matters of marriage, inheritance, and other property issues, with the fatwas given by 'media muftis' on a weekly radio 'fatwa show' (Messick 1986). The authority of the Islamic religious specialists might have been transformed by the establishment of state legal systems but, as Clarke (2010) also found in Lebanon, it has by no means disappeared.[29]

What was Islamic law?

As Schacht (1964: 210–11) says, Islamic law, as encompassed by the shari'a, was regarded as divinely-ordained, its authority provided by God; this law was the product of a marriage between revelation and reason (Hallaq 2009a: 15). God's law was not, however, the same as the human law of the fiqh. The role of the scholars was to provide a link between the human mind and the divine. The laws spelled out in the fiqh, which ruled the lives of Muslim people, were not coextensive with pure Islamic law; they could only be an interpretation of that law (Weiss 1998: ch 6).[30]

Western scholars have not been entirely consistent in what they term 'Islamic law'. The term can be used to refer to divine law—associated with shari'a—or to fiqh, or a combination of the two, that is, to law as a matter of principles, rules, categories, and doctrine (Gleave 2010). Alternatively, it can be used to refer to any number of different aspects of legal practice, governmental or judicial, or simply the activities of the Muslim community. However, even those, like Hallaq, who emphasize the influence of legal practice on the development of Islamic law, talk of the 'textual and technical' exposition of the shari'a and shari'a law (2009a: 164). As Gleave (2010: 10) says, we can assume that most authors use the term to refer to the theoretical legal system

[29] It is not only through the work of the qadis and muftis that Islamic legal thought could shape the practical course of events. Messick (1993) describes an 'Immamate', a shari'a-dominated polity in the highlands of premodern Yemen in which the realms of religious ideas and authority, texts and their interpretations, scholars and scholarship intersected with the world of power and politics. As he suggests, two research activities need to be brought together—local-level ethnography and textual analysis of the works of Islamic jurisprudence—in order to capture the life of what he terms a 'calligraphic state'.

[30] Weiss uses the past tense to describe Islamic law in order to capture the sense of a long historic tradition. The relationship between Islamic law and society has changed drastically, as he points out (1998: 188) since the Muslim world has been engulfed by the west's modernity. Nevertheless, the jurists' law is still regarded as part of the Muslim heritage. The study of Islamic law and its transformations in the contemporary world is an important and extensive topic for empirical study, but one which must build upon an understanding of the Islamic law of the jurists (Hallaq 2009b, Clarke 2010).

described in works of doctrine, *furu' al-fiqh*. Calder (2010: 47), for example, emphasizes the juristic discipline in which the legal system is grounded, likening it to an Aristotelian science, which achieves permanence by dealing with species, not individuals. It is legalistic, dealing with abstracts, not particulars. A work of Islamic law, Calder says, 'offers its readers a literary experience—diverse, various, profound. It is not like a manual of instruction' (2010: 99).

However we characterize it, Islamic law enjoyed a prestige and authority that was essentially independent of any political or governmental power and authority. The authority of the jurists was declarative, deriving from the legislative authority of God, and it depended upon the validity of what they derived from the foundational texts. In practice, the respect they enjoyed was primarily based on their erudition, legal knowledge, and religious and moral distinction (Hallaq 2009a: 165–66). As Schacht (1964: 209) says, Islamic law came into being not to satisfy the political needs of the early caliphs, but in response to the religious zeal of the growing body of Muslims, who demanded the application of religious norms to all problems of behaviour. It was what he characterizes as 'an extreme case of jurists' law' (1964: 4–5). From nearly the beginning, the elaboration of law was the work of private scholars, who vindicated their independence vis-à-vis the caliphs' regimes and established a monopoly over the exposition of the law. At least in theory, the scholars were in a position to make the regime answerable to them and the caliphs were primarily instrumental in the implementation of the scholars' law. 'Something on the order of an Islamic rule of law became for all time the normal state of affairs' (Weiss 1998: 16). As Messick (1993: 39) puts it, in Shafi'i states interpretation and command were decisively separated into an interpretive authority, controlled collectively by the scholarly community, and a temporal authority, held by the sultan or king. Juristic doctrine gave far more attention to matters of private than of public law: Muslim juristic thinking does not regard the state as a legal entity. Rather, the ruler represents the rights of God, himself, which is what gives him absolute authority (Weiss 1998: 181–82).

The shari'a is, then, concerned with God's vision for the world and the doctrines, principles, and practices of Islamic law are concerned with people's duties towards God. Its texts and doctrines spell out how that vision is to be achieved and the ways in which people may lead principled lives, resting firmly upon the scholarly endeavours of its experts. Their authority stems directly from Islam, not from the power or authority of any caliph or sultan.

LAW AS SCHOLARSHIP

In all three of these cases laws and legal codes developed in the context of centralized polities, and complemented, or even supported, the activities of kings and other rulers. But the laws were, for the most part, not created by rulers; and they were not primarily instruments of government. They were the intellectual output of jurists and religious scholars and were supposed to derive from a source of authority that bound the ruler as much as his people.

Law was the product of scholarship, then, an intellectual exercise that was often esoteric and legalistic, although also concerned with the conduct of daily life: the work of the Hindu scholars was to interpret the ethical and religious system that constituted the dharma, something rooted in the divine and revealed through the ancient Vedas; in Rome, the jurists' work was primarily a scholarly activity applying Greek dialectical methods to the *ius civile*; Islamic legal scholars, meanwhile, were interpreting God's law, something that had only been partly revealed, through the application of intellectual and literary methods.

As intellectual processes, each of these essentially hermeneutical activities tended towards the complex and esoteric. It was scholarly expertise, as exercised in the process of discovering, elaborating on, and refining the law, that revealed its substance. The task of creating rules for, and giving meaning to, the activities of daily life was a matter of jurisprudence, then, more than codification, and produced an esoteric body of scholarship that it was the task of experts—the jurists, brahmins, and muftis—to explain for layman or the judge. This was not just an academic exercise and the work of the scholars was respected and regarded as authoritative in many different ways.

What does this mean for the study of law? It suggests that we should look for law in the activities of scholars, as well as in those of judges and rulers.[31] And it confirms that in order to understand law, even as an empirical matter, we may need to engage in the study of a jurisprudence and its interpretive techniques. In concluding his discussion of Islamic muftis, Messick (1993: 116) suggests that their work provides an example of 'a higher level system of indigenous interpretation'. The anthropologist's task must include analysing the ways in which laws, as systems of meaning, interpretation, or theory, shape the world.

The empirical study of law, as the study of a form of reasoning, may, therefore, find its subject in the activity of scholars, concerned to provide a model for how the world can and should be, as well as the codes or rules they produce. In the case of ancient forms of law the law-makers may remain shadowy figures, but we can trace the thought of the dharmaśāstra authors, the Roman jurists, and the early Islamic scholars through their texts. We can also examine the way in which a family of Brahmins in Kerala was influenced by dharmaśāstra thought when creating rules for other castes, and how a Roman advocate played with ideas about the authority of the law and its interpreters in order to construct a legal argument for his client. In more contemporary cases we can trace the context and work of Islamic scholars and the influence of muftis in a changing, modernizing world, or the influence of Hindu texts within the reasoning of India's Supreme Court.[32] In order fully to understand and appreciate all these activities we need to understand the systems of thought that lie behind them.

This is not to say that the role of judges, or qadis, or Roman magistrates, is not important. But the principles and reasoning of the law may not be those of the courts. The relationship between

---

[31] Of course, law is by no means always the product of scholarship, as I discuss in the next chapter in the context of ancient Greece. However, this does not mean that it was, therefore, either an instrument of government or an indistinguishable part of its socio-cultural milieu.

[32] Courts in the Islamic world are the subject of considerable interest, as already mentioned, and anthropological studies that take seriously the intellectual authority of Islamic legal principles and legal specialists can only enrich the analysis of a world complicated by modernity.

jurist and magistrate, or mufti and qadi, like that between the authors of the dharmaśāstras and the brahmins who drafted judicial rules for local use, may be indirect. In order to explore what law does, means, and is, in any particular case, we need to ask about its styles of reasoning and interpretation, its specialists, and its relations with judicial activities and daily life, as well as its relations with governments and rulers. We must also take seriously the influence that the ideas, principles, categories, and rules produced by legal scholars might have on subsequent generations and in far-flung societies. I develop these themes further in later chapters.

5

IDEALS, TRADITION,
AND AUTHORITY

Hindu and Islamic law are, as I have described them, essentially religious or theological systems. Their provisions are concerned with the ways in which *dharma*, or God's law, can be realized in daily life. Law, like religion, can present the activities of daily life in relation to a higher order of things. But this need not always be a religious or cosmic order: the activities of the Roman jurists also put mundane activities into a system that transcended daily life, one that more simply promised fairness and equity; they presented the law as a personal privilege, guarantor of life and liberty. In the modern world secular systems may invoke the ideals of socialism, or human rights, or the values of economic liberalism. Historically, we often find claims that the law represents custom and tradition, or derives from the authority of an ancient law-giver. As Dresch (2012:15) puts it, law tends to invoke an order that outlasts the moment and context of the particular case.

Law can, thus, construe the activities of daily life in relation to a higher order of things, to produce rules about how the world ought to be and how people ought to behave within it: it can be idealistic. But the nature of that vision varies: it may be religious or secular; it can be directed at individualistic or at political ends; it may invoke ancestry, or else a utopian future. In this chapter examples from traditional China, ancient Greece, and the English common law illustrate some of the different visions evoked by law. As scholars have noted, despite claiming to embody rationality and reason, the appeal of tradition is a recurrent theme, even within modern law, along with the invocation of an ancestral law-giver. In such cases the authority of the law transcends that of any known, or contemporary law-maker, and presents the author of legal texts as primarily an interpreter of the law, whose task it is to explain or renew an ancient tradition.

PENAL LAW IN CHINA

The ancient Chinese legal tradition, with its emphasis upon penal law and imperial authority, contrasts sharply, in many ways, with the legal histories of the Hindu, Roman, and Islamic worlds. The existence of law in China dates back over three millennia: there are references to laws having been made during the Shang dynasty (c.1570–1045BC) and the early Zhou period (c.1000BC) when King Wu issued the Kang Kou, a set of instructions for government, which included criteria for the just application of the law (MacCormack 1996: 146). Codification of the law began at least by the middle of the fourth century BC, following debates between what have been termed the Confucianists and the Legalists about the nature, origins, and value of laws and legislation (Johnson 2009). In this important controversy there was disagreement over whether society needed to enact laws in order to maintain proper order. The Confucianists were suspicious of law as the ad hoc creation of modern men and compared the mechanistic nature of law unfavourably with the proper and ritualistic behaviour enshrined in the traditional and unwritten rules of behaviour, the *li*. The Legalists, meanwhile, regarded rules of law, *fa*, as the basis for stable government, since they could be fixed and known to all, providing standards against which conduct could be measured. Like Hobbes, the Legalists regarded a strong state as necessary for the imposition of law upon men, who were inherently selfish (Bodde and Morris 1967: 19, 49). Their legalism was opposed to the idealism of the Confucianists and the third to sixth centuries BC were characterized by a bitter controversy between these two schools of legal thought.

It was the Tang who are said to have successfully 'Confucianized' the law in the seventh century AD, effectively closing the breach between *li* and *fa* (Bodde and Morris 1967: 29). As Huang (1996: 105–06) puts it, the Chinese codes began as legalist-inspired administrative and penal laws, which came to be infused with Confucian notions of civil hierarchy and moral relations. Chinese scholars have, thus, been engaged in sophisticated jurisprudential debates for well over two millennia and their legal systems were complex and highly developed. In what follows I highlight just some features of the legal thought evident in the structure and content of the penal codes dating from the Tang period onwards, although inspired by the thought of more ancient origins.[1]

The Tang legislation has been described as more important historically than that of any other dynasty (Johnson 1979: 5). It had an immense influence on the laws of all subsequent dynasties, synthesizing and making public a group of rules that embodied and justified the major principles of Chinese culture, and its prestige was such that it was adopted, practically without modifications, during the subsequent Zhou (950–960) and Song (960–1268) periods. A major reorganization of the code was undertaken by the Ming in the fourteenth century and there was another revision and expansion under the Qing (1644–1910). However, it has been estimated that 30–40% of the Qing code consists of articles taken, unchanged, from the Tang code (Bodde and Morris 1967: 59–63; Johnson 1979).[2]

As Bourgon describes it, the Chinese were concerned with the systemic nature of their laws, from even before the Tang period, and since at least the Song they have conceived of their law as a 'unified, coherent system of norms' (Bourgon 2011: 176); they used the image of a 'legal net', which should have holes of an appropriate size to catch the big fish, while not retaining so much as to become unmanageable. The true legal expert, meanwhile, knows how to manipulate the main cord so as to play with the layout and flexibility of the netting, and the sage ruler must shake it so as to straighten out the knots and tangles and unfold the smaller lines of the mesh (Dardess 1983: 196). The penal codes, themselves, contained what Bourgon describes as an almost mathematical system for evaluating punishments, based upon a taxonomy of human acts, established according to criteria of individual responsibility and social dangers. As he puts it, using language that recalls the work of the Roman jurists, Chinese imperial law was founded upon the art of qualification,

[1] I am concentrating on the codified law rather than court processes, for which there is limited evidence until the Qing period.

[2] The Tang code also had an enormous influence beyond China: the code and statutes were adopted by Japanese emperors; in the tenth century Korean law was influenced by the code; and in the fifteenth century a large part was taken over, without alteration, by the Vietnamese Le dynasty (Johnson 1979: 9).

of correctly naming things and acts (2011: 177). Jones (1997) suggests that the Chinese urge to codify human relationships and their consequences was quite beyond anything seen elsewhere and that there was a tendency towards abstraction and conciseness, which rivalled that of the German pandectists of the early nineteenth century.

There are, nevertheless, some fundamental features of these Chinese codes and the principles behind them that differ strikingly from the scholarly law described in the previous chapter. Codified Chinese law was dominated by penal and administrative concerns. Some aspects of property relations were dealt with in the codes, but all other 'civil' matters, including almost all contractual relations and issues of debt and inheritance, were characterized as 'insignificant' or 'minor', supposed to be governed by the moral 'rule of man', as opposed to the harsh 'rule of law' (Brockman 1980; Huang 1996: 1–2). At the same time, penal sanctions were attached to a remarkably wide range of behaviour, including unfilial activities and breaches of mourning regulations (MacCormack 1996: 59).[3] As McKnight (1997) and Macauley (2000) point out, a considerable body of subsidiary rules and regulations relating to contractual relations and other civil matters developed, particularly during the Qing period. However, the penal codes formed the core of the legal system. As Bodde and Morris (1967: 3) put it, the law of pre-modern China was overwhelmingly penal in emphasis, consisting of a legal codification of the ethical norms long dominant in society.[4]

Alongside this emphasis on penal law, the emperors were generally regarded as enjoying absolute authority, combining legislative, executive, and judicial powers: the emperor was the source of all law (Huang 1996: 76). Indeed, measures were taken to limit

---

[3] As Bourgon points out (2011: 177) the mourning tables indicated degrees of kinship, thus exemplifying an important aspect of the social order, something achieved elsewhere through the specification of compensatory payments, as discussed in chapter three.

[4] In practice, at least during the Qing period, magistrates routinely protected the legal claims of common litigants to property, contracts, inheritance, and old-age support. They had rights in practice, if not in theory, even if this did not extend to their relations with the state (Huang 1996: 235). Moreover, as Brockman (1980: 78–79) describes, there was a clear sense of contractual rights among merchants, something different from individual rights against the state.

the discretion that could be exercised by judges, while the penal codes all opened with a list of the 'ten abominations', offences of disloyalty to the emperor or his officials, and lack of respect for superiors, parents, and other senior relatives (MacCormack 1996: 5, 44). Like their Roman counterparts the Chinese emperors declared themselves to be supreme and above the law.

Respect for the ancestral past

The laws contained in the penal codes were, nevertheless, regarded as embodying Confucian ideals concerning human relations, setting out the proper way to behave. They emphasized the importance of personal relations, exemplified in the bonds between ruler, minister, and subject; father and son; husband and wife; elder and younger brother, and so on.[5] As MacCormack puts it, many aspects of the penal codes, and of legal processes in general, stemmed from a concern for the preservation of the ancient moral traditions of humanity and from a great respect for the traditions of the ancestors (1996: xv, 32).

The Tang code accordingly acquired a sacrosanct quality, evident in the extent to which it was reproduced during the following ten centuries, even by Ming and Qing legal reformers. Legal change and development were largely undertaken within each dynasty through the issue of sub-statutes and supplementary provisions, especially during the later periods (Huang 1996: 14–15; Bourgon 2009).[6] The prestige of the Tang code was such that some of its provisions were reproduced, even when the system of landholding they prescribed had long since been abandoned (Johnson 2009: 457), while other provisions seem never to have been intended to be enforced, for example the prohibition of marriage between people with the same name (MacCormack 1996: 46–47). MacCormack describes Chinese attitudes as 'conservative', shaped by a concern to preserve the ancient moral traditions of humanity. As he points out (1996: 41), Confucius

---

[5] This provides an interesting contrast to medieval Europe, where the law was regarded as replacing feudal bonds (Clanchy 1983).

[6] The basic framework set out by the Tang already contained a high level of abstraction, while the legislators worked on the basis of 'economy of means', in order to produce a small number of rules that could be used in different combinations to calculate a large number of punishments (MacCormack 1996: 15).

himself stated that he was merely conserving and re-establishing the good customs of the past, and appeals to the very earliest mythical rulers of China became a standard feature of Confucian rhetoric. This led to a form of legal reasoning by analogy, which recalls the Islamic jurists' hermeneutical methods (MacCormack 1996: 166–74; Bourgon 2011: 183–85).

Maybe reacting against the charge of 'conservatism', some doubt has been cast upon this depiction of the spirit of Chinese law. Macauley (2000) emphasizes the legal changes enacted through the formulation of the myriad of sub-statutes, especially in the Qing period, when they took precedence in the law courts; as Huang (1996) and Bourgon (2009), among others, have described, the Qing substantially expanded the penal code and supplemented it with sub-statutes, minor provisions, and commentaries of considerable complexity. By the time of the last revision in 1863 there were 1,892 sub-statutes and a total of 2,328 laws, which created a form of legal 'chaos' (Johnson 2009: 459). Nevertheless, as Bourgon (2009: 433) puts it, the Qing had inherited a 'millennia-old' legal system, which they substantially retained, along with its difficult, classical language, hallowed principles, and anachronistic stipulations (Huang 1996: 105; Johnson 2009: 459). The content of the historic penal codes, Bourgon (2009: 434) says, represented a pole of coherence and fixity, which the Qing largely reproduced in their own code, while the sub-statutes and supplementary orders represented a pole of flexible and open evolution.

An ideology of ancient legal principles and inherited laws was, therefore, present in some form up until the fall of the Qing dynasty in 1911. The penal code contained a core of settled legal principles, including the classification of punishments, which could be traced back to the Tang period. As Bourgon (2011: 201–02) describes, increased bureaucratization of justice also led to a search for doctrinal principles and a desire to understand the general meaning and spirit of the law. This was in line with a current of thought that regarded the Confucian classics as a directory of fundamental ethical and legal norms. On this view, Confucius had transmitted judgments containing a sort of super-code for judging and correcting the existing dynastic codes in the annals of his native kingdom. Even for the Qing, therefore, the general examination and harmonization of the laws was not a simple, technical exercise but had to follow the principles of the Confucian classics.

The emperors

The emperors were, in theory, above the law. However, despite often being autocratic, they did not, in practice, generally present themselves as being in a position to act according to their own desires. They were conscious that they had been entrusted with the Mandate of Heaven and that they were bound to respect the laws of heaven and the enactments of their ancestors (MacCormack 1996: 21–22). Ming Tai-tsu, founder of the Ming dynasty, for example, was well known for his autocracy and ferocity, but he explicitly sought to revive the 'good practices' of the past. The code he established was presented as an 'ancestral constitution', which would stand as 'the yardstick for one hundred generations' (Yonglin 2009: 430).

Three centuries later, in a valedictory speech issued to the people after his death, the Kangxi Qing emperor (1661–1722) declared that:

The rulers of the past all took reverence for Heaven's laws and reverence for their ancestors as the fundamental way in ruling the country. To be sincere in reverence for Heaven and ancestors entails the following: be kind to men from afar and keep the able ones near, nourish the people ... protect the state before danger comes and govern well before there is any disturbance, be always diligent and careful. (MacCormack 1996: 22)

The reference to 'Heaven's laws', MacCormack explains, is a reference to the fundamental social relations enshrined in the 'Three Bonds'—those between ruler and subject, father and son, husband and wife—which were regarded as given in nature and endorsed by Heaven. In a similar way, in his preface to the 1740 code, the Qianlong emperor declared that he had personally relied upon an 'estimation of heavenly principles and consideration of human compassion'. He had based himself 'solely on the most just [of principles]' and 'aimed to attain the most [morally] correct'. Like the Ming code, his revision of the law was meant to be immutable, 'not to be changed in ten thousand generations' (Huang 1996: 225–26). In practice, too, it has been said that the emperors' absolutist tendencies were tempered by the legal system. Even if they did not amount to a real check upon his power, the bureaucrats, in particular those with judicial functions, could present a significant resistance towards extreme imperial activities (Bourgon 2011: 186).

Respect for ancient texts and legal principles is also found in the *dharmaśāstras'* evocation of the fundamental cosmic order enshrined in the ancient Vedas, and in the evocation by the *shari'a* of the word of God, as presented in the Quran. Bodde and Morris (1967: 10) stress the non-religious nature of Chinese law, contrasting the Judaic and Islamic systems. However, the Chinese emperors' references to the mandate of heaven do imply a sense of divine or, at least, cosmic sanction behind the imperial laws. The idea that the Confucian classics enshrined fundamental ethical and legal norms was accompanied by explicit appeals to ancestral values.

LAW IN ANCIENT GREECE

Reverence for the past and appeals to the sanction of ancestral laws are also found in arguments concerning the nature and authority of law in ancient Athens. Such claims are strikingly evident in arguments made by the oligarchs during the revolutions of 411BC and 404BC, as well as by those who opposed them and advocated the restoration of democracy. Following a disastrous war between Athens and Sparta, the Athenian democracy, established a century previously, was swept away in an oligarchic coup. A commission was instructed to create new instruments of government; among other things they were to look for the laws that had been enacted by Cleisthenes when he instituted the democracy. When democracy was (temporarily) restored in 410, a recodification of the laws was ordered and the authors were instructed to write up the laws of Solon. These had been created almost two centuries ago, in around 594BC (Rhodes 2011: 18). After the subsequent coup of 404, when democracy was again restored, a decree provided for an interim government 'in accordance with tradition'. It declared that 'the Athenians shall be governed in the ancestral way, using the laws, weights and measure of Solon and also the regulations of Draco, which had previously been in force' (Finley 1971: 39).

Draco's regulations were even older than the laws of Solon, having been created in around 621BC, and both Finley and Rhodes comment that the Athenians must, in practice, have been able to distinguish between what had actually been enacted by these early law-givers and the subsequent laws developed in their polity; they cannot have intended that the latter should be completely ignored. Nevertheless, one of the authors of the new laws was later criticized for having omitted some of the traditional laws and replaced them with new ones. As Rhodes (2011: 29) puts it, the invocation of Cleisthenes and Solon formed part of the propaganda of the oligarchs, who were evidently trying to assure people that they were not promoting a dangerous revolution. But when the democrats, in turn, laid claim to the past and advocated a recodification of what they called the laws of Solon, they were invoking him as an older and even more heroic ancestor. As Finley (1971: 40) says, it was assumed that the argument from antiquity was a valid and persuasive one; in the references to named law-givers the distant past was concretized and personalized, as it had been in the myths and legends of Greece's archaic societies. Finley continues by comparing the arguments of Sir Edward Coke during the English constitutional crisis of the seventeenth century, as well as appeals to the American constitution in the twentieth, to which I return later in this chapter.

The new Athenian constitution, drawn up after the second coup, defined the power of the assembly, council, and magistrates; it laid down penalties for assault and theft, established the calendar of festivals and sacrifices; and it contained specific decrees, for example declaring war against Sparta (Hansen 1991: ch 7).[7] It also placed the laws on a firmly democratic basis, declaring that only written laws could be used by magistrates and that laws—with general application—should be distinguished from decrees—which might only apply to a particular person or event—and containing provisions governing the ways in which the laws

---

[7] The terminology did not, however, distinguish clearly between what we might refer to as laws, as against a constitution, and it was only in the subsequent century that the term *nomos* came to be identified more firmly with what we might call law (Hansen 1991: 161–62; Thomas 2005: 50–51).

could be revised or repealed (Hansen 1991: 166–71). It implicitly accepted the idea of man-made laws, that is, which had to originate in the work of the *nomothetai*, a legislative board, and which could also be scrutinized by the People's Court, thus conforming to contemporary political (democratic) ideals (Hansen 1991: ch 7). Nevertheless, subsequent orators frequently attributed to Solon any laws which they claimed ought to be upheld and applied, even if they were of demonstrably later origin (Rhodes 2011: 26). As Thomas (1994: 129) suggests, later statements betray hints of deep unease with recent law-making and nostalgia for a simple legal past and the single authority of Solon.

Idealism and the ancient law-givers

As Carey (1994: 183), among others, points out, the Athenians regarded respect for impersonal law as one of the main features that distinguished them from non-Greeks. Laws had been made all over the Greek world, dating back to at least 650BC, and were often inscribed on stone, bronze, or wooden tablets displayed in public places (Gagarin 2005: 37). The writing of law by different city-states was probably undertaken for a variety of different purposes (Thomas 2005: 42): some seem to have imposed checks upon the powers of *polis* officials, while many were presented as rules to be applied in judicial proceedings. Nevertheless, the creation of law seems to have had a strongly idealistic aspect from the earliest days. Solon, for example, is described as having written down the laws for rich and poor alike, in the interests of justice, and as having presented his reforms as saving the polis from civil strife, creating good order, and preventing any faction from gaining unjustly (Thomas 2005: 43). In Euripides's fifth-century drama, *Suppliants*, Theseus, the king of Athens, declares that when law is written down it provides equal justice to both the weak and the rich (Thomas 2005: 42–43). As Allen (2005: 387–89) describes, Theseus also suggested that law must be divine, or at least public, rather than the creation of an individual mortal. In Euripides's writings the laws of Greece,[8] the laws of the gods, the

---

[8] The idea of a panhellenistic law was, in practice little more than an aspiration.

laws of mortals, and the laws of the community are all presented as acceptable, and implicitly equated; they are all publicly, not privately 'owned', while the tyrant who rules by means of his own laws is a disaster for his city. In Aeschylus's *Prometheus* even Zeus was criticized for using his own private laws: true law was public law. As Thomas (2005: 43) summarizes it, law was widely regarded as in itself conducive to fairness, justice, and equality, achieved by being made public through writing.

By the fourth century, that is after the reforms described earlier, people in many Greek cities claimed that their laws had been issued long ago by law-givers whose names were remembered, although many were mythical (Sealey 1994: 25–30). During this period Greek commentators, especially Plato and Aristotle, were attributing a grand, creative, even heroic, vision to the law codes introduced by the early Greek law-givers. These men were said to have travelled widely, to have been (on occasion) divinely inspired, and to have borrowed from one another, such that ancient communities progressed from *anomia* (disorder) to the rule of law and lasting *eunomia* (good order) (Szegedy-Maszak 1978). In fact, as Hölkeskamp (1999) explains, the early law codes often had limited aims and apparently specific intent, providing individual solutions to particular problems. They do not indicate a broad process of compilation, codification, or grand constitutional purpose.[9] Nevertheless, the tendency to attribute the ancient laws with idealistic, constitutional consequences and to present contemporary laws as their successors continued to characterize Greek legal thought, even after the democratic reforms of the late fifth century.[10]

In the courtroom, too, there were oratorical appeals to ancient law-givers. Thomas's (1994) explanation is that laws, especially an authoritative code, always require interpretation if they are to be applied in practice. In the absence of a developed jurisprudence,

---

[9] Robinson (2003) suggests that Hölkeskamp is somewhat too extreme in his depiction of their narrow, precise, and limited scope, regarding the laws from Chios and those of Cleisthenes as having some constitutional importance. However, he does not dissent from the overall argument.

[10] The extent to which Greek political thought can be characterized as 'rational' and the continuing adherence to mythic elements is the subject of considerable debate (Murray 1987).

that is rules and principles about how the laws are to be interpreted, the Athenian orators appealed to tradition, morality, and the intentions of the law-giver to support their arguments. As has been recognized by many writers, uniform application of the laws was not regarded as the primary task of the Athenian courts. Almost all cases that came before the courts were based on an alleged breach of a specific law, but the jurors' oath allowed them to vote according to their conscience in areas in which there were no laws; the accused regularly made pleas for pity; and the Athenians disapproved of legal professionalism, with litigants accusing their opponents of excessive legal knowledge or excusing their own (Carey 1994). The Athenian courts have often been compared unfavourably to Roman legal processes, which developed a sophisticated jurisprudence. However, the Greeks were not concerned, in the way that the Romans and their successors were, about the substance of the law as a coherent and rational system. Rather, the Greek court procedures were intended to arrive at just decisions based upon the facts of the specific case before them; dispute settlement was more important than the enforcement of justice in any objective sense (Todd and Millett 1990: 14; Nightingale 1999: 113).[11] It should probably not surprise us, then, that orators appealed to the authority of tradition and to the idealistic intentions of the ancient law-givers in the midst of their courtroom speeches. Reference to the substance of the laws was only one of many rhetorical resources available to them.

It seems as if there were two distinct, though related, strands in Greek legal thought. The first is found in the legalistic provisions of the Athenian constitution, which contained what we could regard as 'rules of recognition'—to use Hart's terminology—that is a set of secondary laws determining what was to be counted as primary law (Kantor 2012: 72). These and related issues concerning the relation between written and unwritten laws, the dangers

---

[11] Laani (2005) talks of the highly individual and contextualized nature of justice. The fact that written laws and judicial processes bore only a loose relationship has troubled some scholars. However, it is now generally recognized that the fact that there was not a simple relationship between the two was not a concern for the Athenians. The examples of the Hindu and Islamic worlds should make this seem less surprising.

of needless legislative change, and the theory and justification of punishment continued to be debated over the following century (Hansen 1991: 176; Cohen 2005; Thomas 2005: 59). The second strand of thought, found in courtroom rhetoric and in the myths surrounding the origins of the laws, involved generalized appeals to the authority of the ancient law-givers and invoked the heroic and idealistic nature of their intentions. As Thomas demonstrates, these approaches and arguments were not entirely consistent; they were respectively characterized, we might say, by the idea that law should be rational and legalistic, and a sense that justice was founded upon tradition. In any event, despite the apparently democratic basis of their laws, the idea of ancient origins remained rhetorically persuasive; ideals of justice were linked to a sense of ancestry and tradition. As Finley (1971) demonstrates, similar arguments recur in seventeenth-century England and even twentieth-century America.

THE ENGLISH COMMON LAW

An all-too-brief outline of the shape and development of the common law is necessary in order to appreciate Finley's comparison fully. Moreover, the history of the common law, unusual though it is when compared to the other great legal systems of the world, has rarely been considered in any detail by anthropologists. It thus represents an astonishingly under-used resource, whose comparative potential is amply demonstrated by historians such as Finley.[12]

What has come to be referred to as the English common law has its roots in the codes of the Anglo-Saxon kings, but took its shape from developments in the late twelfth century, when Henry II took a series of largely successful steps to centralize his government. A great variety of manorial and feudal courts was, at the time, responsible for local government, including the hearing of disputes, and these were gradually amalgamated into a centralized system, with the king's court at the top, later fixed in London. The king's court could deal with cases brought to it by

---

[12] In this section I largely draw upon the classic studies by Pollock and Maitland (1968), Baker (1971), and Milsom (1981).

any section of the population and from any part of the country, thus representing a form of 'common' law (Milsom 1981: 31).

In the early days it was the writ system that effectively defined the remedies that could be granted to litigants and, hence, the substantive content of the law applied by the courts. A writ was issued, on the petition of the plaintiff, from the royal Chancery, which specified the circumstances that, if proved, would entitle him to judgment. A jury then decided whether the necessary facts had been proved.[13] As Milsom (1981: 43) emphasizes, in the early days the judges did not regard the common law courts as applying a system of substantive rules at all. Such explicit law as there was might be found in single rules, generally cast in procedural terms. Nor was law regarded as a matter of conscious social regulation; when they needed to, the judges were making the law explicit, not making it (1981: 80–81). In Maine's (1861: 375) famous phrase, law was 'secreted in the interstices of practice'. It was only gradually that the judges came to think in terms of rules and abstract rights (Milsom 1981: 3).

It was effectively the systematization of judicial practices that led to the development of the English common law, but there was also a sense that the law already existed. In the early twelfth century the *Leges Henrici Primi*, compiled in an older tradition of law codes, had collected together English laws of various kinds, emphasizing royal jurisdiction, although also noting differences amongst local legal practices and complaining of confusion and uncertainty in the law. More generally, it was said that the courts should apply justice and reason (*ius et ratio*) in accordance with the law of the land (*per legem terrae*) (Tubbs 2000: 3). In 1258 it was spelt out that justices were to 'do what belongs to justices according to the law and custom of the kingdom of England' (Brand 2012: 186). After the establishment of the king's courts some scholars and judges, notably the authors of the treatises known as Glanvill (*c.*1189) and Bracton (*c.*1230s), attempted to set out the English common law in a system of substantive rules. But these treatises remained more in the order of textbooks

---

[13] The importance of the writ in initiating a legal case and specifying the remedies sought, of course, recalls the formulary system of Roman law, although there was apparently no connection between the two (Stein 1999: 63).

than authoritative laws.[14] The authors of Bracton, for example, set out to describe the substantive common law, as found in the common law writs, asserting that England used both unwritten law and custom (Bracton 1968: 19). The authors of both treatises were obviously aware of the learned law of the rest of Europe—in Italy and France in particular, Justinian's corpus of laws had been rediscovered and was becoming the basis for extensive scholarship—and wanted to defend the validity and prestige of the unwritten English law in the same terms (Tubbs 2000: 4–6).

Subsequent generations of English lawyers were not so keen to systematize and rationalize English law. The records in the Year Books, from which much of our knowledge of the legal thought of the next two centuries is drawn, indicate that courtroom argument generally proceeded as if Bracton's treatise did not exist (Tubbs 2000: 15). The substance of the law was generally only implicit in the argument. Nevertheless, judges and lawyers were making distinctions between types of crime and culpability, types of dispossession and distraint, the formalities needed for conveyances, types of tenure and the bundles of rights and restrictions that they entailed, relations of lord and tenant, and rights of wardship (Brand 2005; 2007; 2012: 181–85). Courtroom argument was legalistic.[15] After its flirtation with civil law at the time of Bracton, as Stein (1999: 87) puts it, the English common law became a sophisticated discipline in its own right, with its own well-trained core of lawyers.[16]

---

[14] The author of Glanvill's treatise seems to have been heavily influenced by Roman jurisprudence and was obviously concerned to depict the writs and procedures as based upon a form of law. In his introductory remarks he declares that 'although the laws (*leges*) of England are not written, it does not seem absurd to call them laws' and he states that 'the king is to be guided by the laws and customs (*leges et consuetudines*) of the realm, which had their origins in reason and have long prevailed...' (Glanvill 1965: 2).

[15] Milsom's (1981: 83) assertion that even by the fourteenth century 'there was no law of England, no body of rules complete in itself with known limits and visible defects' overlooks the legalism of these processes.

[16] Although the universities taught the principles of the civil (Roman) law, among other things training the scholars who would staff the Church's canon courts, the lawyers and judges who practised in the king's courts were trained at the Inns of Court where they learned the procedures and principles of the common law.

There was, however, no conceptual separation between law and equity. There was 'no body of substantive rules from which equity could be different. And the idea that law could be unjust, if comprehensible at all, would have been abhorrent; failures were mechanical' (Milsom 1981: 84). These remarks recall Kern's (1939) generalized, but evocative depiction of law in medieval Europe. As he puts it, no fundamental distinction was drawn between law, equity, *raison d'Etat*, and ethics: law and equity were almost the same thing, and what existed from time eternal was equitable. Law had been planted by God in men's conscience and public opinion, in custom, and in sound human understanding. It could be presented as an end in itself, standing 'at one and the same time for moral sentiment, the spiritual basis of human society, for the Good' (1939: 151–53, 178). While the study of Roman law had, he says, taught medieval scholars to work out a notion of positive law, as something different from and complementary to natural law, this distinction was not the popular one. *Juste et rationabiliter* (right and just) was a favourite combination in medieval legal phraseology.

Antiquity and the ancient constitution

Medieval common lawyers differed among themselves about the nature of the common law and how it was to be known. It was variously depicted as being founded upon common custom, on the common erudition of the legal elite, on case law, and on reason (Tubbs 2000: 23–52). However, as Tubbs suggests, two strands of jurisprudential thought are apparent amongst lawyers during the medieval and early modern periods. One, made famous by the later arguments of Sir John Davies and Sir Edward Coke, attributes the qualities of the common law firmly to its antiquity and immemorial usage. The other attributes the authority of the law to reason. In 1259 a disagreement arose between a group of English barons and the Pope, concerning the appointment of Aymer de Valence as bishop of Winchester. The barons invoked 'the law' (*lex*), which they said they possessed by the favour of God's grace, which had been used time out of mind in England, 'which their ancestors had used and they wished and were obliged to use' (Brand 2012: 194–95). As Brand comments, 'the customary nature of English law was being used here as at least a rhetorical shield against papal demands'.

Later lawyers praised the common law for its wisdom and excellence in the context of other political tensions. In the fifteenth century, for example, Fortescue claimed that the English laws were the most ancient. In 1612, Sir John Davies declared that 'the Common Law of England is nothing else but the Common Custome of the Realm...being continued without interruption time out of mind, it obtaineth the force of a Law'. Sir Edward Coke picked up these ideas in a series of writings produced during the constitutional crisis of the early seventeenth century and explicitly directed towards the limitation of royal sovereignty. Most famously, he argued against James I that the king's activities were bound by the common law. His arguments placed the emphasis less upon custom and more upon the activity of the judges in constantly refining the law, but the law that the judges declare, he said, is immemorial and embodies the wisdom of generations (Pocock 1957: 33–35).

In his famous study, Pocock argues that Coke's depiction of the authority of the common law was a general and powerful one. It was the idea of custom, he says, that convinced men that the law was ancient and that it had always been what it was now (1957: 36, 50). For hundreds of years before Davies and Coke it had been accepted that English law was *ius non scriptum*, and that the function of the courts was to declare the ancient custom of the realm; even statutes were interpreted as declaratory judgments (1957: 37). As Pocock points out, the Normans themselves had felt that they must rule by ancient law and declared themselves to be governing according to the *laga Edwardii*, the laws of Edward the Confessor (1003–1066), while in the twelfth and thirteenth centuries claims to the throne were made in the form of promises to restore the good old law of St Edward. The 1308 coronation oath, used until the seventeenth century, incorporated a promise to observe the laws of St Edward (Pocock 1957: 42–43; Greenberg 2001: 42–43). In the seventeenth century, Pocock says, the 'fundamental law' of England was still regarded as ancient and representing immemorial custom (1957: 48–49). The idea of an ancient constitution was obviously attractive for the lawyers and parliamentarians concerned to make a political case against royal sovereignty and absolutism; the concept of antiquity satisfied the need for a rule of law which would have no sovereign (1957: 52). But the belief in immemorial law was not just a clever legal argument, Pocock says; it was the near universal belief of Englishmen, such that even arguments put forward by crown lawyers would also, on occasion, appeal to antiquity (1957: 53–54).

Tubbs's (2000) careful historical study casts some doubt on both the universality and the history of the ideas Pocock is describing, showing how alternative strands of thought recognized the law-making prerogatives of the ruler and argued for the foundation of law upon reason. The links between law and custom were but one strand within the historic attitudes and understandings about what the law was. He suggests that in early medieval times the standard theological and juristic view of law was based upon the classical tradition that all law is derived from reason (2000: 148). Common lawyers of the fourteenth and fifteenth centuries also seemed to hold that reason was the basis of the authority of custom (2000: 188), while seventeenth-century lawyers called legal reason 'artificial', meaning that it was the product of artifice and skill, particularly the art of argument, which had been passed down to them in a long tradition from Aristotle.

Concentrating more closely on ideas about the ancient constitution, on the other hand, Greenberg (2001) traces the claims made by Coke and Davies back to ideas prevalent in the middle ages, even the tenth century (2001: 3). The idea of the ancient constitution she says, was not just a seventeenth-century invention, although it was first fully formulated in Reformation England. The foundations had been laid by the monks and magnates who promoted the notion of the ancient constitution for their own purposes; and even in the middle ages it could serve the same political purpose as the early modern version, that is to justify resistance against the king. The attraction of the 'laws' of St Edward, along with other supposedly ancient—likewise more recently confected—sources, was that they pointed to continuity across the great divide of 1066 (2001: 9–14).

The ancient constitutional view of law and government was thus both ahistorical and inimical to contractual theories of law and government (Greenberg 2001: 21). Coke's arguments, in particular, were not entirely consistent and he could associate the common law with divine right monarchy, as well as arguing that it imposed a limit upon royal power. Nevertheless, there was an intellectual and historical tradition that taught that the origins of the ancient constitution lay in the period before 1066, to which the laws of St Edward stood witness. Some writers described the constitution as being in perpetual flux and likened it to a ship which retained its essential form, even though its planks and sails had been continuously replaced over the years. This tradition thus encouraged the use of the past for present purposes (2001: 21–34). Historians can critique this view of history as selective and errone-ous but, as Greenberg points out (2001: 34), it was not the simple anachronism of imposing the present upon the past. It was based upon a reverence for custom and tradition, which reflected and reinforced the common memory of how society was organized and social relations were conducted.

As Finley emphasizes, the language of antiquity was employed in England by royalists, parliamentarians, radicals, and even the Levellers, alongside their appeals to 'natural right and reason' (1971: 41–42). As in Athens, he says, it was assumed that the argu-ment from antiquity was a valid one, while the distant past was concretized and personified in the image of St Edward.

ANCESTRY, CONSERVATISM, AND LEGAL THOUGHT

Appeal to the ancestral past to justify the application of a rule or principle is often a feature of non-literate societies. As Clanchy (1970) points out in his discussion of early English legal history, remembered law, like myth, is not enacted or annulled, so it is timeless: 'When law is called "old" it is rather a description of its high quality than a strict determination of its age' (Clanchy 1970: 172, citing Kern 1939: 160). Ancestral law thus tends to be invoked with the needs of the present, rather than truth about the past, in mind. When a change is made from oral to written modes, as it was in twelfth and thirteenth-century England, many of the old ways, such as the oral presentation of a case in court by a professional pleader, may continue, albeit modified and sometimes even rendered meaningless. In common law England the practice of law had become thoroughly literate by the fourteenth century but, as Clanchy describes, the sanction of ancestry was not abandoned. In twelfth-century Wales, too, new law codes were attributed to the tenth-century Hywel Dda (Pryce 2000: 40, 54).

An appeal to the ancestral constitution can even be found within the political argument of twentieth-century America, as Finley (1971) goes on to discuss. The American constitution had been written down but it was later invoked, along with the image of Thomas Jefferson as the paramount Founding Father, in ways that recall the Athenians' appeals to Solon, the Welsh references to Hywel Dda, and Coke's invocation of St Edward. Roosevelt, in particular, contributed to a series of myths that grew up around Jefferson by compiling a large dossier of Jefferson's speeches and sending an aide to lay a wreath annually at his tomb. As Finley (1971: 43) says, the American argument from the ancestral past had to differ from the Athenian and common law arguments because history was too well documented: selective quotation had to replace forgery as the operational device. But, as in the other cases, the past was personalized, while even those who stressed rational and moral arguments during political debates could not resist adding an appeal to the ancestry of the constitution.

More recently, an ideology of traditionalism has been noted in both colonial and post-colonial Africa, where symbolism of the traditional world of tribal ways and practices has been widely employed as a means of political and legal legitimation (Chanock 1985: 238). In post-apartheid South Africa, Oomen (2005) has noted calls to restore 'traditional' law and governance, as part of an increased emphasis, in both politics and everyday life, on roots, belonging, and cultural difference. Paradoxically, it is migrants who profit from the modern economy and largely work elsewhere, who have been the most active promoters of a patriarchal vision of 'traditional law and governance' in their home communities. She notes how the Bafokeng 'nation', aided by transnational capital, migrant knowledge, and the enthusiastic endorsement of the royal family, has aimed to restore 'traditional laws and customs', while in another region the migrants sought to draw up a tribal constitution telling their new king how to rule his people. In both cases the emphasis was essentially on reinstating a patriarchal, hierarchical set of norms, often at odds with the equality clauses within South Africa's constitution (2005: 106).

The appeal to tradition can, therefore, be political, but it recurs widely, presenting a vision of a higher order lying behind the authority of the law, promising justice and equity, and inviting commitment. A link with divine origins may be claimed, but is not indispensable: as Finley (1971: 48) puts it, a generalized, but not necessarily explicit, reference to God's will seems to serve almost as well. A tendency to invoke cosmic order is also apparent, as we have seen, on the part of the Chinese emperors, even as they claimed absolute authority as law-makers. Some scholars have emphasized the disenchantment of subsequent western legal traditions. As Witte (1991: 1623–24) describes, Olympic mysticism faded from Greek consciousness; Greek and later Roman writers came to view justice, order, and peace not as divine but as secular legal principles; Christian spiritualism gave way to Romanized institutionalism, while its spiritual ideals were reduced to human rules; and biblical theology gave way to 'juristic' or 'political' theology. But, as he also points out, this secularization can be exaggerated and historiography has confirmed the view 'that religious ideas and institutions—in Olympic, Judaic, Germanic, and Christian forms—have had a remarkably enduring and embracive influence on the Western legal tradition' (1991: 1636). Just (2007), for example, highlights the sacred symbolism in the architecture of US courthouses, which may evoke a Greek temple, or the authority of Moses. Their iconography, he suggests, is designed to satisfy a deep-seated desire to see the legal, civil order as corresponding to a cosmic order (2007: 121–22).

It is as if, in all these cases, the law and its proponents seek the sanction and authority of something or someone transcendent, who stands above and beyond the activities of the known law-makers. Finley suggests that it is a desire for something that will create a feeling of continuity and permanence. In other contexts there is clearly a need to find a source of authority above that of the ruler, an issue I discuss further in chapter eight. This might involve an appeal to the divine, but it might also be found in an ancestral constitution or the sense of a legal tradition.

A sense that law is traditional or ancestral may also serve to explain what some writers have remarked upon as its inherent conservatism. There is, for example, a tendency for established laws to be retained and recopied long after their utility can be supposed to have lasted. As well as the provisions of the Tang code in imperial China, the laws of Hammurabi, king of Babylon (ruled 1792–1750BC) were copied and recopied over the following millennium (Bottéro 1987: 196), the Irish codes created in the seventh and eighth centuries were copied, with glosses and commentaries, until the collapse of the Gaelic order in the seventeenth century (Kelly 1988: 225–31, 250–63), and a fourteenth-century code was still being presented as Tibetan 'law' in the early twentieth century (Pirie 2010: 214–15).

Alan Watson maintains that a legal tradition can be an essentially conservative social force, as exemplified by the legacy of Roman law in medieval and later Europe. Social pressure may cause the law to change, he argues, but the nature of that change will be determined primarily by the lawyers and the legal tradition (2001).[17] A dynamic tension then tends to arise between jurisprudential tradition and social purposiveness in law (Frier 1986: 900). As Watson puts it, law is generally treated as existing in its own right. The means of creating law and its sources come to be regarded as a given, something almost sacrosanct. Law has to be justified in its own terms; its authority must already exist (2001: 264). Drawing a parallel between the longevity of Roman law and the classical literature of Hindu law, which presents itself as all but timeless, Skoda (2012: 40) argues that complex legalism seems to be characterized by a peculiar tension between the

---

[17] His arguments, in particular as set out rather schematically in the original text of 1985, have been subject to critical comment. Gagarin (1985/86) points out that his emphasis on the role of the lawyers stems from his concentration on post-Roman examples, a point that Watson recognizes in the renamed second edition of 2001, while Frier (1986) suggests that Watson sets up too great a dichotomy between the different reasons for legal change, arguing convincingly that it must occur for a variety of reasons and in a variety of ways. Nevertheless, Gagarin (1985/86) acknowledges a widespread view that law is inherently conservative, as well as general respect for legal tradition, while Frier considers that Watson is right to emphasize the fact that abstract patterns of jurisprudential thinking can have a powerful influence on law.

claim to contemporary relevance and the claim to authority on the basis of historical longevity.

In practice, a sense of tradition might explain certain legal anachronisms. Lambert (2012) describes the way in which the institution of legal sanctuary ossified in late medieval England, outlasting the interests of the king, church, and people. The Anglo-Saxon practice of sanctuary, whereby a felon might seek refuge in a church for forty days and then leave (abjure) the realm, developed within the context of legal insecurity surrounding the early reforms of Henry II in the 1170s; but it remained unchanged for 300 years, while other legal institutions evolved. Lambert suggests that the explanation must be sought beyond the centralization and bureaucratization of the legal system, in the power and influence of the church. We must not, that is, expect to find a simple pattern of legal change, nor the uniform adherence to tradition, in any particular case.

In his work on ancient Greece, Sealey (1994: 22–23) argues that law is not just a response to social and political factors and that the historian should look beneath the rules for the ideas that underlie and inspire them. We ought, he argues, to regard the history of law as a branch not of social, but of intellectual history.[18] Legal scholars like Krygier (1986) have also emphasized the sense of the past within a legal tradition. Glenn (2008, 2012) uses this concept as a basis for characterizing and describing the 'legal traditions' of the world. This, he argues, produces 'a more inclusive and just approach to the law', which should be studied as a history of ideas (2008: 427). However, as Twining et al. (2006) have pointed out, the concept of legal tradition does not distinguish legal from other ideas.[19] Moreover, other currents

---

[18] Sealey focuses on the internal logic of the law and regards the process of change as a primarily intellectual one, drawing upon the work and approach of the German historical school, exemplified in the writing of the nineteenth-century jurist, Friedrich Karl von Savigny. Other scholars have emphasized the need to understand Greek legal practices in their social contexts, arguing that Athenian law, as found in judicial practice, should be regarded as a response to social and political needs (Todd and Millett 1990; Carey 1994).

[19] Glenn's (2008) description of tradition as 'normative information that has been passed on over time' is even more problematic. As I have argued here, law may be regarded as a matter of meaning, as much as norms.

of thought have often run alongside a sense of tradition. The idea of a *nomos*, law based upon human reason, has a legacy reaching back to the time of Plato, and the pre-eminent figures of seventeenth-century English political thought (including Hobbes and Locke) argued from the natural rights of all humanity, not from the historical rights of Englishmen (Kelley 1990; Goldie 2001). Meanwhile, in China the emperors were acknowledged as law-makers, while in Athens the fourth-century constitutions explicitly acknowledged the law-making powers of the democratic polis. We should not expect to find a single, consistent, or coherent strand of legal theory during this, or any other period of history.

Anthropologists, with their focus on social practice and the particularity of individual examples, have tended to explain legal processes by reference to their immediate social and political contexts, including the interests of powerful groups. It is the argument of this book that an anthropology of law needs to be a study of thought and ideas as much as a description of practice. The ideas that come to be regarded as integral to a legal tradition may have considerable social influence, both geographical and historical. As anthropologists of law, we should not seek to explain the nature or force of law as a response to its immediate social context alone. We must also be careful not to dismiss an appeal to the ancestral past as irrational or to characterize it as conservative in a pejorative way; nor should we be tempted to compare it unfavourably with more modern, apparently flexible, and ostensibly more socially responsive law-making.

What this chapter has shown is that there is a widespread tendency for laws and law-makers to claim or invoke some transcendent form of order, whether divine, cosmic, or traditional, and that this can endow their laws with an unchanging, sometimes sacrosanct, quality. In many cases it is also the sense of a higher order that provides the basis for commitment to the law—as an interpretation of the words of God, or of Vedic principles, as the reflection of immemorial custom, the legacy of a heroic ancestor, or simply as a guarantor of life and liberty. It is this idealism, as we might characterize it, that is in many cases the basis for law's authority. Contrasting tendencies are evident in the history of legal thought: as Witte

(1991) points out, Olympic mysticism, Christian spiritualism, and biblical theology seem to have given way to secular legal principles, human rules, and juristic theology. Appeals to tradition and cosmic sanction may then come into tension with an emphasis on the rationality of the law—with its legalism. It is to this that I turn in the next chapter.

6

LEGALISM

Legalism is a way of thinking and acting; it is what could be said to be distinctive about legal, as compared to other schemes of meaning. It is apparent in many of the examples already discussed, for example the legal codes produced by the ancient Greeks and Anglo-Saxons, but also in the scholastic forms of law which tend to jurisprudential complexity and self-consciously erudite forms of reasoning. A legalistic approach to the world describes and prescribes human conduct in terms of rules, categories, and generalizations. Explicit rules may prescribe or authorize penalties, compensation, and other consequences of specified behaviour, both positive and negative—they set out the way the world ought to be, whether or not anyone actually behaves that way. The formulae of the Romans and writs of the English common law were also legalistic: they specified the precise terms in which a legal action could be formulated, giving rise to arguments about categories, connections, and exceptions, and to the use of precedents, analogies, and other specialized forms of reasoning. More simply, legalistic thought separates fact and law, or what is presented as the 'is' and the 'ought', promising answers in cases of dispute and lending itself to a distinctive form of judicial decision-making, one that appeals to rules and generalities beyond the facts of the particular case. In this chapter I discuss some of the different contexts in which legalistic thought emerges—in courts, at the hands of lawyers and rulers, and under the pen of religious scholars.

LAW AND CUSTOM

In studies of general social norms or processes of conflict resolution, anthropologists have not tended to focus on legalism.[1]

---

[1] I am indebted to Paul Dresch for many of the ideas and examples of the early sections of this chapter.

However, in their debates over the contrast between law and custom we glimpse something of what is distinctive about this aspect of law. Paul Bohannan (1965) looked to the institutions of dispute settlement to examine the distinctive characteristics of law and concluded that 'law may be regarded as a custom that has been restated in order to make it amenable to the activities of the legal institutions' (1965: 36). Custom, he said, must be 'doubly-institutionalized' in order to make it justiciable: 'law is specifically recreated, by agents of society, in a narrower and recognizable context—that is, in the context of institutions that are legal in character and, to some degree at least, discrete from all others' (1965: 34). Socio-legal theorist Denis Galligan proposes a similar model of judicial decision-making: behaviour that is regarded as reasonable and normal is the basis on which rulings are made about how someone should behave in a particular circumstance. As society becomes more complex, notions of what is reasonable need to be replaced by uniform rules as the basis on which such rulings can be made (2007: 70–75). This 'institutionalization' and the creation of uniform and explicit rules are characteristic of legalism.

Such models suggest a relatively smooth transition between custom or notions of what is reasonable and rules of law, a transition that is driven by the judicial institutions faced with the problems of decision-making in a complex society. Taking issue with Bohannan's theory, Stanley Diamond (1973) makes a strong case for a sharper disjunction between law and custom. Considering a number of historical and anthropological examples, he concludes that in the early state laws arise 'in opposition to the customary order . . . they represent a new set of social goals pursued by a new and unanticipated power in society' (1973: 327). Law is formulated as states expand, he says, when they need to conscript labour, muster armies, levy taxes, maintain a bureaucracy, and monitor the population (1973: 332). Like Roberts (2005), he links the development of law firmly with the rise of government. The imposition of laws by a state does, in such circumstances, seem to represent a rupture with custom and practice. As Geertz also notes (1983: 217), laws are not commonly generated out of a shared commitment to moral or social norms: they are more generally needed when there is no consensus or to facilitate new, potentially contested, forms of social practice. However, as previous chapters have shown, the emergence of legalistic thought and the elaboration of law can be associated with the work of scholars, as well as being traced to the rise of a state, and at times it appears that there might have been a general attempt to record and regularize custom. Diamond's analysis only seems able to account for some examples of law.

Law might, then, emerge from custom, but it might also express a ruler's ambitions, or facilitate a new form of social practice, not to mention expressing religious ideals. Its subject matter and origins do not seem to explain very much. We need, rather, to understand legalism as a distinctive form of social thought.

Legalism in the courts

In a detailed study of the Basoga, in what is now Uganda, anthropologist Lloyd Fallers (1969) discusses what he describes as the 'legalism' of their courts. The Basoga had lived under colonial rule for over seventy years and their local courts had undoubtedly been inspired by colonial models. However, they had no explicit laws, writs, or rules of procedure. Rather, litigants and judges reasoned orally with what he terms 'categorizing concepts', often about the appropriate behaviour of married couples, or those who were not, and what defined a marriage. A mistreated wife had remedies under Soga law, for example, but she could not simply return to her family without exposing her father to a charge of 'harbouring'. In such a case the court might have to consider whether the husband had demanded the return of the bride-price, which would indicate an end to the marriage, absolving the father of the charge. The categories of harbouring, bride-price, and various kinship terms thus served as a means to order cases before the courts, narrowing the issues to provide a 'moving system of classification', as Fallers puts it, which is characteristic of law. The courts 'reason legally with categorizing concepts that narrow and frame the issues for decision' (1969: 20–21). Once a case opened in the courts on the basis of a recognized cause of action the judges concentrated upon finding a yes-or-no answer in terms of that rubric (1969: 28).

Rules, Fallers suggests, are needed to arrive at simple dichotomous moral decisions. He follows Hart (1961) in arguing that a

legal mode of social control requires that values with respect to
human conduct be reduced to normative statements, which are
sufficiently discrete and clear so that it may be authoritatively determined whether or not, in a particular case, a particular rule has
been violated (1969: 17–22).[2] Where, on the other hand, courts do
not make use of legal concepts, the judge is faced with a welter
of blame and counterblame, with all the moral ambiguity that is
present in any situation of interpersonal conflict. To put this in
anthropological terms, he says, to classify is to disturb, and legal
concepts disturb in order to define; an issue may then be decided
simply in terms of inclusion or exclusion (1969: 32). As Bourdieu
(1987: 820) remarks, law transforms irreconcilable conflicts of personal interests into rule-bound exchanges of rational arguments.

The legal system and the everyday system of morality may,
however, reach different conclusions about the same events,
giving rise to a tension between law and popular morality. As
Fallers points out, this may induce change in either or both, but
it also reflects a more general and complex interplay between the
logic of ideas and the exigencies of social relations within society
at large: neither can be reduced to the other (1969: 14–15). In
the case of the Basoga, it was apparent that litigants sought the
advantages of both narrow legalism and moral holism, tending
to argue either legalistically or moralistically, depending on
whether they had a good legal case or not. The same tendency has been noted in other judicial processes: Cicero indulged
in highly legalistic arguments in *pro Caecina*, when the merits
of the case were against his client (Frier 1985). In the homicide
courts and maritime cases in ancient Greece, the judicial process
involved the regular application of abstract, standardized rules,
while in the popular courts 'extralegal arguments' provided information about the context of the dispute to assist the jury in
reaching a just verdict, one that took into account the particular
circumstances of the individual case (Laani 2005). In the Middle
Ages the English manorial courts tended to favour appeals to
equity over the application of substantive laws (Bonfield 1989).
The organization of a Balinese village, on the other hand, was
strikingly legalistic: the villagers were committed to the idea

---

[2] In this, he follows Levi's (1948) *Introduction to Legal Reasoning*.

that certain behavioural rules had to be followed, on pain of expulsion, much though they may have sympathized, as individuals, with the plight of the outcast before them (Geertz 1983: 186). Rules and categories transform social relations, that is, according to explicit and objective standards, and in even such localized and relatively simple cases of legalism the rules can acquire an autonomy that transcends the power of the community, including that of the Balinese village council, not to mention the visiting king. The rules stand apart from practice.

The codification of custom

The dramatic development of laws, legal processes, and texts in early medieval Europe provides a wealth of historical examples with which the rise of law and legalism, and its relationship with custom can be explored. After the 'rediscovery' of Justinian's *Corpus Iuris* by Italian scholars, medieval jurists were faced with the task of reconciling the laws and principles of the Romans with the practices of their own courts and, in particular, with the structure of feudal relations that had by then come to dominate the major part of European society (Stein 1999: 62–67). Throughout Europe courts of all sorts were dealing with disputes, among other things (Reynolds 1997). However, the *Corpus Iuris* represented an obviously more sophisticated and, in their eyes, superior form of law to that of the 'barbarian' codes, created in the shadow of Rome (Wormald 1999; Barnwell 2000).

By the thirteenth century scholars in several European countries were setting down local laws in writing, often using Roman categories. Glanvill's and Bracton's compilations of English laws, discussed in chapter five, seem obvious attempts to rationalize English laws in emulation of Justinian's great codifications; the Emperor Frederick II promulgated the *Liber Augustalis* for his Sicilian kingdom; and King Ferdinand III in Spain created the *Siete Partidas*. At more local levels, too, there were moves to write down the customs applied by local courts, particularly in northern France, including Philippe de Beaumanoir's well-known treatise on the custom of Beauvaisis (Stein 1999: 64–67).[3] Other

---

[3] Stein (1999), particularly in chapter three, provides an excellent summary of these complex developments.

custumals abounded, often derived from one another, as well as inspired by the *Corpus Iuris* (Cohen 1993).

This generated considerable debate concerning the relationship between law and custom, which continued through the middle ages, ranging over the differences between written and unwritten laws and the nature of habits, local customs, and the will of the people as sources of law. Historical studies from the period thus provide insight into how laws and legalistic thought may be locally conceptualized. Albeit that the political and legal landscape was fragmented and varied, Ibbetson (2007) detects two contradictory, and recurrent views about the relationship between law and custom. On the one hand, custom (*consuetudo*) was regarded as a form of law, sometimes described as *ius non scriptum* (unwritten law), standing alongside the *lex*, as in the phrase *lex et consuetudo*. This was the view expressed by Bracton, for example, in its assertion that the laws of England (*lex et consuetudo*) were not written.[4] On the other hand, custom was described as standing in contrast to law, even in opposition to it, something that could only be recognized in the courts if properly proved.

As Ibbetson describes (2007: 155), a general shift from the first to the second view can be detected during the middle ages. From the middle of the thirteenth century, contrasts were drawn between civil, canon, common, regional, and general laws, marking what he calls a self-conscious 'juridification' of society. Methods for proving custom in the courts were elaborated, including the *enquête par turbe* formulated by Louis IX in 1270, and local customs became integrated, in this way, into the laws applied in France and Flanders, and subject to the control of the Parlements (2007: 158–60). In England the manorial courts dealt with villein tenants who held their land 'according to the customs of the manor'. However, by the fourteenth century the jury had to determine what that custom was and, Ibbetson (2007: 167–69) suggests, behind the guise of discovery, they

---

[4] This was to emerge again, albeit in a more ideological form, in the seventeenth century with Coke's insistence on the ancient origins of English law in the customs of the realm, discussed in chapter five.

would, 'perhaps unwittingly, have been creating the rules that were to be applied by the courts':

> At a very basic level...the values espoused by the common law would have been generally recognised by people in England but the detailed working out of the rules derived from these values would certainly not have had any such populist grounding. This was all the work of lawyers. (2007: 165)[5]

Although the intellectual influence of Roman law is apparent in these European developments, the formalization and transformation of custom that Ibbetson is describing was obviously not imposed in any straightforward manner by a state or governmental authority. It was more the work of the lawyers, representing a new way of thinking and organizing the work of local courts and judges.

Watson (2001: 103) suggests that, to a great extent, customary law does not even derive from what the people of a locality habitually do. Pollock and Maitland (1968, 1: 399–400), for example, observed that in the middle ages German villages might be inhabited by persons of the same race, religion, and language, and subject for centuries to the same economic conditions, yet have very different rules for the central institution of matrimonial property. In each, one form had become fixed as law following a judicial decision, so that the final result in any one place contained some element of the arbitrary. It was not a simple and smooth evolution from custom and habit to law. Eventually, as Ibbetson (2007: 156) describes, medieval scholars drew a distinction between habit, *mos*, and custom, *consuetudo*. The latter could be recognized by the courts, but only on strict conditions and later only if consistent with reason, like the learned law (2007: 172–74). The application of custom, thus proved, to the facts of a case represented a change in ways of thinking and acting.

Seeking to analyse this juridical shift, Cheyette (1970, 1978) discusses the development of law in twelfth and thirteenth-century

---

[5] More recent colonial and post-colonial examples, discussed in chapter two, also indicate that the recognition of custom by a court elevates it into something different: however hard the South African judges try, they cannot help but transform 'indigenous law' into a more explicit set of rules and principles in order to give it legal effect in the court.

France, contrasting the changing forms of judicial process. Examples from the early part of the period, he found, indicate that solutions were being reached by arbitration and compromise rather than adjudication. The object was overwhelmingly to secure agreement and satisfy honour: in order to broker a compromise courts and mediators would take into account insults to status and invoke general principles, rather than specific, universally applicable rules (1970: 291–95). Such cases were decided or resolved without recourse to impersonal rules of law; they were characterized, rather, by moral holism. Justice would address individuals, their particular situations, complaints and demands. Notions of law, ideals of behaviour, political rules, and social mores were expressed together as statements about particular people doing particular things (1978: 158–61). In medieval courts the jurists' task was to tell stories: they were authors of literature as much as of law (Bloch 1977: 5).

The emergence of written laws in thirteenth-century France, Cheyette continues, involved the development of more abstract and objectively definable categories: 'movables' and 'immovables', 'inheritance' and 'gift', 'tenant' and 'lord'. These are categorizing concepts akin to those with which the Soga were reasoning. As Cheyette found, the appeal to such concepts was accompanied by the development of rules with atemporal force, abstracted from the immediacy of daily life, from the obstinate opacity, the multiple referents, of individual lived experiences (1970: 289; 1978: 170). Their atemporality led to what Cheyette calls the formulation of 'a consciously constructed system of verbalized rules' (1978: 163), that is, to legalistic means of thinking and disputing.

'Why did this change come about?' Cheyette asks (1970: 289). It cannot be assumed, as many historians have done, that a court whose decisions are more 'rational' is necessarily more attractive to the people; there is no reason to believe that individuals, any more than nations, prefer objective neutrality to partiality in their own favour. 'Neutral, objective order is very much a learned value' (1970: 290). The rise of legalistic thought at this time can, obviously, be linked to the rediscovery of Justinian's code and its prestige: as Cheyette points out (1970: 297), the idea that a system of norms should govern disputes had never completely disappeared from southern Europe, although the Roman legal categories had become cloudy. Nevertheless, the influence of Roman law was too vast and generalized to be the sole explanation for the sudden change that occurred in the decades around 1250. Bloch (1977: 8–10) links these developments to the expansion of the royal domain and power in France. The kings installed their own officers in newly acquired lands, but permitted them to govern according to the practices that had traditionally prevailed. Hence the necessity of fixing such practices in writing. But they were also concerned to replace a feudal system of private vengeance with a judicial structure and to establish a system of appeal, with the Parlement of Paris at its centre: 'through a gradual shift in judicial institutions monarchy gained mastery over the language as well as the institutions of law'. Cheyette traces the changes to more local factors: political developments had led to the breaking up of the groups that had gathered around local powerholders; village inhabitants, city consuls, and lords all discovered that the court machinery provided by the monarchy allowed them to fight those who would impose some kind of dominion over them. The courts, in turn, with their special intellectual techniques, led to further legalization of social relationships. By 1300 men thought first of their rights as objectively defined and then strove to have them sanctioned by a court, the king's court if possible (1970: 298–99). Within a matter of decades the whole system was worked out.

The intellectual, the social, and the political all combined, therefore, to change the nature of court processes and arguments in medieval France, and ultimately to change the ways in which people thought of their social, political, and economic relations—or some of them—outside the courts. The emergence of legalistic thought and practice must always be understood within its particular social context, that is, and we should not expect the same (complex) patterns to repeat themselves the world over. Nevertheless, legalism emerges widely, in very different contexts.

RULES AND CATEGORIES

If legalism is a tendency to describe the world in terms of generalizing rules and abstract categories, what does this involve?

Rules are at the centre of Hart's (1994) seminal work of jurisprudence and have been a theme for legal theorists ever since. As he develops the argument, in chapters six to ten, Hart tends to treat rules as if they were always prescribing and proscribing individual behaviour; the model of a law that his account evokes is one that makes certain behaviour illegal. As Honoré (1977) points out, however, in an examination of 'real laws' within the common law system, laws rarely prescribe or proscribe conduct in any direct way. Rather, they tend to create categories and define their ambit, they specify the position—including the rights and duties—of the persons and things in different categories, and they define the scope of other laws, providing for exceptions and limitations. Laws are at once general and subject to actual or potential exceptions. Further rules govern matters of evidence and procedure, providing for the ways in which a court is to decide how the substantive law applies (1977: 112). Laws defining categories and positions are rarely directly normative, specifying or proscribing conduct; they are more often designed, as Honoré puts it, to protect people against exploitation or their own folly, for example providing criteria for the validity of wills and contracts. The law concerning consideration, the reciprocal promise needed to make a contract valid in England, is 'an item of legal paternalism'. Even the law concerning *mens rea*, the mental state that must be proved before an accused is found guilty of a crime, primarily operates so as to excuse those who might otherwise be held responsible for the consequences of their actions (1977: 105). It is worth quoting Honoré's summary in full:

The law is concerned with the relations between human beings and between them and animate or inanimate objects viewed from a special point of vantage. To attain this point of vantage requires the transformation of the data of ordinary life into those of a special drama with its own personages, costumes and conventions, not to mention the invention of new personages and relationships not found in the state of nature. To set the stage for this drama the law categorizes actions, events, personalities, and conditions in a special way and then, from their subsumption into the appropriate categories, draws conclusions as to the legal position of the *dramatis personae* and *res*, their possibilities of acting and suffering, and their mutual relations. (1977: 112)

As Finnis (1980: 283) puts it, law provides the 'costumes and relationships' into which the situations and circumstances of real life must be fitted.

Legalistic thought describes the way the world can be—the categories of property ownership that feudal lords could enjoy—as well as the way it ought, or ought not, to be—a Soga man should not carry off an unrelated woman on his bicycle. It also routinely makes provision for how its own categories and concepts are to be interpreted: it provides a framework for common deliberation about courses of action and reasons for them (Postema 2002: 618).

Legalism is not wholly a matter of rules, however. Bourdieu (1987: 820, fn. 28) notes the use of the indicative mood in French legal drafting, to describe what is just, as if it were an objective property of things themselves: 'the legislator prefers to describe legal institutions rather than establishing rules directly'. This is especially so within a common law system, and Hart has been criticized for developing a theory that accounts badly for the common law (Simpson 1987). The Roman *ius civile*, too, was not primarily a system of explicitly stated rules: a writ or formula with precise wording was required to initiate a legal case, but the principles upon which the judges acted and the categories and rules they applied and refined were only implicit in their judgments. As Postema (2002) emphasizes, the common law consists of accepted principles and forms of reasoning more than explicitly stated rules. However, even without explicit rules, in a judicial context implicit rules, principles, and categories can provide the grounds on which authoritative decisions can be made. Within the earliest reported medieval English cases, for example, the argument clarified categories and principles, using explicitly logical argument, analogies, syllogisms, arguments from 'inconvenience' or hardship, the *reductio ad absurdum*, and citation of prior decisions (Brand 2007; 2012: 191). It provided a framework for judicial reasoning, which entailed a different sort of argument from that of particularistic, moral discussion. The Soga use of categories and the principles during a court case formed a similar framework for legal reasoning. As Lucas (1977: 89) puts it, with morals there is an ultimate emphasis on authenticity—individual motives and intentions matter—whereas with the law the ultimate emphasis is on conformity.

Looking further afield, the judicial processes of the Islamic world have been noted for their use of categorizing concepts and sophisticated forms of argument and interpretation. Powers's (2002) study of fourteenth and fifteenth-century documents from the Maghrib (Northern Africa), mentioned in chapter four, describes the course taken by a number of legal cases and the interrelation between the work of the *mufti*, the legal scholar, and the *qadi*, the judge. As he summarizes it, the muftis used authoritative legal texts to define what it meant for a particular society to be Islamic, while men and women used the law to negotiate their status in society: society and legal thought shaped each other (2002: 11). More particularly, he describes how, when a qadi asked a mufti for advice, 'he customarily translated the names of the litigants and their stories into the abstract and impersonal language of the law'; and the mufti's fatwa was equally abstract (2002: 232). During legal proceedings, as he puts it, the ongoing traffic in social relations is reduced to a set of symbols ordered by a specialized mode of logic. This reduction is performed by a notary or jurist who translates agreements and conflicts into legal norms that are expressed in the specialized vocabulary of the law (2002: 295).

Once a set of legal norms and relations has been established, it may no longer be a simple matter of applying categorizing concepts to the factual situation, of the kind suggested by Fallers's (1969) depiction of the Soga courts. The situation can become more complicated, illustrated particularly by the property disputes Powers describes, where not only did the underlying concepts relating to ownership and use determine the nature of the conflict, but theories of linguistic interpretation further refined the arguments. In an inheritance dispute in fifteenth-century Fez, for example, the conflict turned upon the interpretation of a written endowment and the presumed intentions of its founder. According to the accepted theory of textual interpretation, the words of the founder were comparable to God's words, as preserved in the Quran; they were to be treated like the words of the divine law-giver, to be carefully adhered to and executed (2002: 165). Islamic jurists attributed special meaning to ordinary language: 'indeed the technical meanings attributed even to commonplace particles and conjunctions often played a key role in the resolution of disputes' (2002: 165–66). The muftis 'understood their task as the application of a theory of language to a legal instrument and the integration of the results of their linguistic analysis to the facts of the case' (2002: 66).

General and abstract categories, along with both explicit and implicit rules, thus make possible a certain type of argument. The world is represented and analysed in terms of abstract concepts and relations between them, and this allows the development of sophisticated forms of argument, already noted in the development of Hindu, Roman, and Islamic law. Argument is conducted according to rules of interpretation, analogy, and precedent, not to mention the rules of procedure and evidence which may be developed to govern their application to the particular case.

Legalism thus promises definitions, distinctions, and right answers: it claims to produce a specific form of judgment (Bourdieu 1987: 820); it pretends that it is normal for everything to be tidy and straightforward (Leach 1977: 19); it introduces finality (Postema 2002: 613). Even a relatively simple set of rules and categories, as found among the Basoga, can provide a means to make decisions in difficult circumstances. We can contrast examples from the Tibetan region where, without laws to draw upon, it was difficult for judges to make authoritative decisions and judicial processes could only be concluded through agreement between the parties. This meant that in cases where the facts were in dispute the parties might be flogged until one changed his story, or sent to swear an oath in the temple (Pirie 2007b: 159–63). In one instance, reported from the early twentieth century, two parties to a homicide dispute remained at odds even after they had both been flogged. The judge ordered that a yak's skin be placed on the ground, bloody side up, and the parties threw dice upon it, invoking justice from the deities, and the case was determined accordingly (Cassinelli and Ekvall 1969: 176).[6]

---

[6] Asad (1983) discusses the development of judicial torture as a means to extract confessions in thirteenth-century Europe, where it was promoted by the Lateran Council of 1215 in order to replace trial by ordeal, duels, and sacred oaths. The establishment of truth through the spoken word, in this way, has been regarded by some writers as a step towards the rationalization of justice, although Asad suggests that just as significant are the bodily practices of asceticism, penance, and physical hardship that characterized the Christianity of the period.

Law can provide the basis for decision, and the distinction between adjudication and mediation, highlighted by Gulliver (1979), is an important one. Anthropological work has tended to blur the difference, however, presenting legalistic adjudication as just another technique of dispute resolution. Gulliver suggests that adjudication puts decision-making in the hands of a third party who exercises some degree of accepted authority, and that this need not involve applying authoritative rules (1979: 20). The Tibetan case indicates that even judges with political backing might not regard themselves as having the authority to make final judicial decisions, however. It is, rather, the law that provides the resources for adjudication, not political power (Postema 2002: 617–18). Legal rules and principles, when they make categorical statements about how the world should be, make possible the discovery of a right answer, just as the forms of reasoning found in the early common law courts provided a framework for judicial rulings.[7] It is the authority of the law, rather than the authority of the judge, that makes a final decision possible.

Literacy

The development of legalism in medieval France is associated by Cheyette with the rise of literacy. In a 'non-literate' society, that is one in which literacy is restricted to certain classes, the rules or principles to which the courts can appeal have to be memorizable; in practice, they often take the form of narratives, concerning individuals rather than abstracts (1978: 158–61). The task of the law, on the other hand, is to make rules and categories explicit. 'In the (written) contract we find men struggling for exactness of statement and clearness of diction...Every phrase is technical and legal, to an extent that often defies translation' (Johns 1904: iv, cited in Goody 1986: 147). It is not surprising, then, that the emergence of law is very often associated with the rise of literacy. As Goody (1986: 129) points out, reviewing a large

---

[7] One might also reflect upon the difficulty faced by both lawyers and judges when they try to encourage the parties to a legal case to opt for mediation, as promoted in the UK following Lord Woolf's recommendations in 1996. Once litigation has been initiated the parties are relating to each other as adversaries in a process directed towards a definitive answer: if the system promises an answer compromise seems unsatisfactory.

number of historical and anthropological examples, written law represents a 'new modality' by which a society can organize its affairs. 'Writing helps to transform ideas of how we can use the past (by precedent) and arrange the future (by legislation)' (1986: 154). Even without a high level of abstraction and formality, he says, writing encourages generalized statements of norms; it makes explicit and public what might otherwise remain implicit; it encourages a process of universalization and generalization. Written law can also become the subject of further elaboration, generating a jurisprudence (1986: 166). As he summarizes it, such processes of generalization and abstraction can be seen in the early codes of Mesopotamia, the treatises of Theodosius and Justinian, the legal procedures of medieval Britain, and the colonial codifications of the twentieth century (1986: 168).[8]

Goody's emphasis on the universalizing capacity of written rules echoes Bourdieu's discussion of written law:

writing adds the possibility of universalizing commentary, which discovers 'universal' rules and, above all, principles; and writing adds the possibility of transmission. Such transmission must be objective... it must also be generalized—able to reach beyond geographical (territorial) and temporal (generational) frontiers... written law fosters the process by which the text becomes autonomous. It is commented upon; it interposes itself between the commentaries and reality. At that point what the inhabitants of the legal world call 'jurisprudence' becomes possible: that is, a particular form of scholarly knowledge, possessing its own norms and logic, and able to produce all the outward signs of rational coherence. (Bourdieu 1987: 844–45)

Like Bourdieu, however, Goody perhaps overdraws the determinative effect of writing, particularly when he suggests that there is no distinction between law and custom in a non-literate society. He argues that when legal cases are reported and legislation is written, the notion and nature of concepts and rules changes, both as regards form and content (1986: 142).

We must not ignore the possibility of legalistic thought without writing, however. The courts that Fallers was describing

---

[8] Goody's earlier 'literacy thesis' (Goody and Watt 1963), alleging that writing makes possible a certain type of logical thought, has been subject to considerable criticism (Halverson 1992; Parry 1985), but his work on law is more cautious.

employed largely oral processes, nevertheless making use of explicit categorizing concepts. These might also be found in oral
categories, oaths, set formulae, and repeated phrases. As Thomas
(1995: 63) notes, there is a surprising amount of evidence for
early Greek laws being sung, even at a time when they were
already being written down, and it seems as if oral transmission
continued to be important, even after the laws were recorded in
writing. I have already noted the insistence on the superiority
of oral transmission in the Hindu and Islamic worlds, in which
literacy and the textual form are highly respected (Messick 1993;
Fuller 2001). The written tradition of the *dharmaśāstras*, for
example, is held to be based upon an originally spoken revelation of the gods. The Vedas should be, and still are, preserved
by direct transmission from teacher to pupil, a process involving endless repetition and an elaborate system of mnemonic
checks and phonetic rules to ensure exact replication of the
proper sounds (Parry 1985: 207–08). As Parry says, the apparently
paradoxical prestige of the written word arises from the fact
that although oral transmission has ideological pre-eminence,
memory is regarded as fallible and the written text has become a
more reliable guide to ancient wisdom. Nevertheless, the authoritative 'text' is not conceptualized as a purely literary document
and its 'authentic version' is an original and sacred revelation,
the recovery of which may require recourse to both written and
oral sources (1985: 213). The Icelandic Lawspeaker had to recite
the law at regular intervals and Kern (1939: 168) notes that in
Scandinavia there was a custom of declaring the law by word
of mouth at set intervals, 'in order to fix it'. On the other side
of the world, the Amish community of the US insists that their
'doctrine' or teaching 'is supremely certain and clearly known,
being safeguarded to each generation by means of an *oral tradition*
which contains and repeats the essential teachings' (cited in Cover
1983/84: 30, who comments that this is law in all but name).[9]

In an example from Mustang, on the margins of the Tibetan
region, Ramble (2008: ch 9) found what he analyses as two

---

[9] We might also consider that in the British courts, until recently, proceedings
were fundamentally oral and all documents, including authorities (reported
cases), were read out to the court.

forms of law. A written constitution was subject to review on a twelve-yearly cycle, but there was also an oath, repeated orally every year, which set out the various offences against the community that might attract divine sanction. The unchanging nature of both, he suggests, imbued them with a transcendent quality. The oath, in particular, was

not amenable to modification based on rational assessment: it was not formulated in public debate, and it is locked up in poetic form, a fixed number, an inaccessible past, and divine curatorship. It exhibits the principle—beloved of myth—that it is the most intangible things that are the most binding. (Ramble 2008: 310)

The constitution was different. As Ramble remarks, the twelve-yearly review ensures that the community, as far as it is represented in the constitution, never makes the transition from autonomy to hypostasis. After twelve years of being a constraining social factor, the document loses its status as a collective representation and becomes the property of the individuals who created it. It is brought close again, into the sphere where the conscious preferences of individuals can radically change it and, after suitable modification, set it apart from themselves again to get on with its constraining work (2008: 308–09). 'Verbalized rules', to go back to Cheyette's definition, are capable of being articulated and repeated, regarded as transcendent and respected as binding, in oral as well as written forms.

Work on law and literacy in Europe has noted the interaction of literate and non-literate forms of legal practice and instruction, with the survival of oral forms, such as the 'counting' performed in English common law courts, long after their function has been superseded (Clanchy 1979: 272–78). Esther Cohen (1993: 7–8) notes that in medieval Europe law and literacy were eminently oral forms based upon formulae, gesture, and ritual. The procedure of the feudal court resembled a literary performance involving the affirmation of an acknowledged set of shared beliefs and aspirations through the articulation of a collective history, as a prerequisite to the constitution of the legal and social community and the articulation and enforcement of a sanctioned code of conduct (Bloch 1977: 2). The element of orality did not disappear when the customs were written. As Pryce (2000: 32–33) also says, discussing medieval Welsh law books, the written word needs to be related to the mass of non-written practices which surround, envelop, and rival it. Literacy was regarded 'not as a technology for transforming the overwhelmingly oral world of legal procedures, but as a tool for conserving and transmitting native law and for promoting the authority of legal experts by giving visible and tangible form to their learning'. The Welsh law books were written in the vernacular, in contrast to other official documents, which were in Latin: 'legal writing was seen as a means of ensuring adherence to Welsh law as a body of native learning', and 'literacy was valued above all as a servant of legal tradition' (2000: 67). In this case, as in the Tibetan village described by Ramble, the spoken word is associated with a legal tradition, in contrast to the written word of the official documents or the village constitution. Writing may enable legal innovation, precision, interpretation, and jurisprudence, but it may also detract from what Ramble calls the mystique of the intangible. As Kern comments of the Middle Ages, law promulgated in written form was regarded as fixed and rigid, and merely a part of the all-embracing customary law, a fragment and not a complete codification. Statutes and capitularies regularly pointed to the unwritten customary law as the criterion to be followed (1939: 167).[10] There is a recurrent sense, then, that the written law reflects something ideal and intangible; that the legalistic form, whether written or not, can only capture a part of the law.

Formalism and its critics

A recurrent feature of the examples given in previous chapters is a mistrust of legalism: the formulary and writ systems of litigation found in the early Roman republic and the medieval English common law were notoriously formalistic and rigid, often providing what Frier (1986: 894) calls a legal solution to a problem that cried out for greater flexibility; Athenian orators would criticize their opponents for displaying excessive legal knowledge, or apologize for doing so themselves (Carey 1994);

---

[10] As Kern says, those who wrote down the law in the middle ages were very seldom concerned with objective law, and never with a complete and systematic codification of objective law, but rather with determining the subjective rights of individual persons (1939: 176).

Chinese lawyers were denigrated as 'pettifoggers' (MacCormack 1996: 25); and *shari'a* based litigation could be seen as overly procedure-bound (Clarke 2012: 114). In the European courts of the Middle Ages, as Ibbetson has remarked (2007: 169), the 'juridification of custom' and the fixity that this entailed gave rise to a tension between fidelity to the past and the desire to reach the right result in a particular case; and this tension came to characterize the customary law of the manors as well as the common law. The manorial courts described by Bonfield (1989) seem to have resolved disputes more often on the basis of equity than application of substantive laws; the consistency maintained by rules of law was evidently less appealing than a just result.

We can go back to Plato to find a stinging critique of the rigidity of the law. In both the *Statesman* and the *Laws* he criticizes the tyranny of the written law: it is like 'a stubborn and igno-rant man' who does not permit anyone to do anything contrary to his orders, nor to ask any questions; it orders and threatens like a tyrant or despot who writes his decrees down on the wall and is done with it (Nightingale 1999: 114, 117). However, Plato was not thereby implying that it was impossible to be a good law-giver, and the bulk of the *Laws* is devoted to describing the nature of this project, which must involve writing 'preludes' to the laws, couched in persuasive language to instruct and elicit lawful behaviour without threats and commands; the laws must ultimately be the product of divine wisdom.

The dangers of rigidity, thus noted by Plato, are echoed in the criticisms of 'formalism' or 'legalism' found in more contem-porary debates within legal and political theory. According to Chroust (1963), given the plurality of interests and goals within any society, the idea that there could be any supreme or abso-lute value enshrined in an unchanging and perfectly logical law is absurd. Ambiguity is, indeed, indispensable for preserving the dynamic quality of law. Thus, 'to insist that every decision and every law must flow with logical necessity from antecedently known premises is both an impossibility and an absurd propo-sition'. To reduce human experience to a logical or 'legalistic' system would be tantamount to depriving it of its substantial meaning (1963: 6–8). In her book on *Legalism*, political theorist

Judith Shklar (1964) famously criticizes the rigidity of legalistic categories of thought and the tendency to think of law as
'there', as a discrete entity discernibly different from morals and
politics (1964: 8–9).[11] The dangers of excessive legalism have even
been expressed by members of the contemporary British judiciary: in a case concerning the interpretation of human rights
provisions within the Bermuda constitution, Lord Wilberforce
declared that the court must avoid 'the austerity of tabulat-
ed legalism', a dictum often subsequently cited in both British
and Commonwealth courts.[12] What is evident is that normative
debates about the benefits and dangers of legalism have a long
history and show no signs of abating.

As an empirical matter, therefore, legalistic thought—widely
found in different social and political contexts—is often accompanied by theoretical reflection on the dangers of rigid and formalistic rules and categories. Where justice, in particular, is the
goal, legal rules and categories are inevitably flawed and fail perfectly to capture the complexity of real life, a point frequently
made by anthropologists. As Schauer (1988: 547–48) describes,
rule-based decision-making is inherently stabilizing, but the
law is inevitably both over and under-inclusive. Or, as Lucas
(1977: 96) neatly characterizes the problem, law is 'in an important sense no respecter of persons. It treats like cases alike, not
like persons'. Laws often promise justice, then, but they are blind
to the particulars of the case. The tension between legalism and
justice is a theme to which I return in the following chapters.

JURISPRUDENCE AND PLURALISM

Legalism enables a certain style of argument and critical reflection (Dresch 2012:12–14). Once we divide up the world into
general categories, different types of contract, for example, we
can argue about different conditions for validity, and types and
consequences of breach; different laws can be set against one
another, limitations and exceptions can be specified, and the rules
and principles concerning legal reasoning and interpretation can

---

[11] MacCormick (1989), by contrast, argues in favour of 'ethical legalism'.
[12] *Minister of Home Affairs v Fisher* [1980] AC 319, 329.

come to dominate a court case. This is inevitable when laws are applied in practical situations. The fit is never perfect and the ambit of a rule may need to be specified when the court is faced with a concrete case, or an obvious injustice might only be avoided by the creation of an exception or limitation to the application of the rule. Further rules need to be elaborated, as Honoré (1977) points out, to define the ambit of primary laws and their relationship one with another. Within the more complex systems of the English common law, Islamic *fiqh*, and Hindu *dharmaśāstra* literature, discussed in previous chapters, precise rules are not central, and forms of juristic reflection and deduction involve reasoning by analogy and refined theories of interpretation.

The juristic form of argument found in all these types of case tends to proliferate. This is especially so in the hands of legal scholars, but it is also evident in the archaic codes discussed in chapter three. Miller (1990: 225) comments upon the complexity of the medieval Icelandic codes. Formal transcription, he says, did not stint the propensity for law-making. If anything, it seems to have encouraged it and within a short time after the writing of the laws there was a need for a citation law. In Rome, too, citation rules were developed in the later imperial period to rank the opinions of the different jurists, necessitated by the proliferation of their opinions and the lack of consistency between them (Nicholas 1962: 37). Kantor (2012: 76) comments on the lack of clear hierarchy amongst the different sources of law in the late Roman republic. As Frier (1985: 194) puts it, the Romans encountered one of the paradoxes of autonomous legal thinking, that the quest for certainty through jurisprudence makes possible an increase in law's complexity and its tolerance of uncertainty.

Another type of proliferation occurs when law is exported. When Romans moved to the conquered lands of the eastern provinces they took their law with them: Roman citizens continued to enjoy the benefits, as they were seen, of their law.[13] In the

---

[13] Initially, the *ius civile* was the proud possession of Roman citizens and could not be extended indiscriminately to *peregrines*. The law applicable to non-Romans was the *ius gentium*. Initially relating to foreigners within Rome, it developed into the idea of law common to all nations, becoming associated with Greek

meantime, as Kantor (2012: 78–79) describes, Rome was keen to preserve the 'ancestral laws' of the provincial cities it had conquered and Roman governors would recognize local laws. A plurality of laws thus persisted into the late second century AD, while knowledge of Roman legal forms became widespread and hybrid laws developed. Nevertheless, the Romans did not devise any conflicts of laws principles in order to determine which laws should apply, to whom, and in which circumstances. Law was a resource that individuals could claim, more than a governing system to be applied by the imperial powers, and supposed to be complete and coherent in its own right. As Kantor remarks, this casts doubt on Raz's confident assertion that 'every law necessarily belongs to a legal system' (Raz 1973: 1), and that law always claims to be comprehensive and supreme (1979: 116–21).

This is not the only place, as Dresch (2012: 14) points out, in which different types of law have been thought to coexist. Premodern Malaya, for example, distinguished *adat perpateh* (customs of the commons or of community) from *adat temengong* (customs imposed by princes), from Islamic shari'a. In England, by the mid-thirteenth century, contrasts were being drawn between civil, canon, common, regional, and general laws (Ibbetson 2007: 155). There was also a great range of courts, including the courts of the cities, boroughs, towns, and ports, as well as the mercantile courts (Basile et al. 1998: 30). Some, like the London courts—as distinct from the king's court at Westminster—were well integrated into the common law system, although they would have preserved and recognized their own set of customs; the forest courts, governed by royal statutes, dealt with particular issues not covered by the common law; the merchants' courts largely applied the common law, but had their own procedural rules; the stannary courts of the tin miners applied their own customs; while the manorial courts tended to merge law and custom (Ibbetson 2007: 170–71).

We should not expect law always to form a tidy and ordered system. When the law is found in judicial precedent, like the

---

ideas about natural law and, by the time of Justinian, it had acquired an extended meaning as the model to which all law ought to conform (Waldron 2012: 33–35).

post-eighteenth-century English common law, we are likely to find a certain amount of inconsistency, and contradictions not yet rationalized by the judiciary. Indeed, in the attempt to give an appropriate remedy in a particular situation the judges may make matters worse by simultaneously complicating the law and unavoidably directing its course for the future (Watson 2001: 58–59). Even within the federal organization of Switzerland, as Watson points out, neighbouring provinces and states built up very different legal rules on matters of fundamental concern. Lack of systemic coherence is a normal and inevitable aspect of all law, especially when it is regarded as tradition: 'a transmitted past is treated by participants as an authoritatively significant part of their present' (Krygier 1987: 34). Law then 'contains deposits made by swarms of contributors of greater and lesser intelligence, foresight and self-awareness' over generations. Mechanisms may exist to reject, prune, and amend the tradition and to make what remains self-referring and reinforcing, but the task is not easy. Doctrine survives, like language and culture, to shape and, to a greater or lesser degree, to constitute what succeeding generations believe, imagine, and practise (1987: 36).

Legal pluralism is, thus, an important and widespread phenomenon, but one that is far more complex than the coexistence of state law and customary practices, normally referred to by the term and now found everywhere in the world; and it involves more than the coexistence of state, international, and transnational laws, discussed in the next chapter. Nor is it particularly a feature of the colonial or post-Roman worlds, as some have suggested. A multiplicity of laws, in the sense of rules and legalistic practices, has characterized European history even, or especially, where there is no state or dominant legal system to encompass and define what else is to count as customary or subordinate 'law'.

Pluralism and authority

The proliferation of juristic thought at the hands of legal scholars can also complicate the issue of legal authority, which was the problem that the Icelandic and Roman citation rules were designed to address. It is a problem that arises in acute form in the Islamic word, in which an intellectual system with great influence spread widely, without being subject to any single territorial authority. For Islamic scholars themselves, the question of authority is primarily a religious one: interpretations of the shari'a tend to derogate from the authority of God's word as enshrined in the Quran. The concern for the Islamic jurists is not so much the authoritative exercise of legal power as fidelity to the 'nominally divine' and, therefore, 'inscrutable' source of the shari'a (Clarke 2010). Indeed, since AD900 juristic activity is supposed to have been confined to the explanation, application, and interpretation of the doctrine. Nevertheless, over the centuries the juristic literature has proliferated, forming what Messick (1993: 1–3) has described as an endlessly open and interpretable field of shari'a discourse. When attempts to modernize and codify the shari'a were undertaken within the Ottoman regime, those charged with its drafting were almost defeated by the vast field of shari'a discourse, which they described as 'an ocean without shores', echoing a metaphor used by scholars from many of the Islamic schools.

In contemporary Lebanon, too, Clarke (2010) describes the 'prodigious intellectual output' and the 'torrent of *fiqh*' produced by the religious specialists. Amongst the Shiite Muslims, he found, prestige continues to attach to a relatively informal hierarchy of specialists, culminating in a limited number of 'sources of emulation', or marja', that is men whose opinions, *fatwas*, can or must be followed. These highly influential and revered authorities are now surrounded by the trappings of bureaucracy, their offices staffed by officials and judges. One Ayatollah has his own 'court', for example, where disputes, chiefly financial, are heard by one of his staff. However, the authority that flows through the structure, Clarke found, is still personal in nature and the work of the officials is linked to individual marja' through the deployment of images, signatures, and seals. Claims to authoritative opinion, he suggests, need to be tied to recognized individuals in order to stand for something meaningful (2010: 379). The bureaucratic formally depends upon the personal, even if the two claims to authority do not sit happily together (2010: 367). Despite attempts by state officials to monopolize the interpretation of shari'a in parts of the contemporary Islamic world, therefore, its openness and interpretability remain, and scholarship continues to proliferate. It is as if to counter an ever- multiplying body of fatwas, opinions, and other interpretative texts, that claims to authority still need to be tied to recognized individuals.

The problems caused by the proliferation of legal interpretation arise in all the great legal traditions discussed in previous chapters. Indian scholars recognized the Vedas as the lost, and therefore inscrutable, sources of the law. The dharmaśāstras then stood as authoritative interpretations of that law. Hindu jurisprudence assigned legal authority amongst different people and groups, resulting in what Davis (2012) describes as a culture of open-ended legal pluralism. In Rome even a small number of jurists could reach different opinions, requiring the device of a rule of citation. Of course, a powerful ruler may order that the law be codified. Both Justinian and Napoleon made imperial claims to be fixing the law forever and banning further interpretations, albeit that their attempts were ultimately and, in Napoleon's case, quickly unsuccessful (Kelley 2002). In common law England, by contrast, calls for codification by Bentham fell on deaf ears and the courts developed instead the principle of precedent, whereby the rule of law implicit in a previous decision is binding on subsequent judges. As Simpson (1987) suggests, before the nineteenth century the common law was essentially a form of customary law, that is a matter of common practices and principles—rules, maxims, and standards—recognized by the lawyers, amongst whom a sense of professional identity and cohesion allowed consistency and consensus to emerge. However, the proliferation of legal materials in the form of case reports and treatises led to the perceived necessity for more formalized principles governing authority and, ultimately, to the system of precedent. Even so, law remained 'more like a muddle than a system' (1987: 381).

Much modern jurisprudential writing has been concerned with the authority of the law, concerned that is, with the attempt to establish a theoretically coherent account for the binding nature of legal rules.[14] This is often presented, for example, by raising

---

[14] Jansen (2010) gives a fine account of the informal sources of authority, often overlooked alongside official legislation and texts in these accounts.

the question, 'why should we obey the law?' or 'what makes judges' rulings definitive?' Austin's theory of the sovereign's commands and Hart's account of primary and secondary rules can both be seen as addressing this issue.[15] Several theorists, including Honoré (1977) and Lucas (1977), have suggested that it is the existence of enforcement mechanisms that identifies and distinguishes law from other sorts of rules. However, as Postema (2002: 616–20) describes, it is not plausible to analyse the common law as a set of authoritative rules, in the sense of directive laws backed by mechanisms of enforcement. The task of the court is not to enforce the laws; it is to specify the positions of the parties, as defined by the law, and determine what remedy is appropriate. The substantive law merely justifies coercion, spelling out when a ruler or state may use its powers to enforce carefully defined criminal penalties or civil sanctions. And this is not all that it does: it is also a system of practical reasoning, which provides a framework for both common and institutionalized deliberation.

What appears to have been a recurrent, if theoretical, problem within the developed legal systems of the world has been to limit the categories and sources of authoritative legal interpretation. The problem has been too much, not too little, authority. A distinction must be drawn between the authority of the law itself, and that of its interpreters. God's law, the Vedas, the shari'a, the *ius civile*, the common law, are all regarded as standing apart from, and transcending, the mundane world of fallible interpretation, while lawyers and scholars struggle to establish the authority of their own interpretations over those of their rivals.

Legalism, at its simplest, establishes rules, principles, and categories, which stand apart from practice, which can be used to order the messy reality of everyday life, which symbolize equivalence and ordered hierarchy, and which create possibilities for social relationships, as well as authoritative judgments. But legalism also makes possible a type of thought, a form of juristic argument that seeks relations between rules, distinctions between categories, and canons of interpretation. When this type of reasoning proliferates, the authority of what is regarded as the basic law

---

[15] Even Luhmann (1988) considers that the issue of the judge's authority is an important, but 'unanswerable', question, as discussed in chapter three.

becomes indistinct and the substance of the primary rules and principles paradoxically less certain. We must not, therefore, be over-impressed by the ideals of authority, system, and coherence into seeking an account of law that is too neat, simple, and systematic. We are aiming to understand law as an empirical phenomenon and this means recognizing the plurality and proliferation towards which legalistic thought tends, as well as the rigidity and formalism that legal categories may acquire. That law can also invoke a sense of higher order and promise justice is a source of recurrent tension, to which I return in the Conclusion. The following chapters discuss further examples of legalistic thought and its relations with morality, community, and the state.

7

MORAL ORDER: ASPIRATION AND EMULATION

Having delved into some of the most sophisticated legal traditions of the world in previous chapters, I turn here to examples of tribal and village laws. This is to ask about the significance and appeal of legalism and to explore patterns and practices that illuminate more familiar examples. If law cannot satisfactorily be explained as an instrument of power, a strategy within power struggles, or the effective norms of a social sphere, then how are we to understand it?

It becomes evident that some laws are bound up with a sense of community, and the ways in which insiders can be distinguished from outsiders, some with assertions of autonomy against more powerful neighbours. The legal form, and even the substance of the rules, may also be borrowed from elsewhere, as if in emulation of superior law-makers or more sophisticated intellectual thought. This is not to deny or ignore the power relations in which law is often entangled, but there is something distinctive about the role it plays within them, something, I argue, that is connected to what is promised or invoked by the legal form: its ideals and aspirations must be studied alongside the power dynamics and practices that surround it.

TRIBES, VILLAGES, AND MORAL ORDER

Tribes can be regarded as distinct groups that have relatively egalitarian internal relations, and whose leaders who are more like chiefs than heads of state (Khoury and Kostiner 1990). Without centralized government, they generally have no means of directly enforcing any laws, yet examples of tribal laws exist. Such laws thus provide an opportunity to ask about the different visions of order that law may promise, as well as the practical arrangements it promotes.

Eastern Tibet

The lush grasslands of the northeastern part of the Tibetan plateau, locally referred to as Amdo, are home to tribes of sheep- and yak-herders, ethnically Tibetan and followers of Mahayana Buddhism. Until the momentous changes wrought by the Chinese government after 1958 many of these tribes, particularly in the Golok area to the south-east, retained a significant degree of autonomy under hereditary ruling families, the *xhombo*. They formed a loose confederacy, but often came into conflict with one another, as well as combining to wage periodic war on their neighbours. The Golok tribes were historically renowned for their violence, a reputation that remains in the early twenty-first century, as I have described elsewhere (Pirie 2008). Accounts by Robert Ekvall from the early twentieth century depict a pattern of feuding and mediation among these tribes: in cases of inter-tribal conflict it was necessary to call upon high status mediators, normally chiefs from other tribes, Buddhist *lamas*, or famous orators, who would exercise their powers of argument, persuasion, cajolery, and appeals to honour and self-interest to bring the parties to accept compensation in lieu of further violence (1964: 1140; 1968: 77–80). There was no question of an adjudicator applying the rules of a code to make a judgment and impose a punishment: agreement had to be achieved through mediation and negotiated indemnity (1968: 76).

During fieldwork conducted in the early twenty-first century, I found that despite the presence of the Chinese state, whose governmental structures, agents, and police force penetrate far into the grasslands, practices of feuding and mediation continue in a form that follows much the same principles as those described by Ekvall. When feuds escalate they may continue for decades unless a high-ranking Buddhist lama or a renowned mediator from one of the ruling families intervenes and successfully promotes a settlement. Just as Ekvall describes it, the process of mediation is tentative and contingent upon the mediators' powers of persuasion; they have to threaten or cajole the parties to accept the solution they are proposing or there can be no final settlement (Pirie 2008). It is a process that recalls Cheyette's (1970) description of judicial practices in early medieval France, characterized by appeals to pride and honour, rather than reference to laws and legalistic adjudication.

It came as a considerable surprise, then, to find a historic law code still being referred to. As I describe elsewhere (Pirie 2009), this code has been reprinted as part of a history of the region.[1] Its main sections contain, firstly, general and directive rules for the making of war, specifying how tribal leaders should organize their forces and select commanders, and secondly, detailed and specific provisions for the making of peace, that is, the amounts and nature of the compensation to be paid after killings and injuries. As I have described, it is inconceivable that these laws were ever enforced. The compensation provisions are impractically complex and the amounts specified far outweigh the sums currently awarded, as well as requiring the use of silver coins that must have been rare. Moreover, neither contemporary informants nor ethnographic accounts from the time have suggested that mediation processes ever took a substantially different form from those that occur now.

The codes might well have been referred to during the lengthy speech-making that characterized such processes, along with appeals to religion, moral principles, and the authority of tradition. There is historical evidence that the people of Golok regarded their laws as ancient, unchanging, and a symbol of their independence. A Russian explorer recorded the boast of a confident and confrontational tribesman: unlike the timid subjects of the Dalai Lamas, he declared, 'we...have from time immemorial obeyed none but our own laws, none but our own convictions...they have never been altered' (Kozloff 1908: 522–28). Appeal to the codes may well, then, have been employed as a rhetorical device during practices of mediation but, more than that, the codes seem to have been, and to remain, important in themselves, as a vision for tribal society. Their specificity, the precise amounts prescribed by way of compensation, is familiar from codes discussed in chapter three, in which rules create a sense of system and order, in and of themselves. In the Golok case, the provisions also encapsulate ideals of honour, revenge, loyalty, and family and tribal solidarity. They provide for increased compensation to be paid in the event of

---

[1] In what follows I summarize the discussion of that paper.

livestock theft from within an encampment, rather than from the pastures, for example, a principle I also noted in contemporary mediation practices (2008: 227). Above all, their provisions repeatedly affirm the need for loyalty towards the xhombo, the tribes' ruling families.[2]

In a society in which conflict was common, and to some extent admired, tribal relations have always, in practice, been unstable. A text that articulates shared principles for both the conduct of warfare and the achievement of peace suggests that the Golok tribespeople, although divided and often antagonistic, participated in a single moral domain. References in the preamble of the text to the laws of the seventh-century Tibetan emperor, Songtsan Gampo, reinforce the code's aspirational qualities. Songtsan Gampo is widely revered throughout the Tibetan region as responsible for the introduction of Buddhism, and law codes made in central Tibet claim to be based upon the laws he created. These could well have provided inspiration for the authors of the Golok code, which claims to have been modelled upon his laws, despite the assertions of uniqueness and independence made at other times by the Golok tribesmen. By appealing to the highest moral and religious authority available to them, the authors were representing their tribes as part of a wider Buddhist civilization, participating in the historic moral world represented by the Dalai Lamas, as heirs to Songtsan Gampo.

Contemporary fieldwork has indicated that this code retains importance in the eyes of the Golok people, both as a historic record and as an indication of enduring tribal values. Its details and aphorisms affirm principles of loyalty and revenge, they provide a partial map for tribal relations that were essentially unregulated, save by shared values; and these are values which are still adhered to in the modern world, dominated though it is by the structures of the Chinese state. The code did not regulate anything, but we could say that it represented an aspiration, an ideal for tribal

---

[2] Curiously, they also repeatedly refer to social status—high, middle, and low—to determine the contributions to be made towards a war campaign, and the amount of compensation payable to the victim of an injury. There is no evidence that such status distinctions were ever marked in practice, below the small class of xhombo. While the specification of rank and status was a feature of Anglo-Saxon and early Irish law codes, it is less common in tribal societies.

society, which it presented as being founded upon recognizable religious and moral principles, sanctioned by historic tradition.

Tribal Yemen

Another, and rather different, set of legal codes, found among the tribes of Barat in northern Yemen, is discussed by Paul Dresch (2006). By the late eighteenth century, the era from which the codes originate, the Qasimi state had already been established but Barat remained substantially beyond the control of its rulers (2006: 60–63).[3] On the whole, relations amongst the tribespeople were unstable and uncertain, characterized by conflict and violence, but principles of honour and revenge, protection, guarantee, and compensation gave them a shape, affirmed in these documents. Throughout the Arab world, as Dresch describes (2006: 6–7), principles recur regarding protection, compensation, and forms of settlement, which are generally attributed to custom, 'urf. Tribesmen are distinct from others—slaves, servants, women, and minors are dependents and protégés, having 'no price' (2006: 35)—and amongst them offences are recuperated by vengeance or compensation. Formal scales of recompense, like those found in the Barat documents, imply equality (2006: 8–9). Asymmetric relations could be created through agreements and practices of protection and guarantee, but these were generally reversible; the same person could find himself as alternately protector and protégé. While the state asserted a monopoly of legitimate power and required obedience to its rulers, the tribes maintained an alternative morality, based upon symmetrical, rather than hierarchical, relations amongst tribesmen (2006: 70–72).

The signatories to the Barat codes, as Dresch describes, formed a dispersed and variegated set of people, and the codes take the form of pacts of fellowship or brotherhood, setting out the responsibilities of their signatories (2006: 2). They set limits to the forms of vengeance that could be taken, and include detailed provisions for the types of compensation that were payable after an

---

[3] In fact, Barat was not entirely isolated, being ecologically dependent upon greater Yemen, and its tribespeople, a mixture of nomadic and settled, were scattered widely; however the tribal documents talk as if Barat and the land of the state were geographically quite separate.

injury or death, for the calling of truces, and for the contexts in which sanctuary could properly be given to a fugitive from justice. Straightforward principles concerning reparations for wrongs, depending upon whether the act had caused shame and disgrace, or simply material damage, were subject to a complex of further rules providing for exceptions (2006: 119–21). In this way, relations of truce, guarantee, and ongoing arbitration created links between the tribes and their sections (2006: 98).

A central principle of the Barat documents was, then, personal protection and the shared responsibilities of families, tribes, and their sections to provide it—it was the ability to offer escort and protection that marked out those of full tribal status (2006: 75–77). As well as women and children, guests were protected, as were travelling companions and refugees (2006: 82). The codes also provided for protection at the market. The common market was important as the nucleus of tribal activity: it was the only shared space in which violence was forbidden, agreements were formed on collective matters, and announcements had to be made of public claims. Protecting it was a means of preserving cohesion amongst tribes and their sections (2006: 25–26). The laws thus represent the market as a sacred space in which violence denied the values of commonality.[4]

The pacts effectively claimed a moral coherence among the signatories in that everyone agreed what his fellows' rights were and how these should be recognized (2006: 124). In effect the signatories undertook to be a single unit in vengeance and to contribute to collective debts: refusal to do so entailed loss of the right of protection (2006: 126). This did not imply unconditional solidarity but moral balance, expressed through tribal identities, each of which had its reputation to maintain as against other tribes and sections (2006: 129). Possessing a pact may have generated a feeling of identity, which reached beyond the obligations of shared descent and residence; it indicated a general acceptance of the categories and definitions which it 'renewed' (2006: 132–33). The tribespeople thus formed what Dresch (2006: 289–90) describes

---

[4] This recalls the Durkheimian (1912) notion of a sacred space, as one that is set aside, marked by beliefs and practices that unite its adherents into a single moral community.

as jural communities: their laws and agreements allowed the possibility for anyone—other than dependants—to participate in the moral field of those willing to live and let live as mutually recognized persons.

These texts are not formalistic in the way that the Roman formulae and common law writs were. Nevertheless, they specify, in legalistic terms, when a man had a right and could claim help from his fellows. Without a body politic, as Dresch (2006: 295) describes, and maybe 150 signatories to one pact, there was no centralized authority to enforce their rules. Rather, the codes and agreements represent a string of practical decisions, making provisions for compensation, guarantees, and protection, without imposing general order. As he puts it, they promise an order of categories and definitions, not an order of statistical or administrative regularity. The same could be said of the Golok code. As in Barat, practices of procrastination and mediation made patterns of dispute untidy and when a feud arose neighbours who might exert a restraining influence on the protagonists stood aside. Nevertheless, as Dresch (2006: 295–97) puts it, the 'custom' represented by the codes was valued as promising just settlement; there was a general idea that peace resulted from justice, although there was no collective means to ensure it. The laws, thus, relate to a moral, rather than a political, domain, providing a moral vision for an uncertain world. Like other varieties of law, early European codes, the law of the early Irish legal specialists, or the Icelandic manuscripts that purported to regulate everything, the Tibetan and Yemeni codes present the world as governed morally by rules, promising answers to the ambiguities inherent in antagonistic tribal relations. The acceptance that there simply was law, that it had always been there, was basic (Dresch 2006: 301).

Boundaries and borders

Like the Golok code, the laws of the Barat tribes present a moral vision for a world without a body politic. They relate to an infinitely wide moral domain, made up not of bounded groups, but of shared assumptions in which other tribesmen could participate. Both sets of tribal rules make provision for a protected space: the encampment of the Golok herders and the markets of the Yemenis are marked by particular rules, which set them apart, but they are not fixed in terms of either territory or time.

A study of Armenian laws by Robert Thomson depicts the way in which a code, indeed the very act of law-making, created an explicit sense of nationhood amongst a politically dispersed people. In the eleventh century Seljuk invasions had led to a loss of political control by Armenian lords and much of the population had come under the control of Muslim emirs. Their religious leaders became concerned that, without a law code of their own, disputes were being adjudicated in Muslim courts, so that Armenians were being subjected to Islamic law. Mxit'ar Goš, an Armenian priest and teacher, compiled a law code ostensibly based upon Armenian practices with the explicit aim of allowing the Armenians to avoid the infidel courts. Having a book, he said, would enable them to recall the right law for any particular situation and would indicate to foreigners 'that we live by a code, so that they will no longer reproach us' (2000: 22). In fact, the content of his code was drawn primarily from the Old Testament, canons from the Armenian *Kanonagirk'*, and an early twelfth-century penitential, although he did occasionally add extra material to reflect local custom or to modify canonical provisions in line with his spiritual aims.

Spiritual concerns, he explained, were to take precedence over written codes (2000: 34), and he emphasized several times that he was only offering guidance, discussing penance as much as laying down penalties. This text was not, then, presented as a definitive law code, describing its rules neither as the redaction of ancient custom, nor as a comprehensive guide to practice. Nevertheless, it was supposed to allow the Armenians to avoid being drawn into the Muslim courts. Over the next century the code was amended, simplified, and arranged more systematically (Cowe 1997: 299–300). It was adopted by Armenian communities in sixteenth-century Poland, where disputes amongst merchants were tried by a local judge, sitting along with Armenian elders, on the basis of Mxit'ar's laws (Cowe 1997). A code, rather tentatively drawn up it seems, with symbolic as much as practical aims, thus came to stand as the law of a dispersed people and an enduring marker of nationhood.

The modern association of law with territory must not, therefore, be allowed to colour our understanding and interpretation of other forms of law. Legal order and moral community do not often map neatly onto territory, nor onto any form of political order, nor even onto a clearly-demarcated social community. In medieval Russia Franklin (2007) depicts overlapping legal, political, mercantile, and religious communities. As he describes it, before 1300 there was no unified polity but princely domains and a diversity of populations, differentiated according to local hierarchies, as well as regional differences. Codes were imported from Byzantium and translated into Church Slavonic, while other documents were written in the East Slav vernacular, but legal complexity in the region went far beyond these categories. Franklin distinguishes three types of law, linked to the three sources of authority the Russians acknowledged at the time: the polity as the source of *pravda*, the community as the source of *obychai*, and the church, or divinity, as the source of *zakon*.[5] As he suggests, early legal history should be regarded in terms of the changing configurations between them (2007: 71). Expansive legal documents, like the *Primary Chronicle*, might acknowledge all three, while asserting that Christians have one zakon.

This plurality of rules can also, he suggests, be related to a plurality of social configurations and associations: translated codes, the statutes of a ruler, the responses of bishops to practical questions, rules set out to govern relations between merchants, treaties with Byzantium and other external trading partners, rules governing monastic life, the foundational documents of the Bishopric of Smolensk, or agreements between Novgorod and its princes. Such laws and codes were mostly distinct, occasionally overlapping or contradictory, but equally there was no hierarchy between them. They did not form part of a single system and nor, says Franklin, should we think in terms of a simple model of discrete communities with their own rules. The rules of the *Russkaia pravda*, for example, were initially little more than a set of penalties concerning those around the prince, but they later expanded to regulate the marketplace, the townspeople, and their relations of exchange and money-lending. The princes extended the scope of their

---

[5] As Franklin (2007: 70) explains, during this period pravda roughly denoted rules stemming from the polity; obychai were rules stemming from the community; while zakon were rules authorized from divinity.

putative community by co-option, associating themselves with systems of rules operated by others: they ostensibly allocated jurisdiction over certain behaviour to the church and also stipulated that disputes between foreign merchants in Rus' should be resolved by the community itself.[6] Meanwhile monastic rules were replicated in new institutions, trade treaties defined their own conditions of membership—like the Yemeni tribal rules—religious canons enjoyed different forms of authority in the hands of a bishop or a priest, and the activities of merchants could be subject to trade agreements and a princely code at one and the same time. As Franklin (2007: 77) summarizes it, law in early Rus' can be imagined as functioning in multiple, diverse, overlapping, intersecting, and generally expanding textual communities.

Laws do not always map neatly on to territory, therefore, and nor are they always concerned with the regulation of social relations within a defined space. The expansion of law beyond national boundaries in the form of international laws, or the idea of a modern *ius gentium*, should not seem surprising or aberrant (Waldron 2012). These are the subject of further discussion in chapter eight. We might recall, in this context, that the Roman *ius civile* was originally a personal law, the property of Roman citizens, which they enjoyed in contrast to the common *ius gentium* of the *peregrines*. Neither was defined in territorial terms and Roman citizens, like their Greek counterparts, took their law with them to the provinces as a personal privilege (Modrzejewski 2005; Rupprecht 2005; Kantor 2012). It was only in post-Roman Europe that a general shift from personal to territorial laws took place (Watson 1985: 28); indeed, this only came to full fruition with the identity between law and nation state established in the nineteenth century.

Laws are obviously useful and appealing in a myriad of practical and symbolic ways, setting rules and standards for communities, defining crimes, penalties, and modes of mediation, seeking to establish or extend authority, as well as indicating participation in an established sphere of civilization or religion. We need to ask about the moral worlds they may be creating, and

---

[6] As Diamond (1973: 324–25) describes, rulers with expansive ambitions often permit in order to command.

the social relations they seek to establish, rather than concluding with the fact of pluralism.

Village communities

In an agricultural village, by contrast with a nomadic tribe or a dispersed nation, the law may be more clearly associated with a sense of physical boundaries. Even here, however, law codes may have aspirational and expressive qualities, their meaning and significance not exhausted by their practical or regulatory functions. Two case studies, from either side of the Mediterranean, may stand as examples.

In the villages of Kabylia, a Berber-speaking region of northeastern Algeria, Scheele (2008) found legal codes which, as she puts it, essentially define the community against outsiders. Like the tribal codes already discussed, they were not obviously enforced as instruments of local regulation but provide glimpses of shared Kabyle notions of justice, community, and communal space (2008: 898–201). They contain lists of punishments and payments, a large proportion of which were concerned with collective action in the village, seeking to ensure that respect was shown towards the village assemblies and their representatives, and making provisions for the activities of officials; others sought to suppress internal dissent; there were sumptuary laws, provisions for dowries and marriage expenses, and for the regulation of other family matters; some envisaged the involvement of the village assembly in life cycle rituals; others regulated land sales to strangers and relations with outsiders. Scheele (2008: 907) comments that the complexity of the codes and the emphasis on abstract categories might seem incongruous in a village in which the inhabitants could have been expected to know each other and in which disputes were reportedly settled through negotiation. There was also an astonishing amount of monetary detail, recalling the complexity of the Icelandic and other early codes.

The laws' ideas about protection, compensation, offences divided into injuries to honour and material damage, responsibility for dependents, and communal guarantees are familiar from elsewhere in the Middle East and North Africa (2008: 914). However, unlike the tribal documents from Yemen, each of the Kabyle codes seems to have been attempting to create a communal (village) space, consciously set apart and distinct from its surroundings. In the event of injuries, for example, reparation had to go to the victim, but an amount also had to be paid to the village assembly, indicating that the honour of the village and its inhabitants were of public concern. The codes thus posit the village as a legal space and community, set apart from the outside world, beyond whose boundaries other norms apply, be they the codes of neighbouring villages, the law of the state, or the *shari'a*. Some codes were, nevertheless, promulgated in the name of God, and included references to local religious scholars. As Scheele (2008: 901–02) puts it, they point to the various layers of legitimacy and justice within which the Kabyles attempted to act lawfully.

More recent codes might name both the Algerian republic and the village assembly as sources of legitimacy, but seem to affirm village autonomy against the encroachment of outside systems of morality, including modern Islamism. As Scheele puts it, the codes publicly claim community in the face of new sources of moral standards, especially militant Berberism and political Islam, which purport to be exclusive and come with their own local elites and independent, exterior sources of legitimacy. Yet, she concludes, the codes are more than just an archaic reaction to change: like their historic antecedents, they appeal to local notions of moral sovereignty (2008: 911–13). The act of law-giving in the villages of Kabylia is not, then, an imperfect or failed attempt to describe or regulate practice. Rather, the act of law-giving constitutes a public claim to moral community and the need and capacity to protect the community and its space (2008: 914).

On the other side of the Mediterranean, villages in northern Spain have a tradition of law-making that dates back at least to the sixteenth century. Behar (1986: 5), in an ethnographic study of one such village, describes what she calls 'a local tradition that had flowed, at its own pace and rhythm, alongside the "great tradition"... of legal thought', that is, alongside the laws created by kings—often inspired by Roman forms. Written ordinances took a similar form in villages throughout the region, containing provisions for meetings and requiring the villagers to provide labour for communal projects. They also concerned religious and moral matters, stipulating attendance at religious events, such as funerals and votive masses, as well as obliging households to take it in turns to harbour the wandering poor (1986: 162ff). Thus, Behar found, they seem to have represented a conscious agreement to maintain moral standards, as well as preserving village customs. Renovation of the ordinances continued into the twentieth century, even after the outbreak of civil war in 1936, when they were expressed as representing the community's desire 'to bring to life again ancient customs of a clearly Christian character', or, echoing the Armenian code, in order to demonstrate 'to those who do not practice such Christian customs faith and human feeling' (1986: 181–82, 280).

In this region, village government historically lay in the hands of the assembly of village citizens, the *concejo*, which functioned as a form of acephalous polity. The assembly was also a juridical and moral presence, as Behar describes it, with the power to coerce individuals to recognize its prescriptions (1986: ch 7). It is clear that the community was, however, both more and less than its rules. Behind the laws were ideals of justice and morality, and a sense of solidarity and autonomy. The villages would, for example, choose their own holy days, thus affirming a certain autonomy against clerical intrusions. But why did the villagers feel impelled to create laws in order to do this, Behar asks, especially in the early days when literacy was limited and the villages used an accounting stick to keep a tally of the amounts contributed to communal funds. As I found in a Ladakhi village, autonomy against both political and religious control, as well as preservation of a sense of moral community, can be created without anything resembling written law (Pirie 2006). Moreover, as Scheele comments on the Kabyle codes, rules formulated in terms of abstract categories seem unnecessary when everyone can be presumed to know everyone else. Behar found that before the nineteenth century there was a constant recycling of earlier texts, which were recopied in order to preserve the 'best and soundest customs' of the village. Villagers, she comments, seem to have welcomed the order created by their ordinances out of the flux of custom, which was 'inscribed in so inconstant a vessel as the memory of men' (1986: 277). With greater literacy, from the second half of the nineteenth century, there was a turn towards revision and modernization, but the old documents were reread, scrutinized, and often renewed, in a deliberate attempt to keep alive 'the ancient traditions of a clearly Christian character' (1986: 280).

Originally, it seems, the ordinances were drawn up in response to pressure by the kings of Castile for locally-enacted laws. Their thirteenth-century forebears had published the law books known as *Siete Partidas*, influenced by the example of Roman law (Stein 1999: 65–66), and peasant customs were being redacted as 'customary law' in other parts of Europe, following the idea that custom, sanctioned by tradition, could have legal force (Behar 1986: 274–75). Codification thus took place in the context of an interaction between state and local community, and on the assumption that the latter had the power to make and enforce its own laws. But it is evident from Behar's account, that over time the codes took on a life of their own, coming to represent the sanctity of tradition and expressing the moral standards by which the villagers sought to live and to distinguish themselves from the alternative moral world of politicians and clerics. As in Kabylia, these laws must be read as an expression of moral community, as much as instruments for internal regulation. Like minor constitutions, the village codes do not seem to be organizing or regulating social life so much as asserting the status of the community as an independent entity, but one that participates morally in the Islamic or Christian world of which it forms part.

The legal form may, then, proscribe and prescribe, specifying fines and other penalties, even in circumstances in which there are no enforcement mechanisms. Tribespeople, amongst whom there are well-established practices of mediation and who approach conflicts as matters of individual honour and reparation may also write down their laws. Law is about more than regulation. Nor can a village or tribal code simply be read as a statement of 'what we do'; the claim to moral community may have to be understood both as expressing a deeper sense of justice and identity, and as a statement of autonomy against the outside world, while also appealing to a set of wider moral and religious values.

Practice and moral order

We should not, on the other hand, assume that such law codes have no practical significance. Rather, they may be invoked or applied in different and varied ways, providing standards for local regulation, establishing pacts and relations between distinct communities, and requiring solidarity and commitment on the part of their inhabitants.

In the Islamic region of Daghestan Kemper (2004) found a set of practically-oriented local laws created by both villages and village confederacies, dating from the eighteenth and nineteenth centuries, that is before the period of the Russian colonial presence. Mostly written in Arabic, rather than in one of the many local languages of the region, the texts contain what is normally described as *adat*, customary law; many are treatises and agreements between different villages, or between villages and larger confederacies, or between either of these and the *khans* who sought to exercise political power in the region.

The adat provisions recorded in these treatises deal with the offences of murder and manslaughter, bodily harm, family matters, calumny, theft, arson and other damage to property, debts, fraud, and so on. Some of the most simple record fines extracted for basic offences, seemingly built up out of records of actual cases. They apparently represent a process by which the recording of particular cases was transformed into a simple form of legalism, that is, into general conditional statements ('he who steals a cow has to give...'). Such documents were produced for use in the village courts and, as Kemper puts it, appear to be a means of transmitting legal experience for future generations (2004: 31–32). They also tend to make provisions for the political organization of the village, including the use and protection of communal resources: many deal with the consequences of dereliction of duty by shepherds. They also seek to enforce religious duties, thus in many ways reflecting the content of the Spanish and Kabyle village codes (2004: 123–24, 145–46). An agreement between the different members of a confederacy of villages, on the other hand, might be more extensive, recording legal rules amongst narratives concerning the history and geography of the region, giving an account of the different agreements made between the various villages and settlements concerning the handling of offences, and recording undertakings between them not to help each other's enemies (2004: 133–34).

Some agreements, thus, establish a confederacy amongst a set of villages, or regulate relations amongst confederacies and with outsiders, by prohibiting the practice of confiscation by creditors amongst their members. They also provide for military defence and the protection of the community, reinforcing a sense of loyalty and identity. In many ways these recall the agreements entered into by the Yemeni tribes and seem to bear witness to an older, clan-based organization; clan loyalty, as Kemper mentions, became important in the event that someone was accused of a crime. However, the primary authority within any legal proceedings was the village community. The whole community, that is the adult men, assembled regularly to appoint elders or leaders, who would serve for one year and take responsibility for public order (2004: 139–40).[7] Parallel structures of authority characterized the village confederacies, but they mostly had limited legal responsibility, and agreements explicitly recognized that the villages were independent in applying their own legal provisions: village adat was more powerful than confederacy adat (2004: 147, 150).

As Kemper characterizes it (2004: 149), these agreements testify to the force of communal principles, requiring solidarity amongst their members against adversaries, and even displaying hostility towards local noblemen.[8] This raises questions. As in the case of the Spanish villages, we can ask why the Daghestani villagers thought it appropriate to write down their laws at all. Agreements between larger units defined relations between groups in terms of loyalty and the restriction of the possibilities for violence. So why, Kemper asks, were agreements regulating village affairs, including religious duties, written in Arabic rather than local languages? We might detect the influence of Islam, its language and texts, which provided a model for law-making, albeit that the agreements themselves can be read as asserting autonomy against clerical, among other, influences.

Kemper emphasizes the active nature of Daghestani law-making and the changing nature of their rules. Only rarely do the

[7] At the end of their year these leaders had to take an oath on the Quran that they had performed their duties correctly, recalling the oath taken by village leaders in Mustang at the end of their term of office (Ramble 2008).

[8] Some recognize, or even require, the presence of a *qadi*, who would administer the religious endowments and collect and distribute the Islamic tax. However, attempts to replace adat by shari'a law were resisted (2004: 144–45).

agreements refer to the example of the 'forefathers', he says; they do not present an ideology of ancient and immutable law, as we find it elsewhere. Adat regulations were set up as voluntaristic acts of collective decision; they can be seen as a confident assertion of autonomy in the face of competing claims to authority, particularly those of the nobility.

The rules were drawn up as if for the purpose of internal regulation and we should not doubt that they were, on occasion, used for this purpose, maybe appealed to by the Daghestani village elders to justify the imposition of fines or to bring recalcitrant villagers into line. It seems possible that the Spanish village concejo did likewise with their code. However, in no case can the imposition of order account fully for the existence and significance of the codes. Maybe they were cited rhetorically, as authoritative precedent, during the persuasive speeches of a Tibetan mediator; they served to record practical decisions made amongst the Yemeni tribespeople, within their complex relations of loyalty, guarantee, and protection; but none of them seem to have guaranteed order in any practical sense and the evidence of enforcement is virtually non-existent. As Dresch puts it (2006: 296), they provide an order of categories, not an order of regularity. Or, as in the Kabyle village, they specify the moral basis of villagehood. Laws can be appealing in a myriad of different ways and we cannot, as anthropologists, ever assume that a set of laws must have been enforced in order for it to have had practical importance, or that the aims of regulation and regularity exhaust its significance.

The laws I have been discussing are expressive and symbolic, then, but of what? There is not always a clearly bounded community to which they relate. Nor do they always reflect a sense of tradition and the immutability of custom, divinity, or cosmic order. A Golok tribesman might boast that his laws were just as ancient as those of the Dalai Lamas, and the Yemeni tribespeople seem to have had a sense that their law was, as Dresch (2006: 301) puts it, 'simply there'. The extent to which law-makers claim the sanction of tradition and appeal to the immutability of ancient custom is variable, however, as already discussed in chapter five. The Daghestani villagers were apparently quite willing to revise and formulate new laws, as was the

Spanish concejo. Scheele (2008) found that in Kabylia it was the act of law-making that was important, in and of itself. The authority of the written word is likewise variable, as discussed in chapter six, acquiring a sanctity of its own, or else being regarded as an imperfect record of something more ancient, or both.

At their most basic, laws create moral standards. They can be read as public statements of the principles upon which their adherents should act—as villagers, as tribespeople, or as members of a dispersed nation—thus village laws require contribution to communal activities and resources, and participation in religious activities, while in the case of the tribes, participation in relations of loyalty and protection define what it is to be a tribesman. It is these moral standards that implicitly distinguish insiders from outsiders, the Golok tribes from the pusillanimous subjects of the Dalai Lama's regime, the Yemeni tribesmen from those who enjoyed no reciprocal obligations with them, the Kabyle villagers from the followers of political Islam and militant Berberism, the Spanish and Daghestani villagers from their neighbours, and the Armenians from the Muslim infidels.

It does not require too much imagination to compare the moral standards invoked by contemporary nation states when they promote the 'rule of law'. The idea of bringing civilization through law is not often explicit in the post-colonial world, but it can provide a convenient way of asserting the superiority of 'us' over 'them'. British prime minister Margaret Thatcher, in 1989, acknowledged a common European commitment to 'the rule of law which marks out a civilized society from barbarism' and a common heritage in which 'Europeans explored, colonized and civilized much of the world' (Fitzpatrick 1992: 117). The implicit association of law with progress and civilization may easily be deployed to justify neo-colonial activities (Comaroff and Comaroff 2006; Mattei and Nader 2008; von Benda-Beckmann et al. 2009). Law, as Fitzpatrick puts it, gives effect to the national interest as a general interest; it subsumes particularity and projects itself beyond the particular bounds of the nation. It presents order as a matter of fairness, justice, acceptability, and practicality (1992: 165). These are broad claims, but distant, historic, and tribal examples highlight the ways in which law invokes a moral order that extends beyond the power or territory of a ruler or community. They can also illustrate a related phenomenon, that of legal borrowing.

BORROWING AND ASPIRATION

The modern era provides many examples of what is often regarded as legal imperialism, not least in colonial situations, for which one can turn to the works of Benton (2002), as well as the studies of Cohn (1989) and Chanock (1985), discussed in chapter two. There is no shortage of anthropological accounts of people having to adapt to new legal frameworks.[9] More recently, Nader (2005) has critiqued the 'Americanization of law', the imposition of law which results from hegemonic transnational efforts at homogenization: 'the law is still the vehicle for legitimizing the take' (2005: 199, 210). It is easy, however, to reach too quickly for a model of domination and to look for imposition by the politically and culturally powerful on the weak or oppressed. As Chanock noted, 'customary law' in Africa was often the creation of an indigenous elite as much as an imposition by colonial powers.

Watson (2001: ch 7) usefully addresses this issue the other way around, asking why communities accept law from elsewhere. As he says, 'with a significance that is hard to grasp, borrowing has been the most important factor in the evolution of Western law in most states at most times' (2001: 193). The spread and influence of laws and legal forms has been commented upon frequently by historians, following Watson's (1974) work on 'legal transplants'—or what Waldron (2012: 203–04), rather more attractively, describes as the 'human curiosity' that leads to legal borrowing—but anthropologists have rarely examined the tendency of people all over the world to borrow legal forms from one another.

Most of the laws discussed in this chapter were produced on the margins of established and expansive legal traditions: the Yemeni tribespeople, like the Kabyle and Daghestani villagers, were all part of the Islamic world; the Spanish villagers were writing their codes after the revival of Roman law and under

[9] A fine study by Monique Nuijten (2005) could be regarded as illustrative, here.

the influence of its spread through southern Europe; the Golok tribespeople clearly knew about the laws produced in central Tibet; Mxit'ar borrowed heavily from canon law; Byzantine codes were translated and imported into Russia with the expansion of the church. One could also think of ancient Greece: as Thomas (2005: 49), among others, points out, the Cretan laws inscribed at Gortyn were admired, emulated, and widely copied elsewhere, and even Plato and Aristotle were convinced of the importance of this legal tradition. Somewhat later, Indic law spread throughout south-east Asia: codes created in what are now Thailand, Burma, Cambodia, and Java were derived from Indian texts and thought.[10] As I describe in chapter eight, the *dharmaśāstras* formed the basis for a Thai legal code known as the *Thammasat*, even though Thailand had not developed a caste system (Hooker 1978). Chinese law was adopted in Japan, influential in Korea, and taken over, in large part without alteration, in Vietnam (Johnson 1979: 9). Rulers, scholars, small communities, and tribes have all borrowed legal forms from elsewhere.

Watson's own focus was on the revival and spread of Roman law in Europe, from the Germanic tribes that settled in Gaul in the sixth century to the humanists of the sixteenth, and the law of reason in the seventeenth and eighteenth centuries. Citing Vinogradoff (1961: 11) on Roman law in medieval Europe, he asks 'how did it come about that the Germans, instead of working out their legal system in accordance with national precedents, and with the requirement of their own country, broke away from their historical jurisprudence to submit to the yoke of bygone doctrines of foreign empire?' Political and cultural imperialism explains very little about the spread of Roman law. That such borrowing may need to be understood in terms of political and cultural aspiration, as much as legal imperialism, is apparent in Wormald's (1999) account of the Germanic codes created between the fifth and eleventh centuries, discussed in the next section. But later examples indicate the widespread nature of the

---

[10] Huxley (2006) comments that at the birth of its literacy, south-east Asia made a deliberate choice to adopt the Devangari alphabet rather than Chinese ideographs, thus allying itself with distant India, rather than the soft power of nearby China.

phenomenon: even kings and modern nation states borrow law from one another.

Early medieval Europe

Patrick Wormald (1999) discusses the Germanic texts created in early medieval Europe. The motives expressed in them, he says, tend to be what we might expect of law codes, that is the promotion of peace and order, the redress of injustice, and the resolution of difficult cases. However, it is difficult to account for their content in terms of the needs of justice and government. Their provisions, particularly in the northern European codes, are often 'mixed up' and 'highly selective', with baffling omissions (1999: 11). Many were drafted in Latin, a language which would not have been familiar to the majority of the local population; some manuscripts wander haphazardly from judgment to judgment, without any apparent principle or organization, or include blatant contradictions (1999: 14–15). Much of this legislation, then, 'gives the impression that its purpose was simply to get something into writing that *looked* like a written code, more or less regardless of its actual value to judges sitting in court' (1999: 13). What mattered in the practical enforcement of the law remained the word of the king or his officers and in the administration of justice the reference to written documents was marginal (1999: 23). As Wormald (1999: 18) says, the texts were largely created by ascendant monarchies, whose conquests had given them the confidence to claim to be empires, and this inspired emulation of the most famous Roman achievement, the tradition of written law: 'Legislation could be a matter of image-building' (1999: 25). Most famously, Charlemagne declared that the Frankish laws of his peoples were lacking in many respects and ordered that the unwritten laws be committed to letters. 'Written legislation', Wormald comments, would seem to have 'represented an aspect of his new imperial dignity, because it was *par excellence* the function of a Roman emperor' (1999: 29–30).

Another inspiration was religious. Christianity was a religion of the book and the Bible was the law book of the heavenly kingdom, so by basing their laws on the Pentateuch other kings could identify themselves as Christian rulers. The example of Moses, along with Solon and other Greek and Roman legislators, helped to develop the conviction, as Wormald puts it, that every people should have its own *lex* (1999: 31–33). These laws are, then, evidence of the image that the Germanic kings, and their advisers, wished to project of themselves and their people: 'king and people as heirs to the Roman emperors, as counterparts to the children of Israel, or as bound together in respect for the traditions of the tribal past' (1999: 37–41).[11] Law can be, and was, a tool of societal self-definition, based upon custom or stemming from a mythical law-giver, allowing the society to perceive itself as the heir to a clearly-defined, authoritative past (Cohen 1993: 5–6).

Contrasting the activities of law-makers in India, Rome, and Ireland, where law was the jealously-guarded preserve of a professional lawyer-class, Wormald describes the making of law during this period as a royal function. It may be, he suggests, that the military conquests of the Germanic kings had destroyed any counterpart to the professional classes, enabling them to assume primary responsibility for law and order and to assert new legal functions. Laws were often created at politically significant moments, suggesting that the motives were, in part, to secure loyalty to the rulers and their dynasties (1999: 35–37). However, even in the hands of a ruler, the act of legislation can have ideological or broadly political, as much as directly practical or administrative, aims.

In the shadow of the shari'a

The universalizing nature of Islamic law is well known and one might expect to find legal forms and shari'a principles wherever Islamic scholars acquire local influence. In the absence of strong political or religious control one would also expect such forms to be adapted, as appropriate, to local concerns and conditions. In practice, however, the borrowing may challenge any attempts at functional explanation, as Scheele (2012) describes in her study of the Touat, a group of Saharan oases in south-western Algeria.

---

[11] Some scholars have been dismissive of what they regard as this 'law as literature' approach, arguing for the more practical application of the laws (McKitterick 1989: 39). However, as Cohen (1993: 5–6) points out, even if the codes were a literary genre they were fulfilling an exceedingly important function.

Here, complex communal irrigation systems are ecologically essential. Historically, state control was weak or absent, but the nineteenth century saw a considerable 'legalization' of local affairs and the creation of documents, largely concerned with property transactions and irrigation arrangements. Many of these have been preserved in the twenty-first century, crammed into hanging baskets in local houses. The documents often use Islamic legal forms and categories, which do not seem to make practical sense in local terms. For example, they specify property in precise and supposedly fixed amounts, even in the case of land that might, and does, revert to desert, or water flowing through irrigation channels that might, and do, silt up. Other document-ed transactions involve precise divisions of property, which leads to such anomalies as the sale of a donkey in fractions.

Adopting Islamic legal categories, Scheele suggests, must have involved considerable cost and effort to no obvious practical purpose. This is a particular puzzle in the absence of a central-ized state or any other institution akin to Watson's legal elite. In certain circumstances, as Scheele comments (2012: 223–24), mastery of writing and the ability to produce legal documents offers to the educated few the opportunity to take advantage over others: an ability to use and apply Islamic law could lead to an ability to manage production activities and control prop-erty. But this fails to account both for the apparently local appeal of the law in the Touat and also for its potentially neutral nature. As an abstract moral standard it was apparently used to both maintain and to question existing power structures—local labour contracts, for example, indicate exceptionally favourable terms for the worker. Moving away from models of imposition, enforcement, and resistance, she says, we should think, rather, in terms of curiosity, acceptance, and negotiation (2012: 201).

The attraction of law might, then, be found in the idea of universality, civilizational requirements, and human striving for perfection. Using Islamic legal categories meant describing the local in terms of a social, economic, and moral whole. In Tunisia, equivalent legal documents do not mention precise amounts of water, leaving this to be decided by custom, explained by Bédoucha (2000) in terms of the fear of state intervention: what can be measured can be controlled. By contrast, the oases of the

Touat were not really threatened by state control at the time these documents were created. Their inhabitants' relationship with the outside world was, rather, conceived in terms of civilization and wilderness. Oasis life was fragile and had constantly to be defended against the encroaching wilderness in moral and civilizational, as well as ecological, terms, and this meant the application of divine law and order. Following the shari'a, God's path, meant modelling everyday interactions on pre-existing and universally valid moral standards, establishing links with the outside and making them permanent (2012: 226–27). Using legal language presented the local as an element of the universal, recreating it as part of a larger whole; it provided a semblance of stability, an aspiration to permanence and fixity. Legal documents stuffed into baskets with little value as proof of anything linked the place to the outside, demonstrating its civilized nature.

After Rome

Later medieval Europe, the subject of Watson's (1974) initial work, offers numerous examples of legal borrowing. From the twelfth century onwards, after what is generally characterized as the 'rediscovery' of Roman law by scholars in Bologna, summaries (*summae*) of Justinian's Digest and his Code, together with glosses upon their content, were produced, copied and circulated widely (Stein 1999: ch 3). When a *summa* had acquired prestige, even if it was a private document, the extent of copying could be remarkable: a text known as *Lo Codi*, for example, containing a summary of the Code, was written in Provençal in around 1149, translated into at least five different languages, and influenced many collections of customary law and juristic work (Watson 1974: ch 9).

Roman (civil) law was admired for its technical superiority and, as Stein (1999: 61) suggests, provided a conceptual framework, a kind of universal grammar that could be used by traditional courts. In the thirteenth century what were regarded as the local or customary laws applied by such courts began to be set down in writing, sometimes at the instigation of a king, notably Emperor Frederick II of Sicily, but also by private individuals, such as Philippe de Beaumanoir, a judge of the Count of Claremont's courts in Beauvaisis. In both cases the civil law provided the organizing categories and principles. As Stein (1999: 64) puts it, without a clothing of Roman law the laws of a kingdom or region would not appear fully authentic.

Cheyette (1970) reminds us, however, that we must not place too much emphasis on the inspiration of Rome in seeking to understand the creation of new laws during this period: we must ask why Roman laws were not only copied and studied by the scholars, but also found their way into local contexts and courtrooms. A study by Esther Cohen (1993) describes how, in Northern Europe, where the Roman influence had not remained strong, legal practice had become essentially oral by the twelfth century; it was a matter of public performance in which shared ideals could be affirmed. Writing represented the letter, but not the spirit, of the law, and was inferior to the living, verbal expression of communal legal feeling. As she describes (1993: 9), the writing down of oral traditions as 'customary law' in the thirteenth century represented a new cultural trend. The idea that customary law might be composed of written texts and that a legal system might be distinct from other functional frameworks emerged largely from the attempt to oppose the influence of canon and Roman law, while also emulating their intellectual backing and systematic coherence. It was thirteenth-century struggles over jurisdiction, she says, that forced lawyers to draw a clear line of demarcation by producing coherent written versions of their own system (1993: 27).

The earliest *custumals*, customary collections, asserted that every *pays* had its own customs. They were generally written as private manuals, supposed to assist local lords in the administration of justice, and to preserve their traditions in the face of change (Cohen 1993: 31–32). They often took a narrative form, recounting particular stories and situations (Bloch 1977: 4–5). However, as royal or ducal officers, their authors made efforts to reconcile their matter with the growing body of royal ordinances. The writers, Cohen (1993: 33) suggests, seem to have been familiar with Roman law, at least to some extent, and to have shared a feeling that Roman law was a far superior system, of greater prestige than customary law. The abstract categories and definitions of law, justice, and right were almost all taken verbatim from the Institutes, for example, while an organizational model was often borrowed from the Digest or the Code. As Cohen (1993: 36) puts it, they probably felt a genuine respect for the learned, written system and the Roman elements endowed their work with an aura of intellectual legitimacy.[12] As Hyams (2000: 64) puts it, in southern Europe, *le pays du droit écrit*, the legacy of Roman law meant that Justinian's corpus could be treated as a treasury of modular legal forms, ready to be slotted into receptive vernacular legal schemes. Even north of the Alps, the new *droit coutumier*, customary law, was often written in Latin and so it inevitably drew minds to the formulations of the *Corpus Iuris*.[13]

What is presented as a record of local customs might well, therefore, have been profoundly inspired by a quite alien tradition, with borrowed forms and categories. Sometimes historians of this period refer to the unwritten 'customary law' applied by the traditional courts as the counterpart to the written codes and custumals, which were supposed to have recorded it. But what was this 'law'? We should be very cautious to assume any close relationship between the written forms of 'customary law' and the local understanding of custom, something that legal writers recognized was processual and shifting (Cohen 1993: 39–42). Written law might well represent a radically new form of social organization and, as Cheyette (1970) emphasizes, facilitated new forms of court process.

Legal borrowing is often aspirational, then, drawing upon what are regarded as civilized and sophisticated traditions, and this may include a simple aspiration to uniformity. In Germany, Watson (1985: ch 2) describes the writing of *Spiegel* (literally 'mirror'), private collections of laws, in the twelfth century, the most famous and influential of which was the *Sachsenspiegel*. This contained private, criminal, constitutional, and feudal laws, following the form of papal decretals but using a variety of sources,

---

[12] As she says, these writers also knew each other's work and borrowed a great deal, for example from Beaumanoir, but they never cited these as sources, rather using Roman forms 'as camouflage for customary matter' (Cohen 1993: 36).

[13] As Hyams (2000: 65) points out, once Roman terms had been adopted for legal institutions, successive lawyers, better educated in the learned laws, might notice and question the dissonance between usage in the *ius civile* and that of their own customs, which set the scene for a further and more profound assimilation of learned legal concepts into local law.

both juristic and religious, only indirectly influenced by Roman law. As Watson (1985: 30–31) describes, even though it was a private work and had no legislative authority, it soon came to be treated as a code with influence that extended well beyond the bounds of Saxony, translated into a number of German dialects and leaving over 200 surviving manuscripts. A work of ostensibly regional significance thus came to represent at least an aspiration towards a more general law.

Another example of legal borrowing from this period is found in the activities of the *Schöffen*, the group of citizens established in each town whose duty it was to find and declare the law. In doing so, they might refer to the town's written ordinances, to custom, to any Spiegel that gave local law, and to their own good sense (Watson 1985: 31–32). By the fourteenth century the Schöffen of certain towns were being looked to by others for legal opinions, a practice formalized by referring to them, respectively, as 'mother' and 'daughter' towns. This relationship was not, as Watson emphasizes, one of political domination and a daughter might change her 'mother' town for another. But, remarkably, the mother Schöffen would make no attempt to investigate the law or customs of the daughter, simply giving replies to queries according to their own local customs and feelings of correctness (1985: 39). Although, then, the Schöffen system nominally recognized and reinforced local control over the law, smaller German towns were voluntarily looking to other, maybe more legally prestigious, urban centres to tell them what their law should be.

Even when law presents itself as territorial, then, as it does within these German towns, or in the *pays* of northern France, and even when it can be regarded as an assertion of autonomy against neighbours or an encroaching state, it may yet need to be understood in relation to larger spheres of moral or intellectual authority. Equally the relationship with the source of the laws may be characterized by borrowing and emulation more than imposition and domination.

Examples of tribes and villagers creating their own laws in the shadow of larger legal systems draw our attention to the subtlety of the processes of borrowing and inspiration. In some cases it is simply that traces of a larger system are apparent in the reference to, or adoption of, known formal standards or texts. Other codes may be drawn up in response to political pressure, while also asserting autonomy and local community. Such dynamics can be traced into contemporary settings.

Financial laws in the British Virgin Islands

The British Virgin Islands (BVI) form a British dependent territory in the Caribbean and Maurer (1995) describes the role of law within the process of nation-building that took place there in the second half of the twentieth century. The islanders distinguish themselves from their neighbours as a 'law and order' people, and one of their main sources of revenue is the tax haven facilities they offer to wealthy businesses and individuals. Their construction of national identity in terms of law thus imitates the European narrative of national development. In practice, however, a tension then recurs over the creation of new laws: there is concern about 'borrowed law', in particular that drafted elsewhere in the Commonwealth and brought to the BVI's legislative council by the British Attorney General for adaptation in the territory: some islanders argue that they need their own laws, as a demonstration of their 'uniqueness'. Nevertheless, in practice such laws always pass through the council. The unease with borrowing does not crystalize into any sustained criticisms of colonial rule.

The all-important International Business Companies Ordinance of 1984, which set up the tax haven facilities, is the most important example of original BVI legislation. Rather as Scheele found in Kabylia, it was the act of law-making or authorship that was important, allowing the islanders to regard the ordinance as 'our own' legislation (Maurer 1995: 275–76). Later, concerns over the reputation of the territory, following scandals surrounding other failed tax havens, led to the drafting of new legislation under the direction of the UK's Foreign Office, however, and a treaty with the US allowed federal investigators to scrutinize its offshore financial records. As Maurer puts it, the BVI's 'own' ordinance, which ostensibly demonstrated autonomy, created difference, and drew boundaries, also served to integrate the BVI more firmly into the world economy, and bring it under the economic domination of the US (1995: 283).

These dynamics are patently more complex than the effects of legal imperialism, or a demonstration of 'the overwhelming hegemonic weight of modern Western law', as Darian-Smith (2000: 818) puts it. Presenting themselves as civilized and modern—as governed by the rule of law and an independent judiciary—has allowed other societies to fend off imperial takeovers (Merry 2003), and in the case of the BVI a process of emulation, more than coercion, was influenced by economic goals and a desire to play a part in the modern global economy. Bhutan provides another example: here a modernizing state, proud of its unique history, drew heavily on Anglo-American legal concepts and traditions to develop a new legal system (Whitecross 2009). To analyse these events in terms of asymmetric power dynamics would be to miss the aspirational and ideological aspects of legal borrowing and their resonance with a long, global history of legislative emulation.

MORALITY AND IDEALS

Law can, as these examples show, be an expression of moral values, as much as an instrument of government, a means of conflict resolution, or a technique of power. Laws may enshrine and express the ideals appealed to during processes of mediation, but in many cases it is not apparent that they were ever applied for the purposes of adjudication. Law codes might, rather, be statements of tribal values or express villagers' assertion of difference. Conversely, adopting a borrowed form of law may indicate participation in a larger religious or moral domain, the truth of the shari'a or the Christian canons, the civilization of Roman intellectual forms, or the badge of 'law and order' evoked by a financial ordinance in the modern global economy.

In each of these cases the act of law-making, or simply the sense of having law, seems important in its own right. What is expressed by the laws is significant, and so is the implicit promise of justice and the affirmation of a superior moral order. The legal form seems to be particularly appealing as a means of representing, not just a higher set of values, but also a sense of participation in a larger, maybe more sophisticated or global, order. This might also serve to distance, or assert equivalence with, those who would encroach or impose their will upon the law-makers.

Of course, to say that law expresses moral values must not be taken to imply that it cannot be used as an instrument of centralized government or oppression.[14] Laws may, indeed, 'legitimize the take' (Nader 2005: 199) or 'launder brute power in a wash of legitimacy' (Comaroff and Comaroff 2006: 31); they may force local dynamics into unfamiliar categories and make individuals appear as little more than 'things' (Fox 1993: 184; Strathern 2004: 233). But this is not all that law is about, and models of domination, power, and control may obscure more than they illuminate. Fitzpatrick (1992) suggests that to equate law with power is to start from the equation between law and sovereignty. The legitimating power of law, he argues, must be regarded as a modern mythology, which needs to be understood in its historic context. As this chapter has shown, law concerns a good deal more than power struggles, government, and the legitimation of plunder. In none of the cases discussed here is law imposed in any straightforward way. It may have been created under the influence of a ruler's activities, or borrow heavily from well-known and highly regarded models, but in many cases the impulse for emulation was an internal one. To borrow laws or legal forms is implicitly to recognize that their authority is rooted elsewhere, at least partially, and that the law, itself, might stand apart from or transcend the power of a ruler.

The consequent ability for law to be invoked against a ruler, as well as employed by him, leads to complex relations between laws, rulers, and the state. It is to these that I turn in the next chapter.

---

[14] Historical examples are numerous. As Clanchy (1979: 25) remarks, the Domesday Book was intended to bring a conquered people under the rule of written law while Bonte (2000) describes how religious tribes succeeded in acquiring ownership of large tracts of farmland and palm groves in nineteenth-century Mauritania because they held a monopoly over the written word, legal scholarship, and litigation. Moreover, one community's morality may not be that of another: the Yemeni world, in which women and children were not full tribespeople, does not conform to the standards of the modern west, while the tribesmen of Golok continue to treat their wives as inferior in many ways.

8

LAW AND THE STATE

In chapter one I suggested that a model of state law has come to dominate much legal philosophy. Austin's assertion that law is a matter of the ruler's commands—and its basis in Hobbes's justification for governmental power—has been influential. This model has also shaped questions in legal anthropology, concerning the maintenance of order, the resolution of disputes, and the nature of non-state law. Few of the many examples discussed in this book have concerned what might be called state law, however. It is obvious that we need to look beyond mechanisms of coercion and structures of power in order to understand the social appeal and significance of legalism. By doing so, we can also rethink the 'problem' of international law, which has long troubled legal theorists, precisely because it is not backed by the authority and enforcement power of any state. Like other anthropologists, I suggest that international law deserves just as much status as a paradigmatic example of what law is, as do the laws of modern nation states.

In this chapter I consider contemporary international laws, including human rights instruments and ideas, in order to explore the power and appeal of the legal form in the modern world—although I also suggest that transnational law is an ancient phenomenon, which can be illuminated by consideration of historical examples. First, however, I consider some of the sociological scholarship on the rise of the state and centralized government, and the place of law within it. This is contrasted with studies of laws that are asserted or invoked against rulers: the relations between laws and rulers are multiple.

STATES AND LAWS

The fact that we have come to view law as a monopoly of the state is a testimony to the success of the state-building project and the ideological views that supported it (Tamanaha 2008: 379). Modern national law, as Fitzpatrick (1992: 114) puts it, was explicitly set against natural law and the objective and universalizing claims of the Enlightenment. The nation's law then takes on a mythic scale as the ultimate form of rule, encompassing lesser and partial legal orders, which it supplants, or which become subordinate to it. For the nation state, government and law are constructed and utilized as instruments to achieve social objectives, and law develops an institutionalized apparatus of power, supposed to achieve collective purposes and to structure and order the government and its affairs (Tamanaha 2008: 381). It also evokes and confirms administration as the nature of things (Fitzpatrick 1992: 163). Historical studies can shed light on the particular role of law within these processes, and on what makes it useful as an instrument of power and state-building.

In his historical review of law and legal complexity, Tamanaha describes the association between law and nation state as a product of nation-building projects, which came to fruition in the nineteenth century. But this was based on earlier developments, when law was deployed to subordinate or supersede other forms of social ordering. The legislative paradigm of the eighteenth century, as Kelley (2002: 301) describes, took the form of enlightened despotism and codification: in Prussia, Austria, and France, codes modelled upon Roman law were intended to organize all private law into a single system. Napoleon's *Code Civil*, based upon the riches of Roman law and designed to enhance his military achievements by bringing law and order to his people, was the most famous realization of this vision. His code was published in 1804, just two months before he had himself proclaimed Emperor Napoleon I. Like Justinian, Napoleon was determined to take seriously the old idea that the will of the prince was law and to give it institutional incarnation through a system of codified laws: as Kelley (2002: 289) says, he was obsessed with a belief in his transcendent mission to master and reorder the world, which meant ruling, Justinian-like, over the lives of his subjects from cradle to grave.[1]

As part of the legal developments in Europe, customary and religious laws had already been banished to a private realm, no

[1] As Kelley summarizes it (2002: 300), each hoped to capture the wisdom of the ages in a single system, to bring the historical process to a close; each had a vision of law and order that would be preserved on every level.

longer really law (Fitzpatrick 1992: 115; Tamanaha 2008: 381). Western legal systems then came to be comprehensive and supreme within their respective communities, with authority to regulate all forms of human behaviour (Raz 1979: 116–21; Finnis 1980: 148). As well as providing instruments of rule, means to implement projects of taxation, centralize resources, and organize military recruitment, they also co-opted subsidiary forms of authority, 'adopting' other rules and normative arrangements in order to give them legal force (Diamond 1973: 327). The English common law, for example, gradually confined the recognition of local custom, while presuming to judge the validity of forest law, law merchant, and manorial laws (Ibbetson 2007: 167ff). In France, the creation of the *coutumes* gave the central court jurisdiction over their application, even before Napoleon's comprehensive codification. The totalizing vision of law can, thus, give ideological support to the totalizing project of a ruler. This can occur even without the backing of a state: Islamic *shari'a* treats local custom, *'urf*, as a material source, more like fact than another form of law. As Dresch (2012:14) puts it, 'the common law and shari'a each evolved means to subordinate or marginalize alternative visions of the world'.

As well as subordinating other forms of social ordering, laws may have systematizing aims, something that is apparent in some of the earliest law codes. As discussed in chapter three, Whitman (1996) comments on the concerns of the Mesapotamian, ancient Greek, and Germanic codes to control the marketplace, specifying values and prices, along with complicated lists of compensation payments. Similar aims are apparent in seventh-century Tibetan documents, which record the early emperors making a census and a law book, marking out fields, and establishing systems of rewards and punishments, weights and measures (Bacot et al. 1940; Stein 1986); the emperors are also said to have equalized rich and poor three times (Petech 1977: 35–36). The complex and detailed rules of the Thai *thammasat*, a legal code heavily based on the Indic *dharmaśāstras*, defined relations between the individual and state and set out the precepts by which relations between people were to be regulated (Engel 1975: 3).

The systematic aims of these codes seem to be steps towards the establishment of a realm that can be administered. Rules for compensation payments, in particular, construct individuals as equals, albeit within specific ranks and classes. As Fitzpatrick (1992: 166) suggests, modern law creates the legal subject as an effective actor, corresponding largely to the subject of administration; the spread of individual legal rights is combined with a rapid spread of governmental control (Fitzpatrick 1992: 125). As Graeber (2011) puts it, rules can, like money, be used to symbolize equivalence, but they also depersonalize people and their relationships. Instead of helping someone out because you are his brother or nephew, or a member of the same age-set or club, you give him something by way of measured exchange; a rule construes you as a purchaser, tortfeasor, executor, employer, or landlord, rather than a patron, say, with ongoing, albeit unspecific, obligations of protection and support.[2] Ideas of contract and the contracting individual can also be associated with the development of state law (Fox 1993: 96–97). The rule of contract law, backed by the power of the state, Fox says, eventually usurped all others in importance, and crucial in this was the replacement of the family as the basic legal unit with the individual contractor. The state, despite its occasional persecutions, is happier with individuals as units than with kinship groups, for the simple reason that they are easier to control (1993: 184).

According to Fox (1993: x), the war between kinship and state, between kinship and contract, and between kinship and individualism has been one of the great movers of history.[3] It is a battle which is still being fought when law is formulated, or invoked, to regulate matters of reproduction and succession. This might include issues of surrogacy (Fox 1993: ch 2), or the

---

[2] This raises the unsettling possibility that compensation tables could form part of a shift towards depersonalized economic relations, including the possibility of credit and debt, whereby the rich could take advantage of the poor. As Graeber (2011: 191) argues, while a patron-client relationship entails continuing obligations, a loan assumes formal legal equality, but with it the possibility for ruthlessness and violence.

[3] The long battle between kinship and state law, he suggests, is exemplified in the fate of Antigone, who defied the law of the mythical Thebes, in which Creon had laws and a police to enforce them, thus claiming a monopoly of the legitimate use of force. By insisting on burying her brother, against Creon's orders, Antigone was putting her duties to her family above her duties to the state (Fox 1993: ch 3).

control of traditional practices, such as the 'head pay' marriage in Papua New Guinea, discussed by Strathern (2004), in which a girl was to be given in marriage as a mortuary gift. Pottage and Mundy's (2004) edited volume illustrates the numerous ways in which state laws, with their categories of property and person, are implicated in complex, often difficult, social relations in the modern world.

State law may, then, construct a totalizing vision, and successfully subordinate other visions of order; it may constitute individuals as subjects of its administration; but it may also be confronted by persistent, alternative forms of social relations, particularly where persons and kinship are involved. However successful projects of governmental regulation may be, and although many rulers have been autocratic in the exercise of power through law, legal history also indicates a recurrent resistance to the idea that a ruler should be able to exercise unfettered legislative power.

LAW ABOVE THE RULER

In China, as I have described in chapter five, the emperors regarded themselves as supreme, and above the law. However, they also acknowledged that they had been entrusted with the Mandate of Heaven and that they were bound to respect its laws, as well as the enactments of their ancestors. Appeals to both ancestry and divinity legitimated the power and supremacy of the Chinese emperors, and created an obligation on their part to acknowledge and conform—at least ostensibly—to the ancestral laws. The ancient Greeks also idealized their laws and Euripides presented the law as an essentially public matter. Whether or not rulers were, in practice, constrained by the laws, the idea that law was binding upon the ruler was at least being articulated.

In Rome, Justinian's Digest famously asserts that *quod principi placuit legis habet vigorem*, what pleases the prince has the force of law. This maxim was widely invoked in medieval Europe, even before Napoleon, to justify the absolute power of the ruler (Nicholas 1962: 17). However, the Roman emperors' assertion of legislative authority had distinctly uncertain beginnings. The jurist Ulpian, to whom the maxim is attributed, explained that each emperor's legislative power was effectively granted by the people at the beginning of his reign (Stein 1999: 59). Gaius, in the second century, asserted that the *constitutiones* of the emperor, although they had the force of *lex*, were only one among a number of sources of law. By the time of Justinian, jurists had formulated the idea that the emperor is free from the laws, *princeps legibus solutus est*. Nevertheless, an enactment of Theodosius, also reproduced in Justinian's Code, states that the emperor should declare himself to be bound by the laws as a mark of imperial authority (Stein 1999: 60). There was even a sense that law was somehow tinged with divine or cosmological authority: the first Title in the Digest affirms that law is 'true philosophy' and that its practitioners are 'priests of the law' (Kelley 2002: 291). Another fragment defines jurisprudence as 'knowledge of things human and divine' (Stein 1999: 46). The Roman emperors' assertion of absolute imperial power sits alongside references to the quasi-divine authority of the law and the jurists, a lingering hint of popular sovereignty, and a sense that compliance with the law was an act of imperial dignity.

Indic law in south-east Asia

Complex and ambiguous relations between rulers and laws recur widely. The relationship between law and political power in south-east Asia, for example, has been the subject of considerable comment and debate. Sanskrit texts and Hindu thought heavily influenced the development of laws in what are now Thailand, Burma, Cambodia, and Java (Hooker 1978). As O'Connor (1981: 225) describes, the Thais borrowed, interpreted, simplified, and universalized the Buddhist form of *dharma*, to create a composite Thai concept of *thamma* or cosmic law. It was the moral order of all things, above the actions of individuals and rulers. The Thai legal text, the *thammasat*, as well as defining the relationship between individuals and the state, also prescribed the norms by which the ruler should govern (Engel 1975: 4–5). There was a concurrent tradition of royal law in Thailand, dating from at least the thirteenth century, and early kings presented themselves as universal monarchs, whose harmony with the cosmic world made them interpreters of its laws. A number of law-like edicts and royal decisions were incorporated into an 1805 restatement of the thammasat, known as the Law of the Three Seals, with the result, O'Connor suggests (1981: 22–28), that Thai law became something like a set of Chinese boxes: the cosmic law encompassed the natural law—the thammasat—which itself contained royal or positive law.

In general the kings of these regions could, and did, issue decrees, but they could not officially introduce primary and lasting legislation. As Lingat (1950: 4) says, they were at once the creature, creator, and protector of the legal system. The Thai king was regarded as embodying the cosmic law (O'Connor 1981: 226); or, as Geertz (1983: 200) puts it, 'the sovereign's commands, when they are proper acts, spell out the law'. The dharmaśāstras and the Thai Thammasat thus codified the royal duty to maintain the behavioural order of society by punishing those who disturbed it, but the ruler was, himself, subject to the principles of dharma, like everyone else.[4] Secular power needed to be governed or directed by the sacred (Geertz 1983: 202, n. 51). Of course, as Lingat (1950: 11) comments, many of the kings were, in practice, absolute rulers, who could and probably did deviate from the religious dictates of the law. Nevertheless, the law, at least theoretically, limited their powers and shaped their actions.

Medieval Europe

In European thought, a long history of debates over the nature and origins of law, the relationships between *physis* and *nomos*, divine law, natural right, reason, and royal authority can be traced back to Aristotle (Kelley 1990; Murphy 2005, 2007). In the Middle Ages, as Fritz Kern (1939: 69–81) describes, the idea of an indefeasible hereditary right to the throne had not yet emerged:

Germanic and ecclesiastic opinion were firmly agreed on the principles, which met with no opposition until the age of Machiavelli, that the State exists for the realization of the Law; the power of the State is the means, the Law is the end-in-itself; the monarch is dependent upon

---

[4] In Thailand the relationship between kingship and law was openly debated in the late nineteenth and early twentieth centuries, under the influence of foreign ideas about the legitimacy of government under law, and Engel (1975) describes in some detail how these ideas worked themselves out in practice over the subsequent years.

the Law, which is superior to him, and upon which his own existence is based.... In the Germanic State law was customary law, 'the law of one's fathers', the pre-existing, objective, legal situation, which was a complex of numerous subjective rights.... The purpose of the State, according to Germanic political ideas, was to fix and maintain, to pre-serve the existing order, the good old law. (1939: 70)

By the later Middle Ages, the idea had developed that the monarch was below natural law, but above positive law, that is, free from the bonds of customary law, in a striking parallel with the Thai monarchs. However, the hierarchy of authority was far from clear. As Kern describes, the king was thought to owe a duty to both justice and equity, and these comprised customary and natural law. Moreover, the law of reason could only be expressed through positive law, so that the monarch, at least in the ecclesiastic view, was subject to positive law, as the embodiment of divine law (1939: 72).[5]

There was also a sense of popular sovereignty: 'Law was the living conviction of the community, which, although not valid without the king, was so far above the king that he could not disregard the conviction of the community without degenerat-ing into lawless "tyranny"'. Although the Frankish kings created laws, these remained technically folklore, found by the commu-nity and ordained by the king (1939: 73). A standard attribute of good medieval government was upholding the ideal of law and justice, which meant ruling people in accordance with their own law (Dunbabin 2001: 117). In practice, too, the princes of the Middle Ages regularly acknowledged that they were bound by the law and an oath to this effect was frequently offered by new rulers, eventually formalized under clerical influence as a corona-tion oath. In the later Middle Ages, as Cohen (1993: 39–42) de-scribes, the coronation oaths made in northern France continued to repeat the idea of good, old custom. The ideal of customary law as pure, old, and good, she says, remained strong, despite the

[5] The history of medieval thought is complex. Dunbabin (1965: 2001) describes how the thirteenth-century ruler's relations with his subjects were controlled by good intention and education, not laws. Civil law, as taught in the universities, carried prestige, but was not thought of as a technique for restricting the power of the ruler.

fact that the authors of the *custumals* knew that custom was, in fact, processual and shifting and was constantly being subjected to new legislation by the rulers. The lay perception insisted that law should, first and foremost, be just. A king achieved the status of just ruler by applying the laws and customs of the past, the ones he shared with his people, not the ones he had invented (1993: 47).

In England, a famous speech made by the judge, Lord Bereford, in 1312 indicated that legislation was merely an internal amendment to the body of custom applied in the king's courts, not something external and above it (Milsom 1981: 177). It was by no means unquestionably accepted that legislation supervened over the custom normally applied within the king's courts (Plucknett 1922). The subsequent rise of equity, as a means of tempering the rigorous application of the law, is only intelligible, Milsom (1981: 25) suggests, if we remember the medieval familiarity with earthly institutions of conscience and the medieval belief in an absolute right. It was only much later that it came to be widely accepted that law could be the creation of the state, whether in the form of the commands of the ruler, as argued by Hobbes, or as the custom, legislation, and professional reasoning that the state's courts enforce. It was this that eventually entailed a theoretical separation of law and morality, of *ius* from *lex*, or *le droit* from *la loi* (Finnis 1980: 208). Even in the eighteenth century 'immense efforts were made…to project the image of a ruling class which was itself subject to the rule of law' (Thompson 1975: 263). The idea that law could be identified with the commands of the ruler, or the enactments of a legislator, has had a chequered history, to say the least (Murphy 2005).

Southern Baptists

The association of true law with some sense of transcendent right has not disappeared, even in the modern west. Legal theorists have long been uncomfortable with the idea of a 'positive law', traced to a single source in the commands of the sovereign or, as Milsom (1981: 25) puts it, that the connection between law and morality should be relegated to the classroom. There is continued attachment to theories of natural law (Finnis 1980) and to normative accounts as proposed, albeit in very different forms, by Dworkin (1986) and Waldron (1995).

Adherence to the view that true law is rooted in morality and natural right is, moreover, not limited to legal theorists. In a study of a Baptist community in the US state of Georgia, Greenhouse (1986) discusses their sense of a superior or divine law that transcends the imperfect legislation of the state. As she says (1986: 120), the Baptists attach importance to avoiding confrontation and feel a need to transcend it in order to achieve salvation. The judicial authority required for the authoritative resolution of a dispute contradicts local understandings of Baptist doctrine: their ideal of harmony implies purity and obviates the need for human authority (1986: 195–96). The Baptists have, as she puts it, accomplished something of what Tocqueville describes as the American dream, that is, a society without overt applications of human authority, built not on obedience but on participation. Like the Armenians and the Berber villagers discussed in chapter seven, the Baptists adhere to a set of moral norms, in particular an ideal of harmony, which connects them with a wider moral world, in this case the Christian brotherhood, and which distinguish them from their non-Christian neighbours and political leaders (1986: 196). As Greenhouse (1982) explains, the Baptists regard themselves as sharing the norms, ideals, and values of the Bible and regard their commitment to these norms as very different from abiding by the rules of the state, which are externally imposed upon them. It is not that they do not respect the state's laws, but they eschew the court process by seeking to re-establish community values and commitments. Thus, the norms that give meaning to their community are not those of the state's legal system but those of their religion (1982: 63).

Reflecting more generally on American ideas about law, Greenhouse suggests that law is, in one sense, regarded as 'the sum of the society's functional and organic qualities' (1989: 266); for the Baptists, more specifically, it helps people live in peace and is located in reason, God, and nature (1989: 257). Official law, by contrast, is often regarded by Americans as man-made, a matter of rules imposed externally by elite institutions (1989: 269) and for the Baptists court use is something distinct and undesirable, which 'violates an ordained equality amongst citizens and believers' (1989: 258). There are two concepts of law here, a very general idea of law connected with ideas about community, divinity, and

justice, and a contrasting notion of legislation and state law as the
imperfect products of human endeavour. Greenhouse is suggesting that Americans generally, and Baptists in particular—and in
specifically religious terms—have a sense of a true law, one that
lies above and beyond the rules and statutes of the state.

It is not just that there is resistance to the idea that rulers can
exercise unfettered legislative power, then. Laws are also thought
to enshrine ideals that supervene the power and authority of the
government.

Tibet

Within the legal thought of the Hindu world, discussed in chapter
four, the ruler was supposed to embody and be guided by the law;
he was also supposed to ensure its realization amongst the ordinary population through the promulgation and enforcement of
criminal laws and penalties (Davis 2010: 116). This was the *dharma*
of the ruler, elaborated upon in the texts known as the *arthaśāstras*.
The king was supposed to exert his coercive authority, his *danda*,
over those who should be punished in order, among other things,
to protect the weak from the strong (Zimmerman 2006: 214–16).

Buddhist thought developed in India from around 500BC and
was closely linked with Hindu thought and ideas, but it rejected violence as wholly unethical. The Buddhist texts, therefore, developed a different ideal of kingship: the Buddhist king,
the *cakravartin*, should rule over the earth without the need for
punishment or violence, simply by persuading his subjects to
live according to the precepts of Buddhism. This hardly represented a practical ideal for rulers faced with the demands of
governance, however. As Zimmerman (2006: 216–17) describes,
Indian Buddhist thinkers struggled to reconcile the imperative of
non-violence with the need and duty of the king—both practical and theoretical—to carry out physical punishment. Buddhist
texts suggest that the king's legal duties were inherently problematic, some even claiming that it was impossible to be a good
Buddhist king, a view expressed in the Jātaka Tales, for example
(Cowell and Rouse 1907: no. 538; Hopkins and Rinpoche
1975: 66–67; Zimmerman 2006: 218–23). Other attempts to
reconcile the conflicting imperatives, appealing to ideas of compassionate punishment, were developed in the Mahayana texts,

which formed the basis for Tibetan Buddhism (Zimmerman 2000). They were never wholly convincing, however, and the result for the ideal of kingship was, as Schmithausen (1999: 62) describes it, a vacillation between two conflicting sets of values.

Many of these texts were translated into Tibetan, along with a huge corpus of other Buddhist material brought from India, in the eleventh and subsequent centuries.[6] This was a time of political diversity and disunity on the Tibetan plateau, following the collapse of the Tibetan empire. During the imperial period—lasting roughly from the sixth to ninth centuries—there had been some law-making and centralization of the judicial system (Thomas 1936; Richardson 1989; Richardson 1990; Dotson 2007). The surviving texts consist mainly of practical lists of compensation payments and punishments. A historiographic tradition, initiated during the late empire, however, claims that they were Buddhist laws, created by the early emperor Songtsan Gampo to replace an earlier tradition of criminal laws, as part of his project to bring civilization, through Buddhism, to Tibet (Bacot et al. 1940).

This narrative tradition developed further during and after the translation of Buddhist texts from India. What the supposedly Buddhist laws created by the emperors might have consisted of was never consistently spelled out, however. Some texts reproduce what appear to be fragments from the empire, which bear no relation to Buddhist ethics or principles, while others set out what are more like lists of exhortations for the organization of a good legal system (Uray 1972; Toussaint 1978; Stein 1986; Sørensen 1994; Dotson 2006). Although they are far from consistent, the texts indicate that it was expected of the kings, even their duty, that they should formulate laws for the guidance of their subjects, while also indicating that punitive laws were immoral. The practically-oriented laws of the empire were thus replaced by a problematic combination of Buddhist morality and Hindu ideas about punishment, influenced by the tensions contained in the imported texts. Over the following centuries, the narrative tradition continued to portray imperial law as having

---

[6] Kapstein (2007) provides a good overview of political developments during this period.

been a Buddhist project, but the general depiction of moral conduct and the vision of a well-organized society that the texts contained tended to be unspecific and unlegalistic. Ultimately, in one well-known narrative, Songtsan Gampo's punitive laws were said to have been mere illusions, created to inspire fear and devotion amongst the population (Uray 1972; Dotson 2006; Mills 2012). It is as if the Tibetan tradition could not, as the Indian texts themselves had indicated, elaborate a system of laws that satisfied the ethical demands of their religion.

What later came to be regarded as Tibet's laws were contained in a text drafted in the fourteenth century.[7] This set of laws explicitly claims to have been derived from the imperial laws of Songtsan Gampo, whose law-making activities were known from contemporary historical narratives. It combines a certain amount of Buddhist imagery and metaphor, at the beginning of each section, with stipulations concerning the conduct of military commanders, administrators, and judicial officers, and provisions for compensation payments and punishments in the event of various crimes and conflicts (White 1894; Meisezahl 1973, 1992).[8] The ideal of compassionate Buddhist laws remained unrealized. This code was preserved and reproduced in Tibet, right up to the twentieth century, but there is no evidence that its rules were ever applied in practice. Rather they appeared as symbolic, ornately bound texts in a twentieth-century courtroom, ceremoniously consulted on difficult points of procedure (Dawa Norbu 1974). They had become a symbol of the continuing legacy of the empire and of the Buddhist origins of the Tibetan government. An ideology of law, or what we might call a jurisprudence, can thus constrain and impede legislative activity.

Within the Tibetan intellectual world, then, a tension between Buddhist ethics and the duties of the king was introduced in imported texts, and the idea that law was essentially a matter of punitive sanctions, imposed by a ruler, was never fully reconciled with religious ideals of non-violence.

---

[7] The earliest surviving copy dates to the seventeenth century, but the laws are attributed to the era of the fourteenth-century ruler, Changchub Gyaltsan.
[8] An unpublished translation prepared in 1917 for the British official, Charles Bell, is in the British library.

The modern state

Idealistic aims are readily apparent in the invocation and creation of laws, even in the contemporary world. The Comaroffs, in a wide-ranging survey of law-making in contemporary society, describe what they term the 'fetishization of law', particularly in the postcolonial world (Comaroff and Comaroff 2006).[9] They remark upon the number of constitutions written or rewritten since 1989, evincing a belief in their capacity to conjure up equitable, just, ethically founded, pacific polities. Faith in these new constitutions, like the establishment of constitutional courts, they suggest, may rest upon the promise of a new beginning, a radical break with the past. We might compare the major human rights declarations in post-war and post-communist Europe, and in post-apartheid South Africa, which represented a dramatic break with the previous regimes (Chanock 2000). The Comaroffs remark upon a shift in the content of such constitutions, from an emphasis on parliamentary sovereignty, executive discretion, and bureaucratic authority, which characterized the constitutions created during the decades of decolonization after the second world war, to an emphasis upon the rule of law and the primacy of rights (2006: 23). However, as we have seen, the idea of a law that binds the ruler is ancient, at least as old as the assertion of parliamentary sovereignty by the ancient Greeks. Even if vague, a sense that the law transcends the government serves to legitimate a regime, and historically it has often hovered in the background to a monarch's claims to law-making authority.

The Comaroffs comment upon the incongruence between ideology and practice in the making and maintenance of these constitutions, when 'both the spirit and the letter of that law are violated, offended, distended, purloined' (2006: 23). But if we consider the Germanic and Tibetan law codes it should not surprise us that modern constitutions are enacted for ideological as much as practical reasons, nor that modern rulers clothe their activities in constitutionality, as the Comaroffs (2006: 24) put it.[10]

[9] It is not entirely apparent why they choose to focus on the 'postcolony', since much of what they describe seems to apply more generally.

[10] The constitution in South Africa has become the populist icon of nationhood, tempting us to compare the medieval law code that long stood as an icon of nationhood for the Armenians (Thomson 2000).

The Comaroffs adopt a not unreasonably critical tone when describing this 'fetishization' of law, emphasizing its capacity to stand as a mask for power, clothing the activities of the elite, or simply powerful, in 'a wash of legitimacy, ethics, propriety' (2006: 31). But has it not been ever thus? We do not have to explain the 'fetishization of law' as an unprecedented modern phenomenon, seeking causes in the neoliberal agenda of modern political powers. As Berman (1983: 45) says, the western tradition has always been dependent on beliefs in the existence of a body of law beyond the highest political authority, whether divine or natural law or, most recently, human rights. It is an ancient, and multi-faceted phenomenon, with parallels in the Justinianic codes, the claims of the Chinese emperors, and the aspirations of Germanic kings in post-Roman Europe.

AGAINST AND BEYOND THE STATE

The Comaroffs comment upon the explosion of law-oriented non-governmental organizations, now commonly regarded as 'the civilizing missions' of the twenty-first century. The language of jurisprudence is ubiquitous, they point out; there may be a genuine regard for the law and repeated appeals are made to the judiciary to restore order, even where all means of enforcement are absent (2006: 25–26). Later they comment on the rise of 'lawfare', the tendency of citizens, subjects, corporations, and governments to litigate against one another and to allege breaches of human and constitutional rights; such claims arise out of contested elections, industrial calamities, colonial 'crimes', struggles over intellectual property, and so on, many involving international activities and legal actions (2006: 26–31). But why, ask the Comaroffs, is the language of the law so attractive? The politics of the present is being judicialized, they say, while the past is increasingly caught up in a dialectic of law and disorder, as colonial governments are criticized for their own use of 'lawfare'.

An extensive anthropological literature on the rise of human rights in the twentieth and twenty-first centuries reinforces this observation. Commenting on these developments, Wilson (2007: 352) suggests that 'the legalization of rights is mystifying insofar as it raises false expectations that the state can solve social and economic problems'. This is to suppose that the purpose and significance of law can always be explained in terms of its capacity to regulate, however. As examples in the previous section, as well as many others in this book, have indicated, law may express a powerful ethical vision in and of itself; it may promise order and moral answers in the midst of chaos and injustice, without being enforced. As the Comaroffs point out, it is sometimes the state that 'conjures with legalities' to act against some or all of its citizens; but law can also be a weapon of the weak, 'turning authority back on itself by commissioning the sanction of the court to make claims to resources, recognition, voice, integrity, sovereignty' (2006: 30–31). Why should it surprise us if the powerless and poor appeal to law and the courts, as much as the rich and powerful? Law sets standards that transcend the authority of government, providing language and argument that can be used against the ruler, the powerful, and the official, and has done throughout its history.

Law can be rigid, formalistic, and esoteric, then, but litigants in the lowest of the US courts squeeze their complaints and problems into legal categories, even as officials try to persuade them to seek practical solutions (Merry 1990). Indeed, the phenomenon of people seeking the law recurs widely at different periods (Dresch 2012: 22).[11] Beattie (1986), in a study of crime and the courts in England in the seventeenth and eighteenth centuries, found that the middle classes were overwhelmingly responsible for bringing criminal cases to the courts, and these included a large number of artisans and labourers, for whom the costs were significant. As he concludes, 'the law appears to have been widely accepted in society as a means of settling disputes and ameliorating public grievances. The courts offered a wide range of individual victims of theft or violence some sense of satisfaction' (1986: 622). During the era of European colonialism, too, Merry (2010: 1068) describes a rush to use the new courts that

---

[11] Humfress (2007: ch 3) describes a range of issues on which legal advice might be sought in the late Roman period, Smail (2003) remarks upon the quantity of litigation pursued in fourteenth and fifteenth-century Marseille, which defies easy explanation, while Bossy describes 'an inpouring of people's disputes into the tribunals of the crown' in the seventeenth century (1983: 291).

the imperial powers had created. 'In many cases', she says, 'this enthusiasm was led by relatively powerless individuals...many saw in the new institutions opportunities to escape the bonds of kinship or unfree status'.

Bossy is puzzled by this phenomenon, at least in early modern Europe: 'quite how the image of the law, or the state or the crown, had managed to acquire a sanctity, a moral force of this order seems rather a problem' (1983: 291). But we should not assume that everyone identified the law and the courts with state or crown. They might also offer the opportunity to contest relations of power, as Merry suggests. In thirteenth-century France, when seigniorial relations came to be expressed in legalistic terms, this allowed opposition to the powerful: 'Village inhabitants, city consuls, lords both minor and great, all discovered that the court machinery provided by the monarchy...allowed them to fight those who would impose...some kind of dominion over them' (Cheyette 1970: 290).

It is not just that laws may be invoked in the courts as a means of resistance. Historical examples indicate that, in some cases, people may equate law with freedom, that is freedom from arbitrary power. This is particularly apparent in a feudal, or quasi-feudal, context. In his classic study, *The Making of the Middle Ages*, Southern (1953: 104–107) suggests that what men feared and resented in serfdom was not its subordination, but its arbitrariness, the fact that they were governed not by rule but by will. Liberty meant being subject to law, rather than to will: 'the knight did not obey more rules than the ordinary freeman, but very many more; the freeman was not less restricted than the serf, but he was restricted in a different, more rational way'. The most highly privileged communities were those with most laws, while the serf had least, if any, recourse to the law against the arbitrariness of his superiors.[12] As Lucas (1977: 94) summarizes what this might mean, 'the law makes me free because it enables me to know of myself what to do without having to be told by a superior on each particular occasion. It makes me a full member

---

[12] It was also a characteristic of the higher forms of law, as he describes, that those who submitted to them had to do so by their own choice, through an oath, a profession, or a contract embodied in a public ceremony.

of the community, able to embody communal standards in my own actions and my own approbation of the actions of others'.

Somewhat later, as E. P. Thompson (1975: 264) describes, law was central to the eighteenth-century gentry and their purchase upon power, to the royal prerogative, and to the definition of their lands and marriages. However, it was inherent in the very nature of the medium which they had used for their own self-defence that it could not be reserved for the exclusive use of their own class. The law, in all its forms and traditions, entailed principles of equity and universality, which had to be extended to all sorts and degrees of men. Agricultural society and relations between tenants, serfs, and peasants were defined by laws, in particular those concerning the use of property, but the people could also, on occasion, use the law in their own interests. Thompson ends his analysis of the Black Act with a discussion of the paradoxes of the law: it provided ideological and instrumental support for rulers, he says, but law and justice are ideal aspirations which must pretend to absolute validity if they are to exist at all. Even the 'atrocious' Black Act could not wholly undermine this ideology, and its legacy was the vision of an ideal, an aspiration towards the universal values of law (1975: 267).

Law might serve the interests of domination, then, but as the Greeks realized, it offers justice for rich and poor alike. Or, as the Comaroffs say (2006: 32) 'a ready means of commensuration', which is what the ancient codes, with their lists and scales of compensation, were doing. Of course, the justice that the law promises may be hierarchical, as it was in Hindu, Chinese, and Tibetan codes, and within the Roman imperial constitution (Pharr 2001: 259). As Graeber (2011) argues, laws, like money, may allow people to interact as equals, but they also allow the strong to prevail over the weak with impunity, without the ongoing obligations of more personal relations. At the same time, it offers a system of objective rules, which can be invoked by those to whom they apply, against those who would transgress them. It may not be too far-fetched to talk about law as promising freedom, even now, if we mean freedom from arbitrary power. We must not be too easily drawn into an analysis that concentrates on the way in which law can act as a mask for power or an instrument of hegemony. It may do these things, but it also depends, for its force, upon a sense of moral order, the invocation of higher ideals, or what we have come to call the 'rule of law', to which, as Thompson (1975: 269) says, even the powerful may ultimately have to surrender.

INTERNATIONAL AND TRANSNATIONAL LAWS

Law is widely invoked against, as well as by, the state, then, but some laws disregard all boundaries. International law, that which transcends the limits of the state, can take many forms. Merchants have always sought to standardize their practices and instruments, and often to develop specialized forms of arbitration or dispute resolution. More recently, legal scholars have argued that common principles and standards exist for the conduct of warfare, amounting to a form of 'customary' international law (Henckaerts and Doswald-Beck 2005), while international organizations, such as the United Nations, the International Labour Organization, and the International Atomic Agency, establish rules in the form of treaties between nation states, generally known as 'public international law'. What are labelled 'private international laws' include labour laws, accounting standards, principles of good governance, and regulations for international sport (Jansen and Michaels 2007: 353).

A feature that has troubled some legal theorists about these forms of law is the lack of enforcement mechanisms. What Barkun (1968: 7–9) calls the 'Austinian view', that law has force or the threat of force behind it, would discount most of these as forms of law. Hart (1994: ch X), for example, hesitates to apply the term 'law' to international rules because they lack any 'rule of recognition', that is, any basic rule providing general criteria of validity. The analogy with municipal law is one of content and function, he says, rather than form (1994: 237). Roberts also maintains that we extend the use of the term 'law' to the international arena as an idiom, to characterize practices and understandings at global level, given its dominance in furnishing meaning at national level (2005: 18). Other scholars are troubled by the fact that the 'customary laws' of merchants engaged in transnational transactions are too vague, too incomplete, and lacking sufficient generality and universality to constitute 'law' (Berman and Dasser 1990).

The many examples of laws and legal codes I have already discussed, which are important without apparently ever being enforced, not to mention being 'incomplete', should cast doubt on those concerns. Indeed, as Berman and Dasser (1990: 59) ask, is the law merchant more vague than the French law of delict; and is the elaborate codification of commercial law in the Uniform Commercial Code[13] 'unstable, uncertain and unpredictable' or quite as 'mulishly unruly' as the uncodified common law has ever been? As several legal scholars have argued, we must transcend the equation of law and state if we are to understand international and transnational laws (Menski 2006; Twining 2009; Berman 2012; Cotterrell 2012). What is of particular interest for the argument of this book is that scholars, merchants, social reformers, and human rights campaigners have all found it useful to adopt the legal form. Legalism, as a mode of thought and social organization, is useful beyond the bounds of the nation state and without any distinct means of enforcement, even, or especially, in the modern world.

Law merchant

Many of the laws developed by merchants for transnational trade can be explained in the most straightforward, practical, and commercial terms: trade has often been facilitated through the elaboration of standard formal instruments and mechanisms for the resolution of disputes, without the sanctions normally associated with state law.

In the twelfth and thirteenth centuries, for example, the rise of local, regional, and international trade in Europe led to new rules, customs, and practices, often centred on markets and fairs. A treatise on *Lex Mercatoria*, apparently based upon the practices of the English mercantile court at St Ives, bears witness to a particular form of court procedure, which reflected the customs of merchants and their forms of loans and pledge, agency and credit agreements, arrangements for the allocation of risk, and so on (Basile et al. 1998). For the most part, the court practices

---

[13] This code sets out recommendations for the commercial laws to be adopted by individual states in the US.

it describes were designed to meet the need for speedy justice between itinerant merchants who could not wait for the processes of the common law courts. They were, to a large extent, modelled upon the forms of action found in those courts, and the writers of the treatises borrowed terms and concepts from other legal texts (Baker 1979: 301). It is apparent that the medieval merchants found it useful to have judicial processes that were more speedy than those of the common law courts, even if they did not enjoy the same enforcement mechanisms. As Baker (1979: 303) puts it, by avoiding common law forms the merchants gave themselves more flexibility; the fact that their instruments could not, in themselves, be enforced was a secondary consideration in a community which depended on good credit and honour.

Elsewhere in Europe, the fairs at Champagne played a central role in twelfth and thirteenth-century commerce, providing a system in which traders could settle their disputes, as did numerous other bodies, including the merchants' guilds, the consulates of Italian city states, and colonies of merchants like the Steelyard in London, which enjoyed local privileges and duties (Milgrom et al. 1990). Milgrom et al. suggest that the merchants' laws provided people with the information they needed to recognize those who had cheated; they obviously also defined what counted as cheating in the first place.

Merchants have often developed sophisticated legal forms, that is, trading agreements with standardized terms, reflecting customary practices, even across long distances and amongst people who probably had no other social or political ties. In nineteenth-century Taiwan, as Brockman (1980) describes, merchants trading across the border with China drew up complex contracts, in which they carefully specified reciprocal rights and obligations. Trade practices generated well-developed and relatively precise rules, which governed the determination and allocation of rights and obligations on the occurrence of various contingencies. As he puts it, this system of contract provided a framework within which merchants could reach agreements, make bargains, carry out transactions, and generally order their affairs, despite the fact that the local courts were not effective in enforcing the agreements or generating contractual rules (1980: 79). Rather, the contracts incorporated mechanisms of self-enforcement and self-execution. As Brockman summarizes it, this highly developed system of contract allowed commerce to flourish through long-range, impersonal bargains, which did not require extensive external coercion to assure performance (1980: 129). Similar phenomena have been noted in the Mediterranean, where traders from the Maghrib, in northern Africa, conducted trade in the eleventh century (Greif 1989). In the modern world, rules have developed to regulate the Internet and to establish standards for international sporting and construction activities, as well as more traditional areas, such as the activities of Jewish diamond traders (Michaels and Jansen 2006: 869–70).

There has been a concern among international lawyers to distinguish these forms of 'customary law', as matters of practice and agreement, from law that is authorized or sanctioned by a sovereign state, including treatises transacted between states (Carbonneau 1990). Goode (2005) argues that what we tend to call modern '*lex mercatoria*' is really international trade usage. But why, we might ask, is it so important to preserve this distinction, along with the assumption that 'true law' is more potent than non-legal *lex mercatoria*? As Barkun (1968) suggests, international relations have been bedevilled by the search for sovereign power and the idea that international law is municipal law blown up to global dimensions. Law, he says, is made up of concepts woven into rules; it is a model, a representation, a sophisticated and highly developed form of metaphor (1968: 85, 87). Laws seek to develop concepts that will organize previously unpatterned empirical data. International law provides a repertoire of conceptual tags, whose application gives definition to a situation in which choices have to be made (1968: 139–42). Many legal scholars, such as Berger (2001), argue that the modern international commercial contract is now a genuine source of law. He suggests that a 'non-positivistic' view is emerging, whereby law is not the public reason represented by the state or by inter-governmental organizations alone, but also consists of the power for self-regulation and coordination amongst individuals and private organizations (2001: 18–19).

Pluralism and formalism

Some anthropologists have discussed the 'globalization' of law as a new, late twentieth-century phenomenon, arguing that it calls for assessment in terms of legal pluralism (K. von Benda-Beckmann 2002; F. and K. von Benda-Beckmann 2007; Merry 2006a; Tamanaha 2008). Others have turned to this concept in order to avoid the recurrent issues which, as Cotterrell (2012) points out, occur when law is thought to need institutional backing in order to be legitimate.[14] It is said to offer an analysis that avoids debates about the nature of law and the 'problem' of the lack of enforcement mechanisms (Berman 2005: 539; 2012). Others simply see the idea of legal pluralism as the best way of explaining and accounting for the multiplicity of laws in the world, both legal traditions and common or international laws of various kinds (de Sousa Santos 2002; Menski 2006; Twining 2009: 226).

The difficulty of identifying what is distinctive about legal norms amidst other customs and practices raises familiar issues. De Sousa Santos (2002: 91), for example, asks—why should complementary forms of social ordering not be designated as law?—and he answers this question by simply asking, in return, 'Why not?' Michaels (2005: 1221–24) points out that many who advocate global legal pluralism are participating in a politics of recognition, as multiple groups claim recognition of their statuses. It is the product, he says, of an ideological desire to raise non-state law to the level of law (2005: 1256). We need a better way of understanding transnational law.

Martii Koskenniemi (2001) suggests that international law both creates power and delimits it, offering a language for the defence of both hegemonic and anti-hegemonic power. Like Barkun, he argues that we should not think of law as primarily controlling the actions of bad men. International law is created in part to advance the repertory of substantive values, preferences, and practices that those in dominant positions seek to realize in the world, but it also gives voice to those who have been excluded from decision-making positions: it provides a platform on which claims about violence, injustice, and social deprivation may be made. Its formalism brings political antagonists together as they invoke contrasting understandings of rules and institutions, providing a shared surface for debate, and allowing them

---

[14] As Michaels and Jansen (2006: 874) describe, German legal thinking, in particular, requires that law has jurisdictional, sociological, and ethical validity.

to disagree within a structure of assumed universality. More than that, international law exists as a promise of justice: law describes the world as a (legal) community, in which questions of just distribution and entitlement are constantly on the agenda, where claims of legal subjects receive an equal hearing, and where acts of public officials are assessed by a language of community standards (Koskenniemi 2011).

The 'formalism' and 'assumed universality' of international law, which Koskenniemi thus emphasizes, is in essence the legalism that characterizes the numerous and disparate examples of law discussed in this book. His remarks about legal community and the promise of justice resonate with many historical and contemporary examples, while the formalism of legal language is undoubtedly important. The historian Postan (1973: 64), for example, identifies the attractions of the 'rigidity and conventionality' of the form of the *tratta*, an early bill of exchange used in medieval European trade, in order to explain its rise and spread throughout Europe. Anthropologist Annelise Riles (2000, 2011) has also discussed 'the transnational appeal of formalism'. Her study concerns the promulgation, by Japan, of a new law to regulate the new financial transactions made possible by the 'Big Bang', the deregulation of Japan's financial market in the late 1990s. Japan's new law, she suggests, must be understood as part of a turn to formalism in international law, as the global economy was 're-regulated' under a system of international rules, to be mirrored or enforced in domestic contexts. But why, she asks, has there been this turn to the law of rules? Asking why legal formalism garners the commitment of both scholars and practitioners, she argues that we need to appreciate the significance of the legal form, in its own right, independent of crude instrumentalist definitions of its political and other functions (2000: 4–5; 2011: 213).

The particular puzzle Riles confronts in the case of the Japanese financial regulation concerns the fact that the policy issue, 'netting', is a fundamentally transnational one and that the Japanese reforms were modelled at every level on American and other foreign regulatory systems. The informal system in Japan, informants told her, had worked perfectly well and the new legislation was not important in practical terms. However, the market required a more transparent, rule-based system. The new legislation was 'a response to foreigners' demands', 'a statement to the outside world' (2000: 31–32). It was important to make Japan strong, 'the best it can be', to have the rule of law, like the US, England, and all the others (2000: 14). As she describes it, both the foreigners and the Japanese involved described their activities to her in highly normative terms, as 'a fight for transparency', for the rule of law, as part of a vision to bring Japan into line with 'global standards' (2000: 34). The new law, Riles comments (2000: 54–57; 2011: 204–07), enabled Japanese people to compare themselves to other 'developed nations' and to think of Japanese domestic legislation as part of a transnational imperative. It was more than the simple outcome of instrumental concerns, then; its advocates were on the side of progress and globalization. As she suggests (2000: 59, 2011: 215), echoing the comments of Barkun and Berger, formal procedures can inspire commitment where there may be no meeting of minds. In a transnational context law can create networks, or a sense of community, and provide standards by which public acts can be judged.

The world of transnational relations—finance, trade, communities, and laws—is a complex one. The 'integrative study of law across cultures' called for by Mertz and Goodale (2012), at the very least, needs to distinguish between the legal and the non-legal. Looking for formalism, or legalism, serves to identify the distinctly legal elements, and helps us to isolate their characteristics and analyse their role and significance, an exercise that is often enhanced by comparison between empirical examples. Anthropological and sociological studies, as I have demonstrated, indicate the significance and appeal of legalism in many contexts, the fact that it may facilitate commercial relations, allow for argument on the basis of assumed universality, inspire commitment, and enshrine aspirations.

Human Rights

The appeal of formalism, or legalism, in the international arena is readily apparent in the context of human rights law. As the Comaroffs note, there is an effort to make human rights into an ever more universal discourse, ascribing it with ever more authority (2006: 33). This has given rise to a huge body of critical scholarly work. Many anthropologists, notably Richard Wilson, have remarked upon the appeal of human rights concepts and arguments, including to those seeking to establish 'rights to culture' and to intellectual property, as well as rights to territory and autonomy. As he puts it, concepts of rights may appeal to those whose historical and indigenous ways of conceptualizing the world may not involve the assertion of rights, at least not a notion of rights centred on the individual (Wilson 1997: 10–14).

Seeking to explain such widespread phenomena, Merry (2005; 2007) employs the concept of 'vernacularization', whereby the universalizing discourse of human rights, in particular, is translated or transformed into local terms and ideas. Goodale suggests that the ontological frameworks expressed through human rights must be reconstituted in terms that resonate culturally and politically, because legitimacy is anchored in social practice (2007a: 26). Many anthropological studies have been concerned with human rights 'in practice', and the ways in which human rights discourse, ideas, rules, and instruments affect people on the ground, or are adopted by them; there is much talk of global (law) and local (practice), of the need to connect them by examining human rights on the ground (Wilson 1997; Cowan et al. 2001; Wilson and Mitchell 2003; Strathern 2004; Goodale 2007a). There are also critical views expressed by those who suggest that positive human rights laws inevitably fail to account for human subjectivity and intentionality (Jean-Klein and Riles 2005). Wilson and Mitchell (2003: 6), for example, critique the 'injustice' that it causes to the complex range of subjectivities that exist in any social or historical setting, by framing people simplistically as 'victims' or 'perpetrators', for example. The Truth and Reconciliation Commission in South Africa, they suggest, 'flattens out' the complex terrain of everyday life during the apartheid period (2003: 5–6).

Framing events in terms of abstract rules and categories is precisely what human rights, like any form of law, must do, however. It is the character of law to present and describe people and events in terms of general and abstract categories and relations. To critique it on this basis is like critiquing a ruler for exercising power. The more interesting question is surely why, given these limitations, the legalistic form of human rights discourse is so widely attractive. Several of the chapters in Goodale and Merry (2007) reflect the symbolic and aspirational appeal of the law, if only implicitly. Goodale's study of a human rights services centre in Bolivia, for example, depicts the way in which the director introduces people to the idea of human rights by revealing certain facts about themselves. He suggests that they 'share a common humanity' and possess 'rights', and claims to equality and dignity (Goodale 2007b: 142–43). The notion of human rights, Goodale explains, does not provide concrete guidelines for action, but is presented to them as being prior to the external forces of legal and political authorities. It is clearly the idea of principles and standards—expressed as 'rights'—lying beyond the particular context of the individual's social and political environment, that the activists find appealing.

Shannon Speed, in the same volume, discusses claims made by Zapatista communities in Mexico in the early 2000s that they could govern themselves without state recognition. In the process, she says, the actors employed notions of 'autonomy' and 'rights', asserting that these existed prior to and independent of their recognition by the state. They were adopting a 'globalized discourse', she says, to challenge the logic of the neoliberal state (2007: 164–65). This presents a paradox, Speed considers, if the language of human rights is closely bound up with and reinforces the role of the neoliberal state as the purveyor and guarantor of rights, law, and order (2007: 176–78). However, this is only a paradox if we equate the law invoked by the concept of human rights with the regulatory norms of the state. The Zapatistas were obviously using the language of the law to express a morality that reached beyond the bounds of the state and the regulatory and controlling aims of government. If anything, it is the state that tends to vernacularize the law into a set of administrative regulations and governmental directions, while those who would resist its power appeal to the transcendent, and universalizing, qualities of rights.

Leve (2007) also describes how Theravada Buddhists in Nepal asserted their 'rights' against the Hindu state in 1994. To do this, she says, was to cast localized issues in a way that made them internationally legible. However, the ontology of identity the Buddhists had to draw upon in order to do so directly contradicted the commitments and ways of knowing that made them

Buddhist (2007: 101). 'It is precisely by disavowing key aspects
of this liberal way of understanding the person that Buddhism
distinguishes itself and constitutes its adherents as Buddhist' (Leve
2007: 79). Nevertheless, she comments, none of the activists seemed
to have any practical problem combining this anti-essentialist understanding of the self with the call for secular human rights. It
is apparent that the Buddhists could appeal to the powerful language of human rights without translating it into more personal
and meaningful terms.

It is apparent, then, that it is the legalism of human rights
claims, their ability to transcend national regimes by framing
demands in terms of abstract rules and values, that makes them
attractive, even if the possibility of enforcement is merely theoretical; it is also what distinguishes them as legal claims. We must
take care not to see human rights laws and their abstract categories
as simply doing 'violence' to local ideas and relations, or requiring translation into indigenous terms. What is more interesting, at
least for the anthropologist, is the difference between the particu-
larized claims that people make to specific resources and better
treatment by power holders, and the claims they make in the universalizing language of human rights.[15] The particularistic often
appears less powerful than the universal. Like the English laws
that could be turned against their rulers by eighteenth-century
citizens (Thompson 1975), human rights laws allow modern citizens to make claims in powerful, abstract, and universal—that is
legalistic—terms.

LAWS AND RULERS

To insist that law must enjoy the sanction of a ruler and the
backing of a means of enforcement does little more than distinguish state or governmental from other forms of law. It distracts
attention from other examples to which we can usefully turn to
explain the nature of law. Equally, to criticize laws for failing to
reflect the particularity of real life, as some anthropologists have

---

[15] Wilson (2007) is also right to suggest that we should pay more attention to
the production of human rights laws, as Merry (2006b) has already done, including
the work of the legal experts (Warren 2007).

tended to do—in particular when discussing human rights—is to distract attention from the widespread appeal of legalistic thought.

Anthropologists have recognized that law may be an instrument of power, particularly in the hands of a ruler, and they have identified many of the technologies, often linguistic, through which it is deployed. Turning to legal history, as I have done in this chapter, offers examples of the ways in which law can subordinate alternative visions of the world and support the totalizing vision of a ruler, but also the fragility of great codifications, and the persistence with which alternative models of kinship and property relations can undermine them. Historical examples of laws and legalism indicate that an idea of law that transcends the interests and power of the ruler recurs widely throughout the world, and long back in time; the ideology of the rule of law has ancient origins (Berman 1983: 9). Even in the hands of an emperor or other ruler, the law may have an idealistic, as much as an instrumental, aspect, whether claiming to embody a higher (religious) scheme or using borrowed forms in emulation of another (superior) civilization. Laws are far more than practical instruments of government or ideological justification for power and domination.

Legalism, the rules and categories through which laws are expressed and legal arguments are formulated, is a source of standards and ideals, whether in practical terms for international merchants, or in idealistic terms for those seeking justice and recognition of their human rights. This idealism also makes sense of the ways in which law can legitimate power and its symbolic role in modern constitutions. There is, however, a recurrent tension between legalistic, particularistic, and idealistic modes of thought. It is to this that I turn in the Conclusion.

9

CONCLUSION

Why should anthropologists ask about the nature of law? How does this add to our understanding of the world, and what does it contribute to the wider field of anthropology? It is the argument of this book that we should take law seriously as a class of social phenomena, one that is defined by its form, rather than its functions. This is law delineated more narrowly than the broad range of social norms, processes of government, conflict resolution, and power relations, which fall within the eclectic field of legal anthropology, although it often plays an important role within them.

Anthropology pays close attention to the detail of empirical examples, embracing variety and inconsistency, exploring the boundaries of the concepts we routinely employ to make sense of the world, and questioning the ways in which we normally use them to simplify and categorize. This is a project that can and should be undertaken in the case of law. Exploring the category of forms to which we normally apply the term tells us something about our ordinary language concept. Empirical examples of the laws that have emerged in different times and places reveal commonalities in form, more than function, and that it is legalism rather than regularity, and language rather than practice, that distinguishes them from the non-legal. This is an inquiry that provides clarity about a concept, a category, and a set of social forms, which have been important for hundreds of years—to emperors, religious scholars, villagers, and tribespeople alike. Historical and anthropological studies reveal contexts in which laws provide meaning without being enforced, in which legal scholarship and scholars are respected as authorities, and in which laws are borrowed as much as imposed; they reveal something about how people think and the basis on which they organize their social lives. They tell us something about how the world is.

LAW AND LEGAL ANTHROPOLOGY

At its simplest, anthropology can unsettle the assumptions we may make if we confine our attention to what is familiar within our own world. An Indic scholar might take advantage of the unfortunate exotic status of Hindu law to reveal underexamined presuppositions in current understandings of the nature of law (Davis 2010: 11–12); empirical examples 'force us to reflect on, and make explicit, our conception of the composition of the standard case' (Hart 1994: 4). It is often the peripheral or marginal that have most to offer here.

Courts and other institutions, means of enforcement, and rules come to the mind of many when asked what law is, particularly those educated within a western tradition;[1] and they also feature within much legal theory. But these are aspects of state law and they do not uniformly characterize the range of examples to which we actually apply the term, particularly when looking beyond the modern west and the many legal systems that have adopted its familiar forms. Indeed, the idea that law must be guaranteed by the state or ruler itself has a history. Law-makers, including modern states, often claim that their laws are the foundation of social order, but we must not take these claims for granted. If we look more widely it is apparent that law is often significant in quite different ways to those who make, preserve, use, and appeal to it. Even the Roman and Chinese rulers invoked some form of divine or cosmic authority.

From the earliest days, anthropologists have recognized that if we confine our attention to what it is that performs the functions that state law claims for itself, we miss much that is important— even about modern state law. But what, then, defines the category of law? Legal anthropologists have generally shied away from categorizing too closely their subject of study and often avoid the term 'law', preferring to focus on processes and social norms, or the phenomenon of 'legal pluralism'. The focus has often been on what law does, its role as a 'controlling process', as a tool of hegemony, or a means of resisting power. These studies are often insightful and revealing, but we can also ask about what

---

[1] Asking law and anthropology students on Masters programmes in Oxford confirms this view of how law is commonly understood.

law is and what, in particular, allows it to perform these very
different functions.

Work on legal language and its role as a technique or technology
of power has taken the legal form seriously, noting the importance of legal categories and schemes of meaning. In this book
I build on that literature, but widen its remit to encompass historical examples. This has included the laws of archaic Greece
and medieval Iceland, the great codes of the Roman and Chinese
emperors, while examples of juristic reasoning are exemplified
by the complex argument of Roman jurists, Hindu legal scholars, Islamic muftis, and common law judges. These provide rich
resources for any scholar engaged in the empirical study of law,
but they have not often been the subject of anthropological study.
It seems, at times, as if anthropologists have regarded legal texts
and doctrines as beyond the scope of their inquiries; but these
are social forms, in and of themselves, with contexts, creators,
and discursive power.[2]

The range of cases to which we properly apply the term—law
as opposed to what are better described as 'social norms', 'judicial
processes', or 'government'—is broad, made up of examples united
by little more than a 'family resemblance'. We do not have to delve
far into legal history to realize that what has been recognized as
law, even within the legal tradition of post-Roman Europe, has
varied considerably. The terms *lex*, *ius*, and *consuetudo* were all used
by early lawyers and in the middle ages no fundamental distinction was drawn between ethics, custom, and law. Ideas about the
sources of law were far from consistent or grounded in theoretical justification; custom, legislation, judicial precedent, reason,
equity, and natural law were all recognized sources of law at one
time or another (Kelley 1990; Tubbs 2000; Murphy 2005, 2007).
The genealogy of the concept of law is not straightforward.

If we look widely, we find that law can be an intellectual as
much as a court or governmental system: what we call 'Roman',
'Hindu', or 'Islamic' laws are as much the product of scholarship
as the reasoning found in judges' decisions or the work of rulers
and governments. Looking even more broadly, we are faced with

---

[2] Riles (2004: 777) is one of the few anthropologists to advocate ethnographic
engagement with lawyers' texts and practices.

a multitude of different social forms that invite analysis as law. Some are associated with religious and cosmic order—in India and the Islamic world—with a sense of 'what we do'—in tribal and village agreements—or 'what others tell us to do'—for those under colonial or state laws; we find authoritative texts and pronouncements relating to a particular style of reasoning—the work of the Roman or Islamic jurists and common law judges— or taking the form of a constitution—in quite small village communities. Law has, at different times and places, been elided with religion or with the commands of the emperor; there have been written and unwritten laws; it has been enforced, or not; it has come to be regarded as an attribute of the modern state, but it is also a term used within international trade relations. We can properly apply the term 'law' to all of these phenomena, in the right contexts, and the categories of other languages are similarly flexible. The question is how to make sense of these as empirical phenomena. Are there shared features? What connections and contrasts emerge through comparison?

LEGALISM

Within these studies we find examples of law as scholarship: Isalmic *fiqh* and Sanskritic *dharmaśāstra* literature are forms of reflection and deduction largely independent of case law, purporting to be ahistorical systems of jurisprudence (Dresch 2012: 21). Striking examples can be given from medieval Europe, where the rediscovered Roman law could be regarded as an authoritative source of legal argument, even though its principles and categories did not fit at all well with customary principles (Wickham 2003: 144–50).[3] We also find moralistic and idealistic elements: some laws allow us to imagine the principled lives that we might lead. In an individualistic society, justice may be expressed in terms of rights, and laws that define rights allow individuals to invoke them in favour of their own interests. But in other societies, laws may define a different type of world, including the *dharma* of the Indic world and the hierarchy of the

---

[3] This example concerns possessory rights at issue in a twelfth-century land dispute. I am grateful to Patrick Lantschner for this reference.

Chinese vision. The legal form promises that this vision can be realized, by setting out practical rules and injunctions. Elsewhere, laws are more practically based, established to facilitate commercial relations, maybe, or to bring clarity to a system of landholding. They can regulate, prohibit, and facilitate social relations.⁴ But it is the legalistic elements that recur: rules, generalizations, abstractions, and categories.

Schauer (1993: xi–xii) suggests that law differs from other forms of social interaction largely because of its generality; it extends over time, over persons, and over events; it has a special form of language, shorn of contextual embellishments. In the context of judicial activity, decisions made according to laws are projected onto a larger and less-known future, we could say a transcendent order. As Dresch (2012: 15) puts it, legalistic thought makes explicit use of generalizing concepts, addressing the world through legal categories and rules that stand apart from the flux of events and personalities. The world can then be classified in a way that allows explicit discussion of moral order. It enables a 'critical reflective attitude' (Hart 1994: 57); or 'organized reflection' (Dresch 2012: 15).

Some laws take the form of explicit rules. As Dresch (2012: 12–13) puts it, simple legalism may comprise little more than a set of rules and categories, about the compensation to be paid for different types of injury to different classes of person, for example, as found in the law codes from early medieval Europe. At its most basic, a law code might present a vision of (moral) order and regularity, associated with a sense of community and belonging, and defining what it is to be a (good) member of the village, or who stands inside or outside the more fluid configurations of a tribal society.

Legalism is not confined to rules, however. The reasoning of the Soga courts, which employed general and abstract categories in order to reach decisions, was also legalistic. As Simpson (1987)

---

⁴ Paradoxically, law often appears at its most practical when it is not associated with government or other means of enforcement. The Daghestani codes, discussed in chapter seven, were practical instruments, while the codes, rules, and standard forms employed in international trade regularize activities in an essentially voluntary way.

and Postema (2002) have pointed out, the English common law cannot properly be described as a system of explicit rules; yet, as Schauer (2009: ch 6) emphasizes, it can be analysed as a set of laws extracted from judicial opinions. Both forms of legalism—that found in rules and that characterized by legal reasoning—employ general categories into which people, events, and objects can be placed, and whose application implies duties or rights, along with limits or restrictions on those rights, as well as defining relations between them. Within the English courts, the reasoning that lawyers employ when discussing the rules of a new statute is not so different from that which they employ when discussing common law principles; both are marked by the use of syllogism and analogy, a combination of formalistic and purposive arguments, the use of hypothetical cases, maxims of equity and so on; these are styles of reasoning that recur from medieval to modern times (Schauer 2009; Brand 2012: 193). When legalism becomes complex, in this way, it develops a jurisprudence, a theory about how its rules and categories relate to one another. Citation rules are a basic example, but complex legalistic and jurisprudential thought eventually leads to the esoteric styles of argument that characterize Islamic jurisprudence, the work of the Roman jurists, and the reasoning of the English common law judges. This type of law tends to proliferate, and we should not expect to find order and coherence in any legal system. The ostensible object of a text or opinion is often to clarify, to make certain and predictable, and implicitly to impose some sort of system and order upon the messy reality of daily life. But scholastic law tends to proliferate, distinctions are piled upon distinctions, commentaries upon interpretations, upon earlier commentaries. Authors borrow, combine, and synthesize. Even apparently simple law codes make fine and complex distinctions between types of wrong and reparation.

Legalism tends towards the complex, esoteric, and scholastic, then, but, as the case studies discussed in this book demonstrate, it is a style of thinking and describing that enjoys widespread appeal. There are those who seem mistrustful of law, as the Ladakhi villagers are, refusing to adopt legalistic forms or confining them to a limited sphere, but in many parts of Eurasia it has been employed by religious scholars and leaders, judges and emperors, villagers and tribespeople, and others simply seeking to do what is right and live principled lives.

Legalism is a style of thought identified by its form rather than its functions; it is explicit in its use of categories and distinctions, propositional rather than tacit, not demanding of judgement, and it often seems removed from the practices of daily life. In this way a concept of legalism serves to distinguish laws from general social norms, adjudication according to law from general mediation, and the laws of a ruler from his commands. It gives us a sense, not a very precise one, but useful nonetheless, of what is distinctive about law amongst other social forms.

LEGAL THOUGHT: LAW AND EQUITY

The nature of legalistic thought, described in this way, resonates with distinctions noted by scholars in other contexts. In his account of general human thought, psychiatrist and philosopher Iain McGilchrist (2009) draws a distinction between schematic, logical, and propositional reasoning, on the one hand, and metaphorical, inclusive, and particularistic thought, on the other.[5] Logical and schematic thought brings things into focus, rendering the implicit explicit, in order that it may become the object of our will, but it also renders what it knows 'denatured and decontextualised' (2009: 181, 195). According to the more metaphorical and inclusive style of thought, by contrast, the world is individualized, changing, interconnected, implicit, incarnate, and living. There is a need for the two types of thought to be harmonized, he says, but there must also be a reason that they remain distinct; as many thinkers have noted, paradoxes are productive (2009: 200). Legalistic thought is logical and schematic, as a distinct mode of understanding the world; it may be regarded as rational, productive, and essential to important social structures and relations, but it cannot eclipse more inclusive and metaphorical understandings.

---

[5] He associates these distinctive genres with the two hemispheres of the brain, but his account is far from deterministic: as styles of thought they have a social momentum, and different political, religious and social movements throughout history can be associated with one or the other.

This contrast resonates with Auerbach's (2003) famous description of literary styles. The Homeric style of the Odyssey, as Auerbach describes it, employs orderly descriptions, clearly outlined and uniformly illustrated, in a realm in which everything is visible. Feeling and thought are wholly expressed, phenomena are fixed in their spatial and temporal relations and clearly placed in relation to one another; there are no gaps, or glimpses of unplumbed depths, and little is implied, or left to the imagination of the reader. In the Biblical story of the sacrifice of Isaac, by contrast, more attention is paid to the multi-layered nature of the human predicament. Some parts of the story are left obscure, time and place are undefined, or call for interpretation, while thoughts and feelings are multi-layered or remain unexpressed. Doctrine and promise are incarnate in the Biblical story, requiring subtle investigation and interpretation, drawing the reader into its structure of history. As Auerbach describes it, the Odyssey is a legend and, as such, detaches its material from the contemporary, historical context. The Bible is historical, presenting the reader with contradictory motives, hesitations, and ambiguity.

Legalistic thought, like legend, is detached and simplified. It makes explicit what can or ought to occur, in terms that transcend the ambiguous and multi-layered nature of reality. It provides abstract categories, standard forms, and precedents into which the daily flux of life can, or must, be fitted, and stipulates relations between phenomena. Like legend, it detaches its material from the contemporary and historical context. Yet the dictates of justice and equity recur and intrude. As de Sousa Santos (2002: 434–37) points out, referring to Aerbach's contrast, legislative phrases may involve reference to the 'common interest', or 'reciprocal trust', judicial processes call for discretion, and allowances are made for context, complexity, and the application of maxims of equity.

The tensions thus illustrated between styles of thought recur throughout legal history, particularly when judgment is called for or justice is at stake. In early medieval Europe, law, in the form of judgment, was often opposed to justice, in the form of mercy. As Koziol (1992: ch 7) describes, justice could be associated with defence of the poor and humble, those who lacked means of self-defence and needed to beg and plead for mercy.[6] Justice for the rich, on the other hand, was found in law and judgment, which also confirmed the proprietary rights of the land-owning classes. Medieval ideas about kingship required 'not the consistent application of rules but the moral authority to decide when to apply judgment... when mercy' (1992: 216–17).[7] Similar ideas are found in the accounts left by the Kangxi emperor of late seventeenth and early eighteenth-century China, who might be motivated by compassion to exercise discretion in capital cases (MacCormack 1996: 162–63).

A more abstract opposition between law and equity recurs throughout the history of jurisprudential thought. It can be traced back at least to Aristotle, who described equity as a correction needed when law is defective owing to its universality (Nicomachean Ethics, 1137b, Aristotle 1980: 133). In Rome, Cicero appealed to the concept of *aequitas* to build a concept of fairness, something he presented as mediating between an abstract, general rule and the concrete, specific case (Frier 1985: 120). In the sixteenth century the principles of equity and their relationship with the law became an important theme in English common law jurisprudence.[8] A tension between law and humanity is evident within the Islamic world. Clarke (2012) discusses the dilemmas faced by *shari'a* court judges in modern Lebanon who, although they are supposed to apply the law, face a widespread view that the notion of merely applying rules is incompatible with the role of a true Muslim religious specialist, whose role demands personal engagement with the morally needy. The need for 'humanity' is rhetorically opposed to the 'formal' aspects of legal practice, with which lawyers are regarded as being overly preoccupied (2012: 107). The rules of law may present an unavoidable obstacle

---

[6] Messick (1993: 169) also describes the way in which the 'weak' were expected to 'kiss hand and knees' when they sought justice from a Yemeni *qadi*.

[7] As Dunbabin (1965: 73–75) describes, autocracy had to be tempered by justice: the king had to justify his position by making himself the noblest in the state. But these were moral, not legal imperatives: the burden of choice was wholly on the shoulders of the monarch.

[8] Equity was initially a matter of the Lord Chancellor's discretion intended to temper the rigours of the law, but eventually came to be formalized in the practices of the Chancery courts (Milsom 1981: ch 4).

to ideal moral engagement. This is a tension, Clarke comments, which is intrinsic to the attempt to judge people according to consistent and predictable legal standards, that is, according to rules (2012: 115).[9]

A similar suspicion of legalism is apparent in the Athenians' antipathy towards advocates and the Chinese denigration of pettifoggers. Max Weber commented adversely upon the courts of the rational and bureaucratic state, in which judges apply laws in a mechanistic fashion (1994: 147–48). More recently, scholars have criticized the inflexibility of a legalistic approach, while also recognizing the appeal captured in phrases such as 'the stern rule of the law', and 'above all men stands the law' (Chroust 1963: 14). As Schauer (1988: 547–48) says, any rule-based system is inevitably both over- and under-inclusive: abstract rules inevitably capture more or fewer cases than appropriate to the legislative purpose. Law is an imperfect tool for achieving justice. Nevertheless, as Conley and O'Barr (1990: 175) note, even after an unsatisfactory experience in the US courts many litigants 'retain a belief in the abstraction of the law as distinct from its everyday reality', ironically joining the discourse of traditional jurisprudence in accepting that the law is impartial and fair. Law can tend towards legalism, but it also promises justice and equity, setting up a tension that is recognized in the distinction often made between the spirit and the letter of the law.

SOCIAL IDEALS

As well as justice and equity, law tends to invoke an ideal order, I have suggested, something that its rules and categories represent, but can never fully realize.[10] This idealism—in the sense of the invocation of, or aspiration to, an ideal—is a feature of many of the examples discussed in this book. Legal borrowing may

[9] These tensions may be locally theorized in different terms. As Clarke (2012: 116) points out, disappointed English litigants may declare that 'the law is an ass', but for Muslim petitioners God's law cannot be wrong, so it must be the judge, himself, who is an ass.

[10] A dichotomy between the ideal and what is achievable is a characteristic of both law and ritual. Just as it is a mistake to regard any ritual as instrumental, intended to make the ideal actually occur (Smith 1982), the social vision promised by law always remains beyond reach.

represent an aspiration to participate in a civilization defined by ancient, religious, or imperial laws. Imperial laws and law-makers may, themselves, invoke a higher religious or cosmic order, or appeal to tradition and the authority of an ancient law-giver, as they did in China, seventeenth-century England, and even modern America. There is a recurrent and powerful idea that the law stands above and beyond the ruler, as divine or natural law, or more recently, human rights (Berman 1983: 45). The law may then come to enjoy an unchanging, sacrosanct quality, its form and ideas outlasting its social utility. It may also become a means through which to express claims to social justice, for example as human rights or international criminal laws. In this way, it can constrain a government's actions, be the basis for demands that the ruler enact or embody the law, and provide the standards against which despots and dictators can be judged.

In some societies laws represent a higher order of things— the *dharma* of the Indic world or the hierarchy of the Chinese social and cosmic order, defining duty more than entitlement— but what I have called law's idealism can, more simply, lie in the promise of justice and equity. This might be identified locally, in the moral standards implicit in the decisions of the Soga courts, or the promises of regularity and order contained in Daghestani and other tribal or village codes. Indeed, it is hard to imagine a social form that we might want to call law that is not, to some extent, idealistic.[11] Without being able to claim to embody a set of ideal standards, law can become problematic, as it did amongst early Buddhist writers.

The legal form is, then, a potent means of invoking a moral or religious order, lifting it beyond personal piety. In his discussion of law and religion, Berman (1974) emphasizes the necessary connections between the two, their 'fundamental unity', and laments their separation in the contemporary world. When the links are broken, he says, a society becomes demoralized; law without religion loses its basis for commitment (1974: 21). On the other hand, religion without law, that is without a framework and structure of effective social norms, dissolves into

---

[11] Donovan (2007: 252) identifies fairness as a distinctive feature of legal norms.

personal piety. Although his arguments are deliberately schematic, Berman identifies what we can regard as two distinct, but related aspects of law.

LEGALISM AND IDEALISM

These tensions between legalism and idealism, as I have characterized them, can often be associated with the generality or universality of the law, on the one hand, and the conflicting, and particularistic, demands of equity and justice, on the other. Mercy, compromise, and equity are qualities or virtues that relate to the particulars of an individual case; they can only be conceptualized in context. We cannot say if the lord really has been merciful unless we understand the case presented before him; as Milsom (1981: 90) puts it, equity acts *in personam* because conscience does. On the other hand, truth, judgment, and legal adjudication must be found or enacted by reference to a general and substantive scheme: we can only judge a decision to be legal if we measure it against a set of objective standards, explicit rules, or forms of reasoning. The use of abstract rules is justified by the impartiality of their application and the goals of fairness and objective order, but the law is an imperfect instrument for realizing the justice or moral order that it promises. Laws serve to represent objective order, then, promising that the messiness of reality really can have pattern and purpose, that it makes sense according to a higher scheme of things. This may simply be a matter of achieving justice and equity, but it can be rooted in anything from a transcendental body to the Confucian ordering of the physical and social world.

It is this idealism, combined with the practical utility of its legalism, that makes law such a widely recurrent tool to enact and legitimate the exercise of power and projects of state-building and imperialism, and also to resist or control them. In conjunction with the standardization of weights and measures, the establishment of maps and population registers, the regulation of property holding, the standardization of language, and the creation of last names, laws simplify and represent, and this facilitates administration and regulation. As tools of modern statecraft, they can be regarded as vital to our welfare and freedom, although they can also be instruments of despotism (Scott 1998: 2–4). At the same time, even in the hands of a ruler, laws may be as much symbolic and aspirational as instruments of regulation. They regularly invoke higher ideals, whether implicitly or explicitly, to legitimate power and government, for both good and evil. Even when law is deployed as an instrument of government, it primarily defines when it is right for enforcement measures to be taken or punishment to be enacted; it does not enable the ruler to exercise power, so much as justify its use, and for the same reason can be used to resist or control it.

Recurrent themes are, thus, apparent in the history of law and legalism, related to the tensions that arise when rules and abstract categories are employed, invoked, or contested in different contexts. The power and appeal of law are inevitably taking new forms in the modern world, but if we look widely it is evident that historic patterns are re-emerging. Law has often been regarded as superior to the ruler, embodying higher standards with which he or she ought to comply: the ideal of the 'rule of law' has ancient roots. But the constraining power of the law has often been associated with religious ideals, or a sense of equity, to which human laws can only approximate: we should not put too much faith in the power of human rights or international criminal laws to bring about social or transitional justice through enforcement and technical perfection alone. If we look beyond the common model of secular, enforced, and state-sponsored laws we find that much of the power and appeal of law lies in its form, its legalism, as a means through which the messy reality of daily life can be represented as conforming, at least potentially, to an ideal order. It is the interplay, often tension, between this legalism and the ideals it invokes that explains much that is contradictory, perplexing, and interesting about the law.

REFERENCES

Abel, Richard. 1995. *The Law and Society Reader.* New York: University Press.

Allen, Danielle. 2005. Greek Tragedy and Law. In M. Gagarin and D. Cohen (eds), *The Cambridge Companion to Ancient Greek Law.* Cambridge: University Press.

Allen, N. J. 2000. The Field and the Desk: Choices and Linkages. In P. Dresch, W. James and D. Parkin (eds), *Anthropologists in a Wider World.* Oxford: Berghahn.

Aristotle. 1980. *The Nicomachean Ethics,* D. Ross (trans.) Oxford: University Press.

Asad, Talal. 1983. Notes on Body Pain and Truth in Medieval Christian Ritual. *Economy and Society* 12: 287–327.

Auerbach, Erich. 2003 [1953]. *Mimesis: The Representation of Reality in Literature,* W. Trask (trans.) Princeton: University Press.

Bacot, Jacques, Frederick Thomas, and Gustave Toussaint. 1940. *Documents de Touen-houang Relatifs à l'Histoire du Tibet.* Paris: P. Geuthner.

Baker, J. H. 1971. *An Introduction to English Legal History.* London: Butterworths.

___. 1979. The Law Merchant and the Common Law Before 1700. *The Cambridge Law Journal* 38: 295–322.

Barkun, Michael. 1968. *Law without Sanctions: Order in Primitive Societies and the World Community.* New Haven: Yale University Press.

Barnwell, P.S. 2000. Emperors, Jurists, and Kings: Law and Custom in the Late Roman and Early Medieval West. *Past and Present* 168: 6–29.

Basile, Mary, Jane Bestor, Daniel Coquillette, and Charles Donahue. 1998. *Lex Mercatoria and Legal Pluralism: A Late Thirteenth-Century Treatise and its Afterlife.* Cambridge: The Ames Foundation.

Beattie, J. M. 1986. *Crime and the Courts in England, 1660–1800.* Oxford: Clarendon.

Bédoucha, Geneviève. 2000. Libertés coutumières et pouvoir central: l'enjeu du droit de l'eau dans les oasis du Maghreb. *Études Rurales* 155/156: 117–41.

Behar, Ruth. 1986. *The Presence of the Past in a Spanish Village: Santa María del Monte.* Princeton: University Press.

von Benda-Beckmann, Franz. 1970. *Rechtspluralismus in Malawi: geschichtliche Entwicklung und heutige Problematik.* München: Weltforum Verlag.

von Benda-Beckmann, Franz and Keebet. 2006. The Dynamics of Change and Continuity in Plural Legal Orders. *Journal of Legal Pluralism* 53/54: 1–44.

___. 2007. Transnationalization of Law, Globalization and Legal Pluralism: a Legal Anthropological Perspective. In C. Antons and V. Gessner (eds), *Globalization and Resistance: Law Reform in Asia since the Crisis*. Oxford: Hart.

von Benda-Beckmann, Franz and Keebet, and Anne Griffiths. 2009. *The Power of Law in a Transnational World*. Oxford: Berghahn.

von Benda-Beckmann, Keebet. 1981. Forum Shopping and Shopping Forums: Dispute Settlement in a Minangkabau Village in West Sumatra. *Journal of Legal Pluralism* 19: 117–59.

—. 2002. Globalisation and Legal Pluralism. *International Law FORUM du droit international* 4: 19–25.

—. 2009. Balancing Islam, *Adat* and the State: Comparing Islamic and Civil Courts in Indonesia. In F. and K. von Benda-Beckmann and A. Griffiths (eds), *The Power of Law in a Transnational World*. Oxford: Berghahn.

von Benda-Beckmann, Keebet and Fernanda Pirie (eds). 2007. *Order and Disorder: Anthropological Perspectives*. Oxford: Berghahn.

Benton, Lauren. 2002. *Law and Colonial Cultures: Legal Regimes in World History, 1400–1900*. Cambridge: University Press.

Berger, Klaus. 2001. The New Law Merchant and the Global Market Place. In K. Berger (ed.) *The Practice of Transnational Law*. The Hague: Kluwer Law International.

Berger, Peter and Thomas Luckmann. 1966. *The Social Construction of Reality: A Treatise in the Sociology of Knowledge*. Garden City: Doubleday.

Berman, Harold. 1974. *The Interaction of Law and Religion*. London: SCM Press.

___. 1983. *Law and Revolution: The Formation of the Western Legal Tradition*. Cambridge: Harvard University Press.

Berman, Harold and Felix Dasser. 1990. The 'New' Law Merchant and the 'Old': Sources, Content, and Legitimacy. In T. Carbonneau (ed.) *Lex Mercatoria and Arbitration*. Dobbs Ferry: Transnational Juris Publications.

Berman, Paul. 2005. From International Law to Law and Globalization. *Columbia Journal of Transnational Law* 43: 485–556.

—. 2012. *Global Legal Pluralism*. Cambridge: University Press.

Birks, Peter. 1987. The Rise of the Roman Jurists: 'Studies in Cicero's pro Caecina' by B. W. Frier. *Oxford Journal of Legal Studies* 7: 444–53.

Black, Donald. 1976. *The Behavior of Law*. New York: Academic Press.

Bloch, Howard. 1977. *Medieval French Literature and Law*. Berkeley: University of California Press.

Bodde, Derk and Clarence Morris. 1967. *Law in Imperial China: Exemplified by 190 Ch'ing Dynasty Cases*. Cambridge: Harvard University Press.

Bohannan, Paul. 1965. The Differing Realms of the Law. *American Anthropologist* 67(6): 33–42.

Bonfield, Lloyd. 1989. The Nature of Customary Law in the Manor Courts of Medieval England. *Comparative Studies in Society and History* 31: 514–34.

Bonte, Pierre. 2000. Droit musulman et pratiques foncières dans l'Adrār mauritanien. *Études Rurales* 155/56: 93–106.

Bossy, John. 1983. *Disputes and Settlements: Law and Human Relations in the West*. Cambridge: University Press.

Bottéro, Jean. 1987. *Mésopotamie: l'écriture, la raison et les dieux*. Paris: Gallimard.

Bourdieu, Pierre. 1984. *Distinction: A Social Critique of the Judgement of Taste*, R. Nice (trans.) London: Routledge and Kegan Paul.

—. 1987. The Force of Law: Toward a Sociology of the Juridical Field, R. Terdiman (trans.) *The Hastings Law Journal* 38: 814–53.

Bourgon, Jérôme. 2009. Chinese Law, History of: Qing Dynasty (1644–1911 C.E.). *In* S. Katz (ed.) *The Oxford International Encyclopedia of Legal History*. Oxford: University Press.

—. 2011. The Principle of Legality and Legal Rules in the Chinese Legal Tradition. *In* M. Delmas-Marty and P.-É. Will (eds), *China, Democracy, and Law*, N. Norberg (trans.) Leiden: Brill.

Bowen, John. 2003. *Islam, Law, and Equality in Indonesia: An Anthropology of Public Reasoning*. Cambridge: University Press.

Bracton, Henry de. 1968. *On the Laws and Customs of England*, S. Thorne (ed.) Cambridge: Harvard University Press.

Brand, Paul. 2005. *The Earliest English Law Reports*, vol. 3. London: Selden Society.

—. 2007. *The Earliest English Law Reports*, vol. 4. London: Selden Society.

—. 2012. The English Medieval Common Law (to c. 1307) as a System of National Institutions and Legal Rules: Creation and Functioning. *In* P. Dresch and H. Skoda (eds), *Legalism: Anthropology and History*. Oxford: University Press.

Brockman, Rosser. 1980. Commercial Contract Law in Late Nineteenth-Century Taiwan. *In* J. Cohen, R. Edwards, and F.-M.C. Chen (eds), *Essays on China's Legal Tradition*. Princeton: University Press.

Burman, Sandra and Barbara Harrell-Bond. 1979. *The Imposition of Law*. New York: Academic Press.

Calder, Norman. 2010. *Islamic Jurisprudence in the Classical Era*, C. Imber (ed.) Cambridge: University Press.

Carbonneau, Thomas (ed.) 1990. *Lex Mercatoria and Arbitration: A Discussion of the New Law Merchant*. Dobbs Ferry: Transnational Juris Publications.

Carey, Christopher. 1994. Legal Space in Classical Athens. *The Classical Association* 41: 172–86.

Cassell, Elizabeth. 2009. Anthropologists in the Canadian Courts. *In* M. Freeman and D. Napier (eds), *Law and Anthropology*. Oxford: University Press.

Cassinelli, C. W. and Robert Ekvall. 1969. *A Tibetan Principality: The Political System of Sa sKya*. Ithaca: Cornell University Press.

Chanock, Martin. 1985. *Law, Custom, and Social Order: The Colonial Experience in Malawi and Zambia*. Cambridge: University Press.

——. 2000. 'Culture' and Human Rights: Orientalizing, Occidentalizing and Authenticity. *In* M. Mamdani (ed.) *Beyond Rights-Talk and Culture-Talk*. Cape Town: David Philip Publishers.

Cheyette, Fredric. 1970. Suum Cuique Tribuere. *French Historical Studies* 6: 287–99.

——. 1978. The Invention of the State. *In* B.K. Lackner and K.R. Philp (eds), *Essays on Medieval Civilization*. Austin: University of Texas Press.

Chroust, Anton-Hermann. 1963. Law: Reason, Legalism, and the Judicial Process. *Ethics* 74: 1–18.

Clanchy, Michael. 1970. Remembering the Past and the Good Old Law. *History* 55: 165–76.

——. 1979. *From Memory to Written Record: England 1066–1307*. London: Edward Arnold.

——. 1983. Law and Love in the Middle Ages. *In* J. Bossy (ed.) *Disputes and Settlements*. Cambridge: University Press.

Clarke, Morgan. 2010. Neo-Calligraphy: Religious Authority and Media Technology in Contemporary Shiite Islam. *Comparative Studies in Society and History* 52: 351–83.

——. 2012. The Judge as Tragic Hero: Judicial Ethics in Lebanon's Shari'a Courts. *American Ethnologist* 39: 106–21.

Cohen, David. 2005. Crime, Punishment and the Rule of Law in Classical Athens. *In* M. Gagarin and D. Cohen (eds), *The Cambridge Companion to Ancient Greek Law*. Cambridge: University Press.

Cohen, Esther. 1993. *The Crossroads of Justice: Law and Culture in Late Medieval France*. Leiden: Brill.

Cohn, Bernard. 1989. Law and the Colonial State in India. *In* J. Starr and J. Collier (eds), *History and Power in the Study of Law*. Ithaca: Cornell University Press.

Comaroff, John and Jean. 2006. Introduction. *In* J. and J. Comaroff (eds), *Law and Disorder in the Postcolony*. Chicago: University Press.

Comaroff, John and Simon Roberts. 1981. *Rules and Processes: The Cultural Logic of Dispute in an African Context*. Chicago: University Press.

Conley, John and William O'Barr. 1990. *Rules Versus Relationships: The Ethnography of Legal Discourse*. Chicago: University Press.

Conley, Robin. 2008. 'At the Time She Was a Man': The Temporal Dimension of Identity Construction. *Political and Legal Anthropology Review* 31: 28–47.

Coombe, Rosemary. 1998. *The Cultural Life of Intellectual Properties: Authorship, Appropriation, and the Law*. Durham: Duke University Press.

Cotterrell, Roger. 1998. Why Must Legal Ideas be Interpreted Sociologically? *Journal of Law and Society* 25: 171–92.

—. 1999. *Emile Durkheim: Law in a Moral Domain*. Edinburgh: University Press.

—. 2012. What is Transnational Law? *Law and Social Inquiry* 37: 500–24.

Coutin, Susan and Barbara Yngvesson (eds). 2008. Technologies of Knowledge Production: Law, Ethnography, and the Limits of Explanation. Symposium. *Political and Legal Anthropology Review* 31.

Cover, Robert. 1983/84. Nomos and Narrative. *Harvard Law Review* 97: 4–68.

Cowan, Jane, Marie-Bénédicte Dembour, and Richard Wilson. 2001. *Culture and Rights: Anthropological Perspectives*. Cambridge: University Press.

Cowe, Peter. 1997. Medieval Armenian Literary and Cultural Trends. *In* R. Hovannisian (ed.) *The Armenian People from Ancient to Modern Times*, vol. 1. Basingstoke: Macmillan.

Cowell, E. B. and W. H. B. Rouse. 1907. *The Jātaka, or, Stories of the Buddha's Former Births,* vol. 6. Cambridge: University Press.

Crook, J. A. 1967. *Law and Life of Rome*. London: Thames & Hudson.

Dardess, John. 1983. *Confucianism and Autocracy: Professional Elites in the Founding of the Ming Dynasty*. Berkeley: University of California Press.

Darian-Smith, Eve. 2000. Structural Inequalities in the Global Legal System. *Law and Society Review* 34: 809–28.

___. 2007. *Ethnography and Law*. Aldershot: Ashgate.

Das Gupta, J. N. 1914. *The Study of Indian History*. Calcutta: Presidency College Magazine, vol. 1, no. 1.

Davis, Donald. 1999. Recovering the Indigenous Legal Traditions of India: Classical Hindu Law in Practice in Late Medieval Kerala. *Indian Philosophy* 27: 159–213.

——. 2005. Intermediate Realms of Law: Corporate Groups and Rulers in Medieval India. *Journal of the Economic and Social History of the Orient* 48: 92–117.

——. 2008. Law and 'Law Books' in the Hindu Tradition. *German Law Journal* 9: 309–25.

——. 2010. *The Spirit of Hindu Law*. Cambridge: University Press.

——. 2012. Centres of Law: Duties, Rights, and Pluralism in Medieval India. *In* P. Dresch and H. Skoda (eds), *Legalism: Anthropology and History*. Oxford: University Press.

Dawa Norbu. 1974. *Red Star over Tibet*. London: Collins.

Derrett, Duncan. 1973. Appendix. *In* R. Lingat (ed.) *The Classical Law of India*. Berkeley: University of California Press.

Dhavan, Rajeev. 1992. Dharmaśāstra and Modern Indian society: A Preliminary Exploration. *Journal of the Indian Law Institute* 34: 515–40.

Diamond, Stanley. 1973. The Rule of Law Versus the Order of Custom. *In* D. Black and M. Mileski (eds), *The Social Organization of Law*. New York: Seminar Press.

Dicks, A. R. 1995. Review of Thomas Stephens, 'Order and Discipline in China: the Shanghai Mixed Court 1911–27'. *Bulletin of the School of Oriental and African Studies* 58: 415–15.

Donovan, James. 2007. *Legal Anthropology: An Introduction*. Lanham, MD: Altamira Press.

Dotson, Brandon. 2006. Administration and Law in the Tibetan Empire: the 'Section on Law and State' and its Old Tibetan Antecedents. DPhil thesis, University of Oxford.

——. 2007. Divination and Law in the Tibetan Empire. *In* M. Kapstein and B. Dotson (eds), *Contributions to the Cultural History of Early Tibet*. Leiden: Brill.

Dresch, Paul. 2006. *The Rules of Barat: Tribal Documents from Yemen*. Sanaa: Centre français d'archéologie et des sciences sociales.

——. 2012. Legalism, Anthropology, and History. *In* P. Dresch and H. Skoda (eds), *Legalism: Anthropology and History*. Oxford: University Press.

Dresch, Paul and Wendy James. 2000. Introduction: Fieldwork and the Passage of Time. *In* P. Dresch, W. James and D. Parkin (eds), *Anthropologists in a Wider World: Essays on Field Research*. Oxford: Berghahn.

Dunbabin, Jean. 1965. Aristotle in the Schools. *In* B. Smalley (ed.) *Trends in Medieval Political Thought*. Oxford: Basil Blackwell.

___. 2001. Charles I of Anjou and the Development of Medieval Political Ideas. *Nottingham Medieval Studies* 45: 110–26.

Durkheim, Emile. 1984. *The Division of Labour in Society*, W. D. Halls (trans.) Basingstoke: Macmillan.

—. 1912. *Les formes élémentaires de la vie religieuse: le système totémique en Australie*. Paris: Félix Alcan.

Dworkin, Ronald. 1986. *Law's Empire*. London: Fontana.

Ehrlich, Eugen. 1936. *Fundamental Principles of the Sociology of Law*, W. L. Moll (trans.) Cambridge: Harvard University Press.

Ekvall, Robert. 1964. Peace and War among the Tibetan Nomads. *American Anthropologist* 66: 1119–48.

—. 1968. *Fields on the Hoof: Nexus of Tibetan Nomadic Pastoralism*. New York: Holt, Rinehart and Winston.

Ellickson, Robert. 1991. *Order without Law: How Neighbors Settle Disputes*. Cambridge: Harvard University Press.

Engel, David. 1975. *Law and Kingship in Thailand during the Reign of King Chulalongkorn*. Ann Arbor: University of Michigan.

Evans-Pritchard, E. E. 1940. *The Nuer*. Oxford: Clarendon Press.

—. 1962. *Essays in Social Anthropology*. London: Faber and Faber.

Fallers, Lloyd. 1969. *Law without Precedent: Legal Ideas in Action in the Courts of Colonial Busoga*. Chicago: University Press.

Finley, M. I. 1971. *The Use and Abuse of History*. London: The Hogarth Press.

Finnis, John. 1980. *Natural Law and Natural Rights*. Oxford: Clarendon.

Fischer, Andrew. 2004. Urban Fault Lines in Shangri-La: Population and Economic Foundations of Interethnic Conflict in the Tibetan Areas of Western China. Crisis States Programme, London School of Economics.

—. 2008. 'Population Invasion' versus Urban Exclusion in the Tibetan Areas of Western China. *Population and Development Review* 34: 631–62.

—. 2009. Educating for Exclusion in Western China: structural and institutional dimensions of conflict in the Tibetan areas of Qinghai and Tibet. Centre for Research on Inequality, Human Security and Ethnicity, Oxford University.

Fitzpatrick, Peter. 1992. *The Mythology of Modern Law*. London: Routledge.

Foucault, Michel. 1976. *Histoire de la sexualité*. Paris: Gallimard.

Fox, Robin. 1993. *Reproduction and Succession: Studies in Anthropology, Law, and Society*. New Brunswick: Transaction Publishers.

Franklin, Simon. 2007. On Meanings, Functions and Paradigms of Law in Early Rus'. *Russian History* 34: 63–81.

Freeman, Michael and David Napier (eds). 2009. *Law and Anthropology*. Oxford: University Press.

Frier, Bruce. 1985. *The Rise of the Roman Jurists: Studies in Cicero's pro Caecina*. Princeton; Guildford University Press

—. 1986. Why Law Changes, 'The Evolution of Law' by Alan Watson. *Columbia Law Review* 86: 888–900.

—. 2003. Sociology of Roman Law. *In* S. Hornblower and A. Spawforth (eds), *The Oxford Classical Dictionary*. Oxford: University Press.

—. 2010a. Roman Law. *In* M. Gagarin (ed.) *The Oxford Encyclopedia of Ancient Greece and Rome*. Oxford: University Press.

—. 2010b. Finding a Place for Law in the High Empire. *In* F. de Angelis (ed.) *Spaces of Justice in the Roman World*. Leiden: Brill.

Fuller, C. J. 1988. Hinduism and Scriptural Authority in Modern Indian Law. *Comparative Studies in Society and History* 30: 225–48.

—. 1994. Legal Anthropology, Legal Pluralism and Legal Thought. *Anthropology Today* 10: 9–12.

—. 2001. Orality, Literacy and Memorization: Priestly Education in Contemporary South India. *Modern Asian Studies* 35: 1–31.

Fuller, Lon. 1964. *The Morality of Law*. New Haven: Yale University Press.

Gagarin, Michael. 1985/86. 'The Evolution of Law' by Alan Watson. *The Classical Journal* 81: 173–75.

—. 2005. The Unity of Greek Law. *In* M. Gagarin and D. Cohen (eds), *The Cambridge Companion to Ancient Greek Law*. Cambridge: University Press.

Galligan, D. J. 2007. *Law in Modern Society*. Oxford: University Press.

—. 2010. Legal Theory and Empirical Research. *In* P. Cane and H. Kritzer (eds), *Oxford Handbook of Empirical Legal Studies*. Oxford: University Press.

Geertz, Clifford. 1983. Local Knowledge: Fact and Law in Comparative Perspective. *In* C. Geertz (ed.) *Local Knowledge*. New York: Basic Books.

Glanvill, Ranulf de. 1965. *The Treatise on the Laws and Customs of the Realm of England, Commonly Called Glanvill*, G. D. G. Hall (trans. and ed.) London: Nelson.

Gleave, Robert. 2010. Introduction. *In* N. Calder and C. Imber, *Islamic Jurisprudence in the Classical Era*. Cambridge: University Press.

Glenn, Patrick. 2008. A Concept of Legal Tradition. *Queen's Law Journal* 34: 427–45.

—. 2012. *Global Legal Pluralism: A Jurisprudence of Law beyond Borders*. Cambridge: University Press.

Gluckman, Max. 1955. *The Judicial Process among the Barotse of Northern Rhodesia*. Manchester: University Press.

Goldie, Mark. 2001. 'The Radical Face of the Ancient Constitution: St Edward's 'Laws' in Early Modern Political Thought' by Janelle Greenberg. *The English Historical Review* 116: 1227–28.

Goodale, Mark. 2007a. Locating Rights, Envisioning Law Between the Global and Local. *In* M. Goodale and S. Merry (eds), *The Practice of Human Rights*. Cambridge: University Press.

—. 2007b. The Power of Right(s): Tracking Empires of Law and New Modes of Social Resistance in Bolivia (and elsewhere). *In* M. Goodale and S. Merry (eds), *The Practice of Human Rights*. Cambridge: University Press.

Goodale, Mark and Sally Engle Merry. 2007. *The Practice of Human Rights: Tracking Law Between the Global and the Local*. Cambridge: University Press.

Goode, Roy. 2005. Rule, Practice, and Pragmatism in Transnational Commercial Law. *International and Comparative Law Quarterly* 54: 539–62.

Goody, Jack. 1986. *The Logic of Writing and the Organization of Society*. Cambridge: University Press.

Goody, Jack and Ian Watt. 1963. The Consequences of Literacy. *Comparative Studies in Society and History* 5: 305–45.

Graeber, David. 2011. *Debt: The First 5,000 Years*. New York: Melville House.

Greenberg, Janelle. 2001. *The Radical Face of the Ancient Constitution. St Edward's 'Laws' in Early Modern Political Thought*. Cambridge: University Press.

Greenhouse, Carol. 1982. Looking at Culture, Looking for Rules. *Man* 17: 58–73.

—. 1986. *Praying for Justice: Faith, Order, and Community in an American Town*. Ithaca: Cornell University Press.

—. 1989. Interpreting American Litigiousness. *In* J. Starr and J. Collier (eds), *History and Power in the Study of Law*. Ithaca: Cornell University Press.

__. 2008. Life Stories, Law's Stories: Subjectivity and Responsibility in the Politicization of the Discourse of '*Identity*'. *Political and Legal Anthropology Review* 31: 79–95.

Greenhouse, Carol, Barbara Yngvesson, and David Engel. 1994. *Law and Community in Three American Towns*. Ithaca: Cornell University Press.

Greif, Avner. 1989. Reputation and Coalitions in Medieval Trade: Evidence on the Maghribi Traders. *The Journal of Economic History* 49: 857–82.

Griffiths, John. 1986. What is Legal Pluralism? *Journal of Legal Pluralism* 19: 1–47.

___. 2006. The Idea of Sociology of Law and its Relation to Law and to Sociology. *In* M. Freeman (ed.) *Law and Sociology*. Oxford: University Press.

Gulliver, P. H. 1963. *Social Control in an African Society*. London: Routledge & Kegan Paul.

___. 1979. *Disputes and Negotiations: A Cross-Cultural Perspective*. New York: Academic Press.

Gutschow, Kim. 2004. *Being a Buddhist Nun: The Struggle for Enlightenment in the Himalayas*. Cambridge: Harvard University Press.

Habermas, Jürgen. 1996. *Between Facts and Norms*, W. Rehg (trans.) Cambridge: Polity.

Hallaq, Wael. 1994. From Fatwās to Furū': Growth and Change in Islamic Substantive Law. *Islamic Law and Society* 1: 29–65.

—. 2009a. *An Introduction to Islamic Law*. Cambridge: University Press.

—. 2009b. *Sharī'a: Theory, Practice, Transformations*. Cambridge: University Press.

Halverson, John. 1992. Goody and the Implosion of the Literacy Thesis. *Man* 27: 301–17.

Hansen, Mogens. 1991. *The Athenian Democracy in the Age of Demosthenes: Structure, Principles, and Ideology*. Oxford: Blackwell.

Harries, Jill. 2006. *Cicero and the Jurists: From Citizens' Law to the Lawful State*. London: Duckworth.

Harrington, Jill and Sally Merry. 1988. Cultural Production: The Making of Community Mediation. *Law and Society Review* 22: 709–36.

Harrison, Simon. 1989. The Symbolic Construction of Aggression and War in a Sepik River Society. *Man* 24: 583–99.

—. 1993. *The Mask of War*. Manchester: University Press.

Hart, H. L. A. 1961. *The Concept of Law*. Oxford: Clarendon Press.

—. 1994. *The Concept of Law*, 2nd ed. Oxford: Clarendon Press.

Henckaerts, Jean-Marie and Louise Doswald-Beck. 2005. *Customary International Humanitarian Law*. Cambridge: University Press.

Hirsch, Susan. 1998. *Pronouncing and Persevering: Gender and the Discourses of Disputing in an African Islamic Court*. Chicago: University Press.

Hobbes, Thomas. 1909 [1651]. *Leviathan*. Oxford: Clarendon Press.

—. 1971. *A Dialogue Between a Philosopher and a Student of the Common Laws of England*, J. Cropsey (ed.) Chicago: University Press.

Hodgson, Marshall. 1974. *The Venture of Islam: Conscience and History in a World Civilization*, vol. 2. Chicago: University Press.

Hölkeskamp, Karl-Joachim. 1999. *Schiedsrichter, Gesetzgeber und Gesetzgebung im archaischen Griechenland*. Stuttgart: Franz Steiner.

Honoré, A.M. 1977. Real Laws. *In* P. M. S. Hacker and J. Raz (eds), *Law, Morality, and Society*. Oxford: University Press.

Hooker, M. B. 1978. The Indian-Derived Law Texts of Southeast Asia. *Journal of Asian Studies* 37: 201–19.

Hopkins, Jeffrey and Lati Rinpoche (eds). 1975. *The Precious Garland and the Song of the Four Mindfulnesses*. London: Allen and Unwin.

Huang, Philip. 1996. *Civil Justice in China, Representation and Practice in the Qing*. Stanford: University Press.

Humfress, Caroline. 2007. *Orthodoxy and the Courts in Late Antiquity*. Oxford: University Press.

Hurlock, Matthew. 1993. Social Harmony and Individual Rights in China. *Columbia Law Review* 93: 1318.

Huxley, Andrew. 1997. The Traditions of Mahosadha: Legal Reasoning from Northern Thailand. *Bulletin of the School of Oriental and African Studies* 60: 315–26.

—. 2001. Positivists and Buddhists: The Rise and Fall of Anglo-Burmese Ecclesiastical Law. *Law and Social Inquiry* 26: 113–42.

—. 2006. Buddhist Law, Asian Law, Eurasian Law. *Journal of Comparative Law* 1: 158–64.

—. 2012. Lord Kyaw Thu's Precedent: A Sixteenth-Century Burmese Law-Report. *In* P. Dresch and H. Skoda (eds), *Legalism: Anthropology and History*. Oxford: University Press.

Hyams, Paul. 2000. Due Process Versus the Maintenance of Order in European Law: The Contribution of the *Ius Commune*. *In* P. Coss (ed.) *The Moral World of the Law*. Cambridge: University Press.

Ibbetson, David. 2007. Custom in Medieval Law. *In* A. Perreau-Saussine and J.B. Murphy (eds), *The Nature of Customary Law*. Cambridge: University Press.

James, Wendy. 2003. *The Ceremonial Animal*. Oxford: University Press.

Jansen, Nils. 2010. *The Making of Legal Authority: Non-Legislative Codifications in Historical and Comparative Perspective*. Oxford: University Press.

Jansen, Nils and Ralf Michaels. 2007. Private Law and the State: Comparative Perceptions and Historical Observations. *Rabels Zeitschrift* 71: 345–94.

Jean-Klein, Iris and Annelise Riles. 2005. Introducing Discipline: Anthropology and Human Rights Administrations. *Political and Legal Anthropology Review* 28: 173–202.

Johns, C. H. W. 1904. *Babylonian and Assyrian Laws, Contracts and Letters*. Edinburgh: T. & T. Clark.

Johnson, Wallace. 1979. *The T'ang Code*. Princeton: University Press.

—. 2009. Sources of Chinese Law: Penal Codes. *In* S. Katz (ed.) *The Oxford International Encyclopedia of Legal History*. Oxford: University Press.

Jolowicz, H. F. 1932. *Historical Introduction to the Study of Roman Law*. Cambridge: University Press.

Jones, William. 1997. 'The Spirit of Traditional Chinese Law' by Geoffrey MacCormack. *American Journal of Legal History* 41: 158–59.

Just, Peter. 1992. History, Power, Ideology and Culture: Current Directions in the Anthropology of Law. *Law and Society Review* 26: 373–411.

—. 2007. Law, Ritual and Order. *In* K. von Benda-Beckmann and F. Pirie (eds), *Order and Disorder: Anthropological Perspectives*. Oxford: Berghahn.

Kāne, P. V. 1930. *History of Dharmaśāstra*. Poona: Bhandarkar Oriental Research Institute.

Kantor, Georgy. 2012. Ideas of Law in Hellenistic and Roman Legal Practice. *In* P. Dresch and H. Skoda (eds), *Legalism: Anthropology and History*. Oxford: University Press.

Kapstein, Matthew. 2007. *The Tibetans*. Malden: Blackwell.

Kelley, Donald. 1990. *The Human Measure: Social Thought in the Western Legal Tradition*. Cambridge: Harvard University Press.

—. 2002. What Pleases the Prince: Justinian, Napoleon and the Lawyers. *History of Political Thought* 23: 288–302.

Kelly, Fergus. 1988. *A Guide to Early Irish Law*. Dublin: Institute for Advanced Studies.

Kemper, Michael. 2004. Communal Agreements (*ittifāqāt*) and 'ādāt-Books from Daghestani Villages and Confederacies (18th–19th Centuries). *Der Islam* 81: 115–51.

Kern, Fritz. 1939. *Kingship and Law in the Middle Ages*, S. B. Chrimes (trans.) Oxford: Basil Blackwell.

Khoury, Philip and Joseph Kostiner. 1990. *Tribes and State Formation in the Middle East*. Berkeley: University of California Press.

Koskenniemi, Martti. 2001. *The Gentle Civilizer of Nations: The Rise and Fall of International Law, 1870–1960*. Cambridge: University Press.

—. 2011. What is International Law for? *In* M. Koskenniemi (ed.) *The Politics of International Law*. Oxford: Hart.

Koziol, Geoffrey. 1992. *Begging Pardon and Favor: Ritual and Political Order in Early Medieval France*. Ithaca: Cornell University Press.

Kozloff, P. K. 1908. Through Eastern Tibet and Kam. *The Geographical Journal* 31: 522–34.

Krygier, Martin. 1986. Law as Tradition. *Law and Philosophy* 5: 237–62.

—. 1987. Critical Legal Studies and Social Theory—A Response to Alan Hunt. *Oxford Journal of Legal Studies* 7: 26–39.

Laani, Adriaan. 2005. Relevance in Athenian Courts. *In* M. Gagarin and D. Cohen (eds), *The Cambridge Companion to Ancient Greek Law*. Cambridge: University Press.

Lacey, Nicola. 2000. Philosophical Foundations of the Common Law: Social not Metaphysical. *In* J. Horder (ed.) *Oxford Essays in Jurisprudence*. Oxford: University Press.

Lambert, T. B. 2012. The Evolution of Sanctuary in Medieval England. *In* P. Dresch and H. Skoda (eds), *Legalism: Anthropology and History*. Oxford: University Press.

Lamond, Grant. 2001. Coercion and the Nature of Law. *Legal Theory* 7: 35–57.

Larivière, Richard. 1987. Law and Religion in South Asia. *In* M. Eliade (ed.) *The Encyclopedia of Religion*. New York: Macmillan.

—. 1989. Justices and Panditas: Some Ironies in Contemporary Readings of the Hindu Legal Past. *The Journal of Asian Studies* 48: 757–69.

—. 2004. Dharmaśāstra, Custom, 'Real Law' and 'Apocryphal' Smrtis. *Journal of Indian Philosophy* 32: 611–27.

Leach, Edmund. 1977. *Custom, Law, and Terrorist Violence*. Edinburgh: University Press.

Leve, Lauren. 2007. 'Secularism is a human right!' Double-binds of Buddhism, Democracy, and Identity in Nepal. *In* M. Goodale and S. Merry (eds), *The Practice of Human Rights*. Cambridge: University Press.

Levi, Edward. 1948. *An Introduction to Legal Reasoning*. Chicago: University Press.

Lewis, Andrew. 2000. The Autonomy of Roman Law. *In* P. Coss (ed.) *The Moral World of the Law*. Cambridge: University Press.

Lingat, Robert. 1950. Evolution of the Conception of Law in Burma and Siam. *Journal of the Siam Society* 38: 9–31.

___. 1967. *Les sources du droit dans le système traditionnel de l'Inde*. Paris: Mouton & Co.

—. 1973. *The Classical Law of India*, D. Derrett (trans.) Berkeley: University of California Press.

Lubin, Timothy. 2010. The Spirit and the Flesh of Hindu Law. *Journal of the American Oriental Society* 130: 445–51.

Lucas, J. R. 1977. The Phenomenon of Law. *In* P. M. S. Hacker and J. Raz (eds), *Law, Morality and Society*. Oxford: University Press.

Luhmann, Niklas. 1988. The Third Question: The Creative Use of Paradoxes in Law and Legal History. *Journal of Law and Society* 15: 153–65.

—. 2004. *Law as a Social System*, K. Ziegert (trans.) Oxford: University Press.

Macauley, Melissa. 2000. 'The Spirit of Traditional Chinese Law' by Geoffrey MacCormack. *Law and History Review* 18: 252–53.

MacCormack, Geoffrey. 1996. *The Spirit of Traditional Chinese Law*. Athens: University of Georgia Press.

MacCormick, Neil. 1989. The Ethics of Legalism. *Ratio Juris* 2: 184–93.

Maine, Henry Sumner. 1861. *Ancient Law: Its Connection with the Early History of Society and its Relation to Modern Ideas*. London: John Murray.

—. 1883. *Dissertations on Early Law and Custom*. London: John Murray.

Malinowski, Bronislaw. 1926. *Crime and Custom in Savage Society*. London: Kegan Paul.

—. 1934. Introduction. *In* H.I. Hogbin (ed.) *Law and Order in Polynesia*. London: Christophers.

Markby, Sir William. 1905. *Elements of Law Considered with Reference to Principles of General Jurisprudence*. Oxford: Clarendon Press.

Masud, Muhammad, Brinkley Messick, and David Powers. 1996. *Islamic Legal Interpretation: Muftis and their Fatwas*. Cambridge: Harvard University Press.

Masud, Muhammad, Rudolph Peters, and David Powers. 2006. *Dispensing Justice in Islam: Qadis and their Judgements*. Leiden: Brill.

Mather, Lynn and Barbara Yngvesson. 1980/81. Language, Audience, and the Transformation of Disputes. *Law and Society Review* 15: 775–822.

Mattei, Ugo and Laura Nader. 2008. *Plunder: When the Rule of Law is Illegal*. Malden: Blackwell.

Maurer, Bill. 1995. Writing Law, Making a 'Nation': History, Modernity, and Paradoxes of Self-Rule in the British Virgin Islands. *Law and Society Review* 29: 255–86.

McGilchrist, Iain. 2009. *The Master and his Emissary: The Divided Brain and the Making of the Western World*. New Haven: Yale University Press.

McKitterick, Rosamond. 1989. *The Carolingians and the Written Word*. Cambridge: University Press.

McKnight, Brian. 1997. 'The Spirit of Traditional Chinese Law' by Geoffey MacCormack. *The Journal of Asian Studies* 56: 482–83.

Meisezahl, R.O. 1973. Die Handschriften in den City of Liverpool Museums. *Zentralasiatische Studien des Seminars für Sprach und Kulturwissenschaft Zentralasiens* 7: 221–84.

—. 1992. Die Ta'i Si tu—Fassung des 'Kodex der 13 Gesetze'. *Oriens* 33: 307–37.

Menski, Werner. 2006 [2000]. *Comparative Law in a Global Context: The Legal Systems of Asia and Africa*, 2nd ed. Cambridge: University Press.

Merry, Sally. 1986. Everyday Understandings of the Law in Working-class America. *American Ethnologist* 13: 253–70.

—. 1988. Legal Pluralism. *Law and Society Review* 22: 869–96.

—. 1990. *Getting Justice and Getting Even: Legal Consciousness Among Working-Class Americans*. Chicago: University Press.

—. 2003. From Law and Colonialism to Law and Globalization. *Law and Social Inquiry* 28: 569–90.

—. 2005. *Human Rights and Gender Violence: Translating International Law into Local Justice*. Chicago: University Press.

—. 2006a. Anthropology and International Law. *Annual Review of Anthropology* 35: 99–116.

—. 2006b. Transnational Human Rights and Local Activism: Mapping the Middle. *American Anthropologist* 108: 38–51.

—. 2007. *The Practice of Human Rights: Tracking Law between the Global and the Local*. Cambridge: University Press.

—. 2010. Colonial Law and its Uncertainties. *Law and History Review* 28: 1067–71.

Mertz, Elizabeth. 1994. Legal Language: Pragmatics, Poetics, and Social Power. *Annual Review of Anthropology* 23: 435–55.

—. 2007. *The Language of Law School: Learning to 'Think Like a Lawyer'*, Oxford: University Press.

Mertz, Elizabeth and Mark Goodale. 2012. Comparative Anthropology of Law. *In* D. Clark (ed.) *Comparative Law and Society*. Cheltenham: Edward Elgar.

Messick, Brinkley. 1986. The Mufti, the Text and the World: Legal Interpretation in Yemen. *Man* 21: 102–19.

—. 1993. *The Calligraphic State: Textual Domination and History in a Muslim Society*. Berkeley: University of California Press.

Michaels, Ralf. 2005. The Re-State-Ment of Non-State Law: The State, Choice of Law, and the Challenge from Global Legal Pluralism. *Wayne Law Review* 51: 1208–59.

Michaels, Ralf and Nils Jansen. 2006. Private Law beyond the State? Europeanization, Globalization, Privatization. *American Journal of Comparative Law* 54: 843–90.

Milgrom, Paul, Douglass North and Barry Weingast. 1990. The Role of Institutions in the Revival of Trade: The Law Merchant, Private Judges and the Champagne Fairs. *Economics and Politics* 2: 1–23.

Miller, William. 1990. *Bloodtaking and Peacemaking: Feud, Law, and Society in Saga Iceland*. Chicago: University Press.

Mills, Martin. 2012. Ritual as History in Tibetan Divine Kingship: Notes on the Myth of the Khotanese Monks. *History of Religions* 51: 219–38.

Milsom, S. F. C. 1981. *Historical Foundations of the Common Law*. London: Butterworths.

Modrzejewski, Joseph. 2005. Greek Law in the Hellenistic Period: Family and Marriage. *In* M. Gagarin and D. Cohen (eds), *The Cambridge Companion to Ancient Greek Law*. Cambridge: University Press.

Monaghan, John and Peter Just. 2000. *Social and Cultural Anthropology: A Very Short Introduction*. Oxford: University Press.

Moore, Sally Falk. 1973. Law and Social Change: the Semi-Autonomous Social Field as an Appropriate Subject of Study. *Law and Society Review* 7: 719–46.

—. 1989. History and the Redefinition of Custom on Kilimanjaro. *In* J. Starr and J. Collier (eds), *History and Power in the Study of Law*. Ithaca: Cornell University Press.

—. 2001. Certainties Undone: Fifty Turbulent Years of Legal Anthropology, 1949–1999. *Journal of the Royal Anthropological Institute* 7: 95–116.

—. 2005. *Law and Anthropology: A Reader*. Oxford: Blackwell.

Mundy, Martha. 2002. *Law and Anthropology*. Aldershot: Ashgate.

Murphy, James. 2005. *The Philosophy of Positive Law: Foundations of Jurisprudence*. New Haven: Yale University Press.

—. 2007. Habit and Convention at the Foundation of Custom. *In* A. Perreau-Saussine and J. Murphy (eds), *The Nature of Customary Law*. Cambridge: University Press.

Murphy, Tim. 2004. Legal Fabrications and the Case of 'Cultural Property'. *In* A. Pottage and M. Mundy (eds), *Law, Anthropology, and the Constitution of the Social*. Cambridge: University Press.

Murray, Oswyn. 1987. Cities of Reason. *European Journal of Sociology* 28: 325–46.

Nader, Laura. 1990. *Harmony Ideology: Justice and Control in a Zapotec Mountain Village*. Stanford: University Press.

—. 1997. Controlling Processes: Tracing the Dynamic Components of Power. *Current Anthropology* 38: 711–38.

—. 2002. *The Life of the Law: Anthropological Projects*. Berkeley: University of California Press.

—. 2005. The Americanization of International Law. *In* F. and K. von Benda-Beckmann and A. Griffiths (eds), *Mobile People, Mobile Law*. Aldershot: Ashgate.

—. 2009. Law and the Frontiers of Illegality. In F. and K. von Benda-Beckmann and A. Griffiths (eds), *The Power of Law in a Transnational World*. Oxford: Berghahn.

Needham, Rodney. 1975. Polythetic Classification: Convergence and Consequences. *Man* 10: 349–69.

Nicholas, Barry. 1962. *An Introduction to Roman Law*. Oxford: Clarendon.

Nightingale, Andrea. 1999. Plato's Lawcode in Context: Rule by Written Law in Athens and Magnesia. *The Classical Quarterly* 49: 100–22.

Nuijten, Monique. 2005. Transnational Migration and the Re-framing of Normative Values. *In* F. and K. von Benda-Beckmann and A. Griffiths (eds), *Mobile People, Mobile Law*. Aldershot: Ashgate.

O'Barr, Richard. 1982. *Linguistic Evidence: Language, Power, and Strategy in the Courtroom*. New York: Academic Press.

O'Connor, Richard. 1981. Law as Indigenous Social Theory: A Siamese Thai Case. *American Ethnologist* 8: 223–37.

Olivelle, Patrick. 1993. *The Aśrama System: The History and Hermeneutics of a Religious Institution*. New York: Oxford University Press.

—. 2009. *Dharma: Studies in its Semantic, Cultural, and Religious History*. Delhi: Motilal Banarsidass.

Oomen, Barbara. 2005. McTradition in the New South Africa: Commodified Custom and Rights Talk with the Bafokeng and the Bapedi. *In* F. and K. von Benda-Beckmann and A. Griffiths (eds), *Mobile People, Mobile Law*. Aldershot: Ashgate.

Parkin, David. 2000. Templates, Evocations and the Long-Term Fieldworker. *In* P. Dresch, W. James, and D. Parkin (eds), *Anthropologists in a Wider World*. Oxford: Berghahn.

Parry, Jonathan. 1985. The Brahmanical Tradition and the Technology of the Intellect. *In* J. Overing (ed.) *Reason and Morality*. London: Tavistock.

Pennington, Kenneth. 1997. The Spirit of Legal History. *The University of Chicago Law Review* 64: 1097–116.

Petech, Luciano. 1977. *The Kingdom of Ladakh C. 950–1842 A.D.* Roma: Istituto Italiano per il Medio ed Estremo Oriente.

Peters, Rudolph. 2003. *Islamic Criminal Law in Nigeria*. Ibadan, Nigeria: Spectrum Books.

—. 2005. *Crime and Punishment in Islamic Law: Theory and Practice from the Sixteenth to the Twenty-First Century*. Cambridge: University Press.

Pharr, Clyde. 2001. *The Theodosian Code and Novels, and the Sirmondian Constitutions*. Union: Lawbook Exchange.

Philips, Susan. 1998. *Ideology in the Language of Judges: How Judges Practice Law, Politics, and Courtroom Control*. New York: Oxford University Press.

Pirie, Fernanda. 2002. The Fragile Web of Order: Conflict Avoidance and Dispute Resolution in Ladakh. DPhil thesis, University of Oxford.

——. 2005. Segmentation within the State: The Reconfiguration of Tibetan Tribes in China's Reform Period. *Nomadic People* 9: 83–102.

——. 2006. Legal Autonomy as Political Engagement: The Ladakhi Village in the Wider World. *Law and Society Review* 40: 77–103.

——. 2007a. Order, Individualism and Responsibility: Contrasting Dynamics on the Tibetan Plateau. *In* K. von Benda-Beckmann and F. Pirie (eds), *Order and Disorder: Anthropological Perspectives*. Oxford: Berghahn.

——. 2007b. *Peace and Conflict in Ladakh: The Construction of a Fragile Web of Order*. Leiden: Brill.

——. 2008. Violence and Opposition among the Nomads of Amdo: Expectations of Leadership and Religious Authority. *In* F. Pirie and T. Huber (eds), *Conflict and Social Order in Tibet and Inner Asia*. Leiden: Brill.

——. 2009. From Tribal Tibet: The Significance of the Legal Form. *In* M. Freeman and D. Napier (eds), *Law and Anthropology*. Oxford: University Press.

——. 2010. Law Before Government: Ideology and Aspiration. *Oxford Journal of Legal Studies* 30: 207–28.

——. 2012. Legal Dramas on the Amdo Grasslands. *In* K. Buffetrille (ed.) *Revisiting Rituals in the Changing Tibetan World*. Leiden: Brill.

Plucknett, T. F. T. 1922. *Statutes and their Interpretation in the First Half of the Fourteenth Century*. Cambridge: University Press.

Pocock, J. G. A. 1957. *The Ancient Constitution and the Feudal Law: A Study of English Historical Thought in the Seventeenth Century*. Cambridge: University Press.

Pollock, Frederick and Frederic Maitland. 1968 [1895]. *The History of English Law Before the Time of Edward I*, 2nd ed. Cambridge: University Press.

Pospisil, Leopold. 1958. *Kapauku Papuans and their Law*. New Haven: Yale University Press.

Postan, M. M. 1973. *Medieval Trade and Finance*. London: Cambridge University Press.

Postema, Gerald. 2002. Philosophy of the Common Law. *In* J. Coleman and S. Shapiro (eds), *The Oxford Handbook of Jurisprudence and the Philosophy of Law*. Oxford: University Press.

Pottage, Alain and Martha Mundy (eds). 2004. *Law, Anthropology, and the Constitution of the Social: Making Persons and Things*. Cambridge: University Press.

Powers, David. 2001. Review of 'The Spirit of Islamic Law' by Bernard Weiss. *Law and History Review* 19: 189–91.

——. 2002. *Law, Society and Culture in the Maghrib, 1300–1500*. Cambridge: University Press.

Pryce, Huw. 2000. Lawbooks and Literacy in Medieval Wales. *Speculum* 75: 29–67.

Ramble, Charles. 2008. *The Navel of the Demoness: Tibetan Buddhism and Civil Religion in Highland Nepal*. New York: Oxford University Press.

Rawls, John. 1971. *A Theory of Justice*. Cambridge: Harvard University Press.

Raz, Joseph. 1973. *The Concept of a Legal System*. Oxford: Clarendon Press.

—. 1975. *Practical Reason and Norms*. London: Hutchinson.

—. 1979. *The Authority of Law: Essays on Law and Morality*. Oxford: University Press.

—. 1996. On the Nature of Law. *Archiv für Rechts und Sozialphilosophie* 82: 1–25.

—. 1998. Two Views of the Nature of the Theory of Law. *Legal Theory* 4: 249–82.

—. 2009. *Between Authority and Interpretation*. Oxford: University Press.

Read, James. 1972. *Indirect Rule and the Search for Justice: Essays in East African Legal History*. Oxford: Clarendon Press.

Reynolds, Susan. 1997. *Kingdoms and Communities in Western Europe, 900–1300*. Oxford: Clarendon Press.

Rhodes, P.J. 2011 Appeals to the Past in Classical Athens. *In* G. Herman (ed.) *Stability and Crisis in the Athenian Democracy*. Stuttgart: Franz Steiner.

Richardson, Hugh. 1989. Early Tibetan Law Concerning Dog-Bite. *Bulletin of Tibetology* 3: 5–10.

—. 1990. Hunting Accidents in Early Tibet. *Tibet Journal* 15: 5–27.

Richland, Justin. 2008. *Arguing with Tradition: The Language of Law in Hopi Tribal Court*. Chicago: University Press.

Riles, Annelise. 2000. The Transnational Appeal of Formalism: The Case of Japan's Netting Law. Standford/Yale Junior Faculty Forum, Research Paper 00–03.

—. 2004. Property as Legal Knowledge: Means and Ends. *Journal of the Royal Anthropological Institue* 10: 775–95.

—. 2011. *Collateral Knowledge: Legal Reasoning in the Global Financial Markets*. Chicago: University Press.

Roberts, Simon. 1979. *Order and Dispute: An Introduction to Legal Anthropology*. Harmondsworth: Penguin Books.

—. 1983. The Study of Dispute: Anthropological Perspectives. *In* J. Bossy (ed.) *Disputes and Settlements*. Cambridge: University Press.

—. 1998. Against Legal Pluralism: Some Reflections on the Contemporary Enlargement of the Legal Domain. *Journal of Legal Pluralism* 42: 95–106.

—. 2005. After Government: On Representing Law Without the State. *Modern Law Review* 68: 1–24.

Robinson, Eric. 2003. Review of Karl-Joachim Hölkeskamp's 'Schiedsrichter, Gesetzgeber und Gesetzgebung im archaischen Griechenland'. *Bryn Mawr Classical Review* 2003.04.16.

Rocher, Ludo. 1984. *Ezourvedam: A French Veda of the Eighteenth Century*. Amsterdam: J. Benjamins Pub. Co.

Rupprecht, Hans-Albert. 2005. Greek Law in Foreign Surroundings: Continuity and Development. *In* M. Gagarin and D. Cohen (eds), *The Cambridge Companion to Ancient Greek Law*. Cambridge: University Press.

Ryan, Alan. 1970. *The Philosophy of the Social Sciences*. London: Macmillan.

Sahlins, Marshall. 1968. *Tribesmen*. Englewood Cliffs: Prentice-Hall.

—. 1972. *Stone Age Economics*. Chicago: Aldine-Atherton.

Salmond, Sir John 1920. *Jurisprudence*. London: Sweet and Maxwell.

Santos, Boaventura de Sousa. 1987. Law as a Map of Misreading: Toward a Post-Modern Conception of Law. *Journal of Law and Society* 14: 279–302.

—. 2002 [1995]. *Toward a New Legal Common Sense: Law, Science and Politics in the Paradigmatic Transition*, 2nd ed. New York: Routledge.

Sapignola, Maria. 2009. Indigeneity and the Expert: Negotiating Identity in the Case of the Central Kalahari Game Reserve. *In* M. Freeman and D. Napier (eds), *Law and Anthropology*. Oxford: University Press.

Schacht, Joseph. 1964. *An Introduction to Islamic Law*. Oxford: Clarendon Press.

Schauer, Frederick. 1988. Formalism. *The Yale Law Journal* 97: 509–48.

—. 1993. *Law and Language*. Aldershot: Dartmouth.

—. 2009. *Thinking Like a Lawyer: A New Introduction to Legal Reasoning*. Cambridge: Harvard University Press.

Scheele, Judith. 2008. A Taste for Law: Rule-Making in Kabylia (Algeria). *Comparative Studies in Society and History* 50: 895–919.

—. 2012. Rightful Measures: Irrigation, Land, and the Shari'ah in the Algerian Touat. *In* P. Dresch and H. Skoda (eds), *Legalism: Anthropology and History*. Oxford: University Press.

Schmithausen, Lambert. 1999. Aspects of the Buddhist Attitude toward War. *In* J. Houben and J. van Kooij (eds), *Violence Denied*. Leiden: Brill.

Schulz, Fritz. 1936. *Principles of Roman Law*, M. Wolff (trans.) Oxford: Clarendon Press.

Scott, James C. 1998. *Seeing Like a State*. New Haven: Yale University Press.

Sealey, Raphael. 1994. *The Justice of the Greeks*. Ann Arbor: University of Michigan Press.

Shklar, Judith. 1964. *Legalism*. Cambridge: Harvard University Press.

Sierra, M.Y. 1995. Indian Rights and Customary Law in Mexico. *Law and Society Review* 29: 227–55.

Silbey, Susan. 2005. After Legal Consciousness. *Annual Review of Law and Social Science* 1: 323–68.

Simmel, Georg. 1955. *Conflict: The Web of Group Affiliations*, K. Wolff (trans.) Glencoe: Free Press.

Simpson, A. W. B. 1987. The Common Law and Legal Theory. In A.W.B. Simpson (ed.) *Legal Theory and Legal History*. London: Hambledon Press.

——. 2011. *Reflections on 'The Concept of Law'*. Oxford: University Press.

Skoda, Hannah. 2012. A Historian's Perspective. In P. Dresch and H. Skoda (eds), *Legalism: Anthropology and History*. Oxford: University Press.

Smail, Daniel Lord. 2003. *The Consumption of Justice: Emotions, Publicity, and Legal Culture in Marseille, 1264–1423*. Ithaca: Cornell University Press.

Smith, Jonathan Z. 1982. The Bare Facts of Ritual. In J.Z. Smith (ed.) *Imagining Religion: From Babylon to Jonestown*. Chicago: University Press.

Snyder, Francis. 1981. Anthropology, Dispute Processes and Law: A Critical Introduction, *British Journal of Law and Society* 8: 141–80.

Sørensen, Per. 1994. *The Mirror Illuminating the Royal Genealogies*. Wiesbaden: Harrassowitz.

Southern, R. W. 1953. *The Making of the Middle Ages*. London: Hutchinson.

Speed, Shannon. 2007. Exercising Rights and Reconfiguring Resistance in the Zapatista Juntas de Buen Gobierno. In M. Goodale and S. Merry (eds), *The Practice of Human Rights*. Cambridge: University Press.

Speed, Shannon, and Jane Collier. 2000. Limiting Indigenous Autonomy in Chiapas, Mexico. *Human Rights Quarterly* 22: 877–905.

Starr, June and Jane Collier. 1989. *History and Power in the Study of Law: New Directions in Legal Anthropology*. Ithaca: Cornell University Press.

Stein, Peter. 1999. *Roman Law in European History*. Cambridge: University Press.

Stein, R. A. 1986. Tibetica Antiqua IV: la tradition relative au début du Bouddhisme au Tibet. *Bulletin de l'Ecole Française d'Extrême-Orient* 17: 169–96.

Stephens, Thomas. 1992. *Order and Discipline in China: the Shanghai Mixed Court 1911–27.* Seattle: University of Washington Press.

Stiles, Erin, E. 2009. *An Islamic Court in Context: An Ethnographic Study of Judicial Reasoning.* New York: Palgrave Macmillan.

Strathern, Marilyn. 1985. Discovering 'Social Control'. *Journal of Law and Society* 12: 111–34.

___. 2004. Losing (out on) Intellectual Resources. *In* A. Pottage and M. Mundy (eds), *Law, Anthropology, and the Constitution of the Social.* Cambridge: University Press.

Szegedy-Maszak, Andrew. 1978. Legends of the Greek Lawgivers. *Greek, Roman and Byzantine Studies* 19: 199–209.

Tamanaha, Brian. 1993. The Folly of the 'Social Scientific' Concept of Legal Pluralism. *Journal of Law and Society* 20: 192–217.

—. 2001. *A General Jurisprudence of Law and Society.* Oxford: University Press.

___. 2008. Understanding Legal Pluralism: Past to Present, Local to Global. *Sydney Law Review* 30: 374–411.

Techera, Erika. 2009. Legal Foundations for the Recognition of Customary Law in the Post-Colonial South Pacific. *In* M. Freeman and D. Napier (eds), *Law and Anthropology.* Oxford: University Press.

Teubner, Gunther. 1989. How the Law Thinks: Toward a Constructivist Epistemology of Law. *Law and Society Review* 23: 727–57.

—. 1992. The Two Faces of Janus: Rethinking Legal Pluralism. *Cardozo Law Review* 13: 1443–62.

Thomas, F. W. 1936. Law of Theft in Chinese Kan-su. *Zeitschrift für Vergleichende Rechtswissenschaft* 50: 275–87.

Thomas, Rosalind. 1994. Law and Lawgiver in the Athenian Democracy. *In* R. Osborne and S. Horblower (eds), *Ritual, Finance, Politics: Athenian Democratic Accounts presented to David Lewis.* Oxford: Clarendon.

___. 1995. Written in Stone? Liberty, Equality, Orality and the Codification of Law. *Bulletin of the Institute of Classical Studies* 40: 59–74.

—. 2005. Writing, Law, and Written Law. *In* M. Gagarin and D. Cohen (eds), *The Cambridge Companion to Ancient Greek Law.* Cambridge: University Press.

Thompson, E. P. 1975. *Whigs and Hunters: The Origin of the Black Act.* London: Allen Lane.

Thomson, Robert. 2000. *The Lawcode (Datastanagirkʿ) of Mxitʿar Goš.* Amsterdam: Rodopi.

Todd, Stephen and Paul Millett. 1990. Law, Society and Athens. *In* P. Cartledge, P. Millett, and S. Todd (eds), *Nomos: Essays in Athenian Law, Politics, and Society.* Cambridge: University Press.

Toussaint, Gustave-Charles. 1978. *The Life and Liberation of Padmasambhava*, K. Douglas and G. Bays (trans.) Berkeley: Dharma Publications.

Tubbs, J. W. 2000. *The Common Law Mind: Medieval and Early Modern Conceptions*. Baltimore: Johns Hopkins University Press.

Twining, William. 2002. Reviving General Jurisprudence. In M. Likosky (ed.) *Transnational Legal Processes*. London: Butterworths.

___. 2009. *General Jurisprudence: Understanding Law from a Global Perspective*. Cambridge: University Press.

Twining, William, et al. 2006. A Fresh Start for Comparative Legal Studies? A Collective Review of Patrick Glenn's 'Legal Traditions of the World'. *Journal of Comparative Law* 1: 100–99.

Uray, Geza. 1972. The Narrative of the Legislation and Organization of the mKhas Pa'i dGa' sTon. *Acta Orientalia Academiae Scientiarum Hungaricae* 26: 11–68.

Vikør, Knut S. 2005. *Between God and the Sultan: A History of Islamic Law*. London: Hurst & Co.

Vincent, Joan. 1989. Contours of Change in Agrarian Law in Colonial Uganda. In J. Starr and J. Collier (eds), *History and Power in the Study of Law*. Ithaca: Cornell University Press.

Vinogradoff, Paul. 1961. *Roman Law in Medieval Europe*. Oxford: University Press.

Waldron, Jeremy. 1990. *The Law*. London: Routledge.

—. 1995. The Dignity of Legislation. *Modern Law Review* 54: 633–65.

—. 2012. *Partly Laws Common to All Mankind: Foreign Law in American Courts*. London: Yale University Press.

Warren, Kay. 2007. The 2000 Human Trafficking Protocol: Rights, Enforcement, Vulnerabilities. In M. Goodale and S. Merry (eds), *The Practice of Human Rights*. Cambridge: University Press.

Watson, Alan. 1974. *Legal Transplants: An Approach to Comparative Law*. Charlottesville: University Press of Virginia.

—. 1975. *Rome of the XII Tables: Persons and Property*. Princeton: University Press.

—. 1985. *Sources of Law, Legal Change, and Ambiguity*. Edinburgh: T & T Clark.

—. 1995. *The Spirit of Roman Law*. Athens: University of Georgia Press.

—. 2001. *The Evolution of Western Private Law*. Baltimore: Johns Hopkins University Press.

Weber, Max. 1949. *The Methodology of the Social Sciences*, E. Shils and H. Finch (trans. and eds) Glencoe: Free Press.

___. 1968. *Economy and Society*, G. Roth and C. Wittich (eds), Berkeley: University of California Press.

—. 1994. *Political Writings*, P. Lassman and R. Spiers (eds). Cambridge: University Press.

Weeks, Sindiso Mnisi. 2009. The Interface between Living Customary Law(s) of Succession and South African State Law. DPhil thesis, University of Oxford.

Weiss, Bernard 1998. *The Spirit of Islamic law*. Athens: University of Georgia Press.

Wheatley, Steven. 2009. Indigenous Peoples and the Right of Political Autonomy in an Age of Global Legal Pluralism. *In* M. Freeman and D. Napier (eds), *Law and Anthropology*. Oxford: University Press.

White, J. C. 1894. Sikhim Laws. *The Gazeteer of Sikhim*. Calcutta: Bengal Secretariat Press.

Whitecross, Richard. 2009. Keeping the Stream of Justice Clear and Pure: The Buddhicization of Bhutanese Law. In F. and K. von Benda-Beckmann and A. Griffiths (eds), *The Power of Law in a Transnational World*. Oxford: Berghahn.

Whitman, James. 1996. At the Origins of Law and the State: Monopolization of Violence, Mutilation of Bodies, or Fixing of Prices? *Chicago-Kent Law Review* 71: 41–84.

Wickham, Chris. 2003. *Courts and Conflicts in Twelfth-Century Tuscany*. Oxford: University Press.

Wilson, Richard. 1997. *Human Rights, Culture and Context: Anthropological Perspectives*. London: Pluto.

—. 2007. Tyrannosaurus Lex: The Anthropology of Human Rights and Transnational Law. *In* M. Goodale and S. Merry (eds), *The Practice of Human Rights*. Cambridge: University Press.

Wilson, Richard and Jon Mitchell. 2003. *Human Rights in Global Perspective: Anthropological Studies of Rights, Claims and Entitlements*. London: Routledge.

Witte, John. 1991. From Homer to Hegel: Ideas of Law and Culture in the West. 'The Human Measure: Social Thought in the Western Legal Tradition' by Donald R. Kelley. *Michigan Law Review* 89: 1618–36.

Wittgenstein, Ludwig. 1958. *Philosophical Investigations*, G.E.M. Anscombe (trans.) 2nd ed. Oxford: Basil Blackwell.

The Lord Woolf, The Right Honourable. 1996. Access to Justice: Final Report. Department for Constitutional Affairs.

Wormald, Patrick. 1999. *Legal Culture in the Early Medieval West: Law as Text, Image and Experience*. London: Hambledon Press.

Yngvesson, Barbara. 1989. Inventing Law in Local Settings: Rethinking Popular Legal Culture. *The Yale Law Journal* 98: 1689–709.

Yonglin, Jiang. 2009. Chinese Law, History of, Ming Dynasty (1368–1644 C.E.). *In* S. Katz (ed.), *The Oxford International Encyclopedia of Legal History*. Oxford: University Press.

Zimmerman, Michael. 2000. A Mahayanist Criticism of *Arthaśāstra*. In *The Annual Report for the Academic Year 1999*. Tokyo: The International Research Institute for Advanced Buddhology, Soka University.

——. 2006. Only a Fool Becomes a King: Buddhist Stances on Punishment. *In* M. Zimmerman (ed.), *Buddhism and Violence*. Lumbini: International Research Institute.

INDEX